R... ...ies: B... ...

Debate

Introduced and edited by
Professor M. E. Beesley

Professor David Currie • Professor Martin Cave
Thomas Sharpe • Dr Alan Bollard
Dr Michael Pickford • Dr Dermot Glynn
Professor Colin Robinson • Dr Stephen Glaister
Professor Michael Beesley • Professor Colin Mayer
Tim Jenkinson

Comments by:
Rt. Hon. Sir Christopher Chataway
Sir Bryan Carsberg • John Bridgeman
Professor Michael Beesley
Professor Stephen Littlechild • Ian Byatt
Clare Spottiswoode • John Swift
Professor Geoffrey Whittington

iea

London
Business
School

Published by The Institute of Economic Affairs in
association with the London Business School
1997

338· 0942 R

First published in August 1997 by
The Institute of Economic Affairs
2 Lord North Street
Westminster
London SW1P 3LB

in association with

The London Business School

London

Business

School

IEA Readings 46
All rights reserved
ISSN 0305-814X
ISBN 0-255 36406-7

Printed in Great Britain by
Redwood Books, Trowbridge, Wiltshire
Set in Times Roman 11 on 12 point

Contents

INTRODUCTION

M. E. Beesley
London Business School

LAST YEAR'S BOOK OF THE 1995 SERIES OF REGULATION LECTURES[1] APPEARED at a time when the UK style of utility regulation – with its emphasis on price caps set by individual officers, embodying increasingly stringent incentives for efficiency – was the subject of much criticism. Hence the title's query 'A Time for Change?'. A year later, the tide of criticism seems to have receded somewhat. This is partly because of a political consensus that the structure allows ministerial influence without front-line responsibility for outcomes; and partly because of the technical difficulties in devising and justifying alternatives. Perhaps it has mainly been because of a greater accessibility to the basis of regulators' decisions. This year's book of the 1996 Series attests to the rapidly increasing appreciation of the business of regulation and how it is conducted, leading to much more sober reflection by would-be reformers.

As RPI-x had a highly controversial and political birth, it was always likely that most radical reforms would be associated with future political change. **Professor David Currie** (Lord Currie of Marylebone), arguing from a friendly but detached viewpoint, subjects the Labour Party's views on regulatory reform to searching analysis. Of the principal items on that agenda, three – profit sharing, requiring utilities to compensate for interruptions to supply through insurance, and rather minor reforms aimed at increasing regulatory accountability – are given a cool endorsement. The fourth, the windfall tax, though not in itself likely to affect the business of regulation greatly, is defended principally on grounds of its once-for-all impact and because it sits well with modest regulatory reform. **Sir Christopher Chataway** vigorously disagrees with David Currie's assessment of the effects of the

---

[1] M. E. Beesley (ed.), *Regulating Utilities: A Time For Change?*, IEA Readings 44, London: Institute of Economic Affairs, 1996.

windfall tax, seeing it essentially as a regrettable but understandable need to assist a change in a political stance.

RPI-x, UK style, is a major UK intellectual export. Controversy at home has, if anything, helped its growth. However, **Professor Martin Cave's** paper underlines the great difference in the UK's approach to telecoms liberalisation and regulation from the regulatory developments involved in EU liberalisation. A most import event in telecoms regulation in 1996 was Oftel's adoption of its own rules for competition, much in the spirit of the Treaty of Rome's Articles 85 and 86, and the failure by British Telecom to resist this through judicial review. The EU, as Martin shows, is far from Oftel's intended transformation to a competition authority. In the slow EU process of developing a division of labour between central and national telecoms regulation, he sees the influence of the World Trade Organisation as encouraging, not least because of the danger he sees in the laggard countries' exploiting liberalisation, a possibility he analyses in depth. **Sir Bryan Carsberg**, drawing on his experiences at Oftel, emphasises the very different attitudes to specific measures of liberalisation which have been taken in different European countries. Nevertheless, he has some hopes for progress through informal exchanges between those having to carry on regulatory processes.

Utility regulators' individual means of devising and enforcing competitive rules, which have developed considerably over the years, were a reaction to what **Mr Thomas Sharpe QC** calls in his lecture the 'weakness of UK competition laws'. His list of defects mirrors the reasons Oftel gave for adopting its new position. He thinks that the keys to UK reform are adoption of prohibitions as typified by Articles 85 and 86. He looks to an enlargement of the Restrictive Trades Practices Court to hear in the UK all UK and EU cases, to escape the undue influence on the process of administrators and politicians, and to encourage private actions before the Court. MMC's powers of examination of the sources of large firm power should be retained. This would in effect repair, for the UK at least, a clear deficiency in EU Law. **Mr John Bridgeman** points out that UK practice affects EU's practice, as well as the reverse. There is convergence in European competition laws, but this does not necessarily imply adoption of the present EU system. There is considerable support in the Community for reform of merger thresholds, and the range of restrictive practices to be captured, especially with respect to vertical agreements. Such changes are needed to make European procedures precise and predictable.

New Zealand's much publicised substitution of competition law for individual utility regulation is put in perspective by **Dr Alan Bollard**, Chairman of New Zealand's competition authority, the Commerce Commission, and his co-author, **Dr Michael Pickford**. The nature of the reforms – the corporatisation of government trading activities, encouragement of competition where deemed efficient, the latent threat of price control for non-contestable activities in utilities – is carefully defined, in a comprehensive and accessible account of NZ policy and its development. Dr Bollard is frank about the drawbacks of reliance on competition law, among them persistence of incumbent advantages. And his paper is unusually detailed on the industrial and commercial scope of the reforms. From the Chair, I noted the remarkable similarities in the underlying problems both the UK and the NZ systems face, notably of restructuring utilities to separate the contestable from the natural monopoly activities, and their behavioural consequences. The paper shows that, despite the apparently very different starting points, long-term convergence of the systems is now a reasonable prediction.

Promotion of competition over utility networks is now a main pre-occupation of regulators, with the opening of the protected and large franchise markets, already underway in gas, where the franchise was lifted in April 1996 in the South West of England, and in other Southern areas later in the year. The deadline of 1998 for a full opening of markets in both electricity and gas is provoking a wide debate among the professional advisers. **Mr Dermot Glyn**, addressing electricity, argues from the neo-classical tradition and methods. How far will markets in 1998 deviate from the competitive ideal? Unless they do so, no case for regulatory intervention can be made. In particular, it is up to Offer to show the Public Electricity Suppliers (PESs) have substantial ability to act anti-competitively. He also sees a threat to competition in price controls to protect small consumers, because PESs will be handicapped thereby; price control and non-discrimination will lead to inefficient competition. **Professor Stephen Littlechild** in reply points to the uncertainty about how the market will develop, and in particular about the speed at which competition arises; incumbents' positions will be strong. Focusing on the need for a price control after 1998, he argues that the prudent regulatory course is to adopt one; it can more easily be dropped if competition is effective than it can be revived if competition is not.

Professor Colin Robinson, addressing water regulation, is undeterred that, compared with other utilities, competition has played little part so far. For him, the burden of proof is firmly against intervention; it is regulation which is on trial, not competition. Argument from models of competitive failure which infer the need for regulation are highly misleading. He thinks the Government's proposals to lower the obstacles to trading water across networks well meaning, but quite inadequate. Separate ownership of water pipes, independent of the rest of the industry, is needed; the inhibitions from other regulators charged with pursuing non-economic aims, which constrain Ofwat's efforts to increase competition, should be lessened, the more so because they seem to be increasing. **Mr Ian Byatt** is basically sympathetic to Colin Robinson's stance, but points to remedies other than network separation, namely legislation to require companies to provide common carriage, and wider, more flexible, use of inset appointments (franchises to operate networks) and unbundling water prices. It will be possible, he hopes, to introduce competition whatever standards outside agencies impose.

One of the under-stressed influences on competition over utility networks is the structure of network prices, partly due, no doubt, to the effort needed to ensure that charges made do not favour incumbents' downstream integrated activities, as against those made to would-be competitors. The worry is not so much cost reflectivity *per se*. Clearly, there are further issues to be explored, bearing on the possible challenge to networks themselves and to more subtle strategies by incumbents to protect profits. **Dr Stephen Glaister** explores TransCo's gas transport charges. He shows British Gas's tendency since privatisation to move towards averaging and uniformity in charging. He demonstrates how the deviations from long-run marginal cost pricing can occur. Taking his evidence from geographical studies of potential gas demand and TransCo's cost models, he explains the opportunity for competitive entry in the domestic market and the 'by-pass' opportunities created, including those open to North Sea pipeline owners. He is particularly critical of the 'capacity/commodity' split in charging, and of the incorrect signals thrown up in the current entry/exit basis system. He finds frequent failure to follow the logic of charging according to long-run marginal costs, the stated and agreed basis for TransCo's charging. **Ms Clare Spottiswoode** stresses the need for correct underlying economic assumptions recognising the gas industry's long tradition of using engineering models. This concern is stimulating further inquiries. An outcome will be a greater need to rebalance charges. New gas discoveries will create important changes in the incentives to build pipe lines, and correct economic signals for both gas and electricity production are at issue.

Railway privatisation is arguably the most challenging of all the transformations from the nationalised industries. My paper takes up the story at mid-1996. The challenge arises in particular from the very large element of continuing government subsidy involved. On the basic question of the prospective future reduction of total subsidy which must come essentially from increased efficiency, the evidence seems to point to gains quite typical of other privatisations. Passenger franchise renewals will arise at times dictated by their varying lengths of up to 15 years. I argue that the regulators' strategy should aim at promoting effective competition for continuing exclusive passenger franchises, despite early ambitions to create effective competition for infrastructure slots. Consistent procedures for cost attribution and permitted mark-ups are also needed. **Mr John Swift**, in reply, points out the boldness of the original approach, which has indeed stimulated significant economies. He believes better services will also emerge. The task of setting Railtrack's prices ahead of franchise letting was difficult; and for the future it will not only be the Treasury which will take the subsidy risk, as I had argued was implicit in the original process, but also the regulator, who will have the complication of subsidy too.

The six years of the regulatory lectures has generated a number of long-running intellectual puzzles connected with RPI-x controls. Because of the effect of regulators' decisions on unallowed revenues and therefore implied company values, there has been a continual search for a means of reducing the consequences of this interdependence, not least in substantially increasing the transparency of the implied 'regulatory contract' between the regulator and the regulated. One such issue is the required rate of return. Regulation has relied a great deal on observations of stock market prices in judging this, though recent amalgamations and mergers have greatly complicated the problem. A possible remedy is to require separate Stock Exchange listings for the affected activities. **Professor Colin Mayer's** lecture, from a paper with Tim Jenkinson, considers how to improve the regulator's ability to generate relevant information. He argues that acquisition is one of a class of problems caused by diversification. Ring fencing is difficult to implement. He considers, in particular, whether partial listing would be useful, despite the industry's opposition when it was proposed for water. Listing a subsidiary will enhance conflict between classes of shareholders and increase transactions costs; but other arguments against are unpersuasive. The information provided would, on balance, assist regulators and should appeal to the companies concerned because it would reduce arbitrary regulatory decisions. **Professor Geoffrey Whittington** has misgivings on the score of the conflict of interest between regulators and minority shareholders, the shareholders' lack of access to information, and the Stock Exchange's not being receptive to the principle of listing minority holdings. In the end, he sees its possible contribution as an empirical issue, but warns about focusing too much on the required cost of capital as opposed to regulators' other tasks in RPI-x regulation.

The introduction to last year's volume expressed the hope that the Series would continue to be in the van of regulatory debate. We hope to keep up the momentum in the 7th Series, to be held in October and November 1997, which will retain the 1996 format of academic papers and regulators' responses. In contrast to the early days, academic interest in regulatory affairs is now widespread. Nevertheless, the focus on issues relevant to current regulation will be maintained.

London Business School **M.E.B.**
July 1997

THE AUTHORS

Michael Beesley is a founding Professor of Economics, now Emeritus, at the London Business School. Lecturer in Commerce at the University of Birmingham, then Reader in Economics at the LSE, he became the Department of Transport's Chief Economist for a spell in the 1960s. His recent work has centred on the issues of deregulation and privatisation in telecoms, transport, water and electricity, and he is currently Economic Advisor to Ofgas and Offer. Much of his work to 1991 in this area was summed up in *Privatisation, Regulation and Deregulation* (Routledge with the IEA, 1992).

His independent economic study of *Liberalisation of the Use of British Telecommunications' Network* was published in April 1981 by HMSO and he has since been active as an advisor to the Government in telecoms, the deregulation of buses and the privatisation of the water industry. For the IEA, of which he is a Managing Trustee, he wrote (with Bruce Laidlaw) *The Future of Telecommunications* (Research Monograph 42, 1989) and (with S.C. Littlechild) 'The Regulation of Privatised Monopolies in the United Kingdom', in *Regulators and the Market* (IEA Readings No.35, 1991). He contributed to and edited the IEA's *Markets and the Media* (IEA Readings No. 43, 1996), and he has edited all four of the previous volumes in this lecture series.

He was appointed CBE in the Birthday Honours List, 1985; from 1988 to 1994 he was a member of the Monopolies and Mergers Commission.

Alan Bollard is Chairman of the New Zealand Commerce Commission, the country's anti-trust and fair trading regulatory authority. He has worked as an industrial economist in the anti-trust area for some years. He was appointed as the Government's economic referee for the reviews of the Commerce Act in 1989 and 1992 and was appointed a lay adviser to the High Court. He has published widely in this area.

Before becoming Chairman in 1994, Dr Bollard was Director of the New Zealand Institute of Economic Research for seven years, where he was involved in advising the Government and companies on a wide range of applied economic work and forecasting. His research interests include small firms, technology, industry regulation, competition law and economic liberalisation. He has written widely on these topics, including a number of books.

John Bridgeman is the UK's Director General of Fair Trading. Prior to becoming Director General in 1995, he was managing director of British Alcan Aluminium plc. He joined Alcan Industries as a graduate trainee in 1966 and worked in Canada and Australia before becoming divisional managing director of Alcan Aluminium in 1981. From 1992 until 1993 he was director of corporate planning and development for Alcan Aluminium plc in Montreal, and in September 1993 was appointed Managing Director of British Alcan Aluminium plc.

Mr Bridgeman graduated from University College, Swansea, with an honours degree in chemistry. He undertook postgraduate training in economics and management studies at Oxford and Montreal and in 1992 became visiting professor of management at Keele University.

Commissioned into the Territorial Army in 1978, Mr Bridgeman is Honorary Colonel of the Queen's Own Oxfordshire Hussars. From 1991 until 1994 he served on the Defence Science Advisory Council as business director on the board of the Military Survey Defence Support Agency and was appointed to the National Employer Liaison Committee for Reserve Forces in 1992. He was awarded the Territorial Decoration in 1995.

He has served as a member of the Monopolies and Mergers Commission and is currently vice-president of the UK-Canada Chamber of Commerce, is a member of London's Canada Club and a Council Member of the Canada UK Colloquia.

He was appointed a Deputy Lieutenant of Oxfordshire in 1989 and was High Sheriff of Oxfordshire for 1995/96. Mr Bridgeman is married and has three daughters.

Ian Byatt was appointed as the first Director General of Water Services on 1 August 1989. He is an economist and an expert on the regulation of public utilities. His previous post was as Deputy Chief Economic Adviser to the Treasury (1978-89). He was born in 1932 and educated at Kirkham Grammar School and at St Edmund

Hall and Nuffield College, Oxford. He also studied at Harvard University as a Commonwealth Fund Fellow. He has lectured in economics at both Durham University (1958-62) and the London School of Economics (1964-67).

He joined the Civil Service in 1967 as Senior Economic Adviser to the Department of Education and Science. His career in the Civil Service also included spells at the Ministry of Housing and Local Government and the Department of Environment, before joining the Treasury in 1972. In 1986 he chaired the Advisory Committee on Accounting for Economic Costs and Changing Prices. He is an Honorary Fellow of the Chartered Institution of Water and Environmental Management. In 1994 he was awarded an Honorary Doctorate by Brunel University.

His publications include *The British Electrical Industry 1875-1914* (1979). For the IEA, he contributed a chapter, 'Ofwat: Regulation of Water and Sewage', to *Regulators and the Market* (IEA Readings No. 35, 1991), and another, 'Water: The Periodic Review Process', to *Utility Regulation: Challenge and Response* (IEA Readings No. 42, 1995).

Sir Bryan Carsberg took up his post as Secretary-General of the International Accounting Standards Committee on 22 May 1995. He held public office over the previous 11 years, first as the first Director General of Telecommunications from 1984 and more recently as Director General of Fair Trading.

Educated at Berkhamsted School and the London School of Economics, Sir Bryan qualified as a chartered accountant and became a member of the Institute of Chartered Accountants in England and Wales in 1960. He gained an MSc (Econ.) with distinction through part-time study at the London School of Economics in 1967. Between 1969 and 1981 Sir Bryan was Professor in the Department of Accounting and Business Finance at the University of Manchester. He was the Dean of its Faculty of Economics and Social Studies, 1977-78; and he was the Arthur Andersen Professor of Accounting at the London School of Economics, 1981-84. In 1974 he was a visiting Professor at the University of California (Berkeley). From 1978 to 1981 he was Assistant Director of the US Financial Accounting Standards Board. Sir Bryan was a member of the UK Accounting Standards Board, 1990-94, and was its deputy chairman between 1990 and 1992.

In May 1988 Sir Bryan was presented with the Chartered Accountants Founding Society's Centenary Award in recognition of his services to society through his work at Oftel. He was awarded a knighthood in January 1989. In December 1992 Sir Bryan was presented with the Bleau award for his work in the field of telecommunications.

Sir Bryan is the author and co-author of 11 publications on accounting, economics and finance. For the IEA, he has contributed to four IEA Readings: No. 35, *Regulators and the Market* (1991); No. 40, *Major Issues in Regulation* (1993); No. 42, *Utility Regulation: Challenge and Response* (1995); and No. 44, *Regulating Utilities: A Time For Change?* (1996). Sir Bryan also delivered the 1995 Wincott Memorial Lecture, *Competition Regulation the British Way: Jaguar or Dinosaur?* (IEA Occasional Paper No. 97, February 1996).

Martin Cave is Professor of Economics at Brunel University. He was educated at the University of Oxford and worked as a Research Fellow in the Centre for Russian and East European Studies at Birmingham, before going to Brunel. He has been a Visiting Professor at the University of Virginia and a Visiting Fellow at the Australian National University and La Trobe University. Much of his early work was in economic planning; this includes *Computers and Economic Planning: The Soviet Experience* (1980), and (with Paul Hare) *Alternative Approaches to Economic Planning* (1981). Recently he has worked primarily on issues of regulation, especially of telecommunications and broadcasting, and the measurement of public sector performance. He has acted as a consultant to various government departments and regulatory bodies including Ofgas, Oftel and the Office of Fair Trading, and was an adviser to the Peacock Committee on Financing the BBC. Since 1996 he has been a member of the UK Monopolies and Mergers Commission.

The Rt. Hon. Sir Christopher Chataway's career has been divided between the public and private sectors. After reading PPE at Magdalen College, Oxford, and four years with ITN and the BBC, he was a Member of Parliament for North Lewisham (1959-1966) and Chichester (1969-1974). He was junior Education Minister in the Macmillan Government (1962-64) and a Minister in the Heath Administration (Minister of Posts and Telecommunications, 1970-

72; Minister for Industrial Development, DTI, 1972-74; appointed PC in 1970). From 1974 he was for 15 years Managing Director of Orion Royal Bank. He has been a non-executive Chairman or Director of a number of companies since 1974. He was Chairman of the Civil Aviation Authority from 1991 to 1996. Sir Christopher contributed a chapter, 'The Charter Airline Industry: A Case History of Successful Deregulation', to *Utility Regulation: Challenge and Response* (IEA Readings No. 42, 1995). He also contributed to *Regulating Utilities: A Time For Change?* (IEA Readings No. 44, 1996).

David Currie is Professor of Economics at London Business School, and formerly Deputy Principal (1992-95), Director of the Centre for Economic Forecasting (1988-95) and Governor (1989-95). Before joining the School in 1988, he was Professor and Head of Economics at Queen Mary College, University of London, and on its Governing Body. Prior to that, he worked in consultancy and in the City. He has held visiting appointments at the International Monetary Fund, the Bank of England, the European University Institute and the University of Manchester, and has acted as a consultant to the European Commission and the OECD. In October 1996, he was elevated to the House of Lords as Lord Currie of Marylebone.

Professor Currie has published extensively in the fields of forecasting and macro-economic policy. His recent research has been in the field of government regulation of industry and competition, and he now heads the Regulation Initiative at London Business School. He is a member of the Retail Price Index Advisory Committee, has recently stepped down from the Panel of Independent Forecasters (the 'Wise Men'), and was formerly a member of the Advisory Board to the Research Councils. Professor Currie holds a BSc in Mathematics from the University of Manchester, an MSc in Economics from the University of Birmingham and a PhD in Economics from the University of London.

His books include *Micro-economic Analysis: Essays in Micro-economics and Economic Development* (1981), *The Operation and Regulation of Financial Markets* (1987), *Macro-economic Interactions between North and South* (1988), *Global Macro-economics* (IMF, 1989), *Policy Rules, Credibility and International*

Macro-economic Policy (1994), *EMU: Problems in the Transition to a Single European Currency* (Lothian Foundation), and *North-South Linkages and International Macro-economic Policy* (1995).

Stephen Glaister, PhD, is Cassel Reader in Economic Geography with special reference to Transport at the London School of Economics. He was a member of the Government's Advisory Committee on Trunk Road Assessment and he has been the Specialist Advisor to the Parliamentary Select Committee on Transport. He was a non-executive director of London Regional Transport from 1984 until 1993. He has acted as advisor to the Department of Transport on bus deregulation, and he developed models for the Department for the cost-benefit assessment of urban public transport subsidies. He has worked on urban transport evaluation for the World Bank. In December 1991 he published *Transport Options for London*, and in March 1993, *Meeting the Transport Needs of the City*, both with Tony Travers. For the IEA, he wrote (with Tony Travers) *New Directions for British Railways?* (Current Controversies No. 5, June 1993), and a chapter, 'The Regulation of Britain's Privatised Railways', in *Regulating Utilities: The Way Forward* (IEA Readings No. 41, 1994). He also contributed a chapter, 'Incentives in Natural Monopoly: The Case of Water', to *Regulating Utilities: A Time For Change?* (IEA Readings No. 44, 1996). He has contributed widely to the journals and to books on transport. He is Managing Editor of the *Journal of Transport Economics and Policy*.

Tim Jenkinson is lecturer in economics at Oxford University and a Fellow of Keble College, Oxford. He was educated at Churchill College, Cambridge (BA), University of Pennsylvania (MA) and Oxford University (DPhil). Thouron Fellow, 1982-83; he has been a Research Fellow at the Centre for Economic Policy Research and Visiting Professor at Dartmouth College, USA, in 1992 and 1995. He is Associate Consultant at Oxford Economic Research Associates Ltd., Managing Editor of the *Oxford Review of Economic Policy*, and an editorial board member of *Oxford Economic Papers* and the *Zagreb International Review of Economics & Business*. His publications include (with Colin Mayer) *Hostile Takeovers* (1994); *Readings in Microeconomics* (1996); *Readings in Macroeconomics* (1996); (with Alexander

Ljungqvist) *Going Public* (1996); and (with Dieter Helm) *Competition in Regulated Utilities* (1997).

Stephen Littlechild was appointed the first Director General of Electricity Supply on 1 September 1989. He has extensive experience of regulation both in the UK and abroad. He advised on the regulatory régime for British Telecom and the water industry. He was a member of the Monopolies and Mergers Commission for six years. Reports in which he participated included North and South of Scotland Electricity Boards, Manchester Airport and British Gas.

He has been Professor of Commerce, University of Birmingham, since 1975. He was formerly Professor of Applied Economics, University of Aston, 1973-75, and sometime Consultant to the Ministry of Transport, the Treasury, World Bank, Electricity Council, American Telephone & Telegraph Co., and Department of Energy. Professor Littlechild holds a BCom from the University of Birmingham and a PhD from the University of Texas.

He is author or co-author of *Operational Research for Managers* (1977), *Elements of Telecommunication Economics* (1979), and *Energy Strategies for the UK* (1982). For the IEA he wrote *The Fallacy of the Mixed Economy* (Hobart Paper 80, 1978, Second Edn. 1986), and contributed to *The Taming of Government* (IEA Readings 21, 1979) and *Agenda for Social Democracy* (Hobart Paperback 15, 1983). More recently, he contributed a chapter, 'Competition in Electricity: Retrospect and Prospect', to *Utility Regulation: Challenge and Response* (IEA Readings No. 42, 1995), and he also contributed to *Regulating Utilities: A Time For Change?* (IEA Readings No. 44, 1996).

Colin Mayer is Professor of Management Studies, Deputy Director (Academic), School of Management, and Fellow of Wadham College, University of Oxford. He was educated at St. Paul's School; Oriel College, Oxford (MA, MPhil, DPhil); and Harvard University. HM Treasury, 1976-78; Harkness Fellow, Harvard, 1979-80; Fellow in Economics, St. Anne's College, Oxford, 1980-86; Price Waterhouse Professor of Corporate Finance, City University Business School, 1987-92; Professor of Economics and Finance, University of Warwick, 1992-94. Chairman of European Science Foundation Network in Financial Markets; Director of

Oxford Economic Research Associates Ltd.; Associate Editor of *Journal of International Financial Management, Journal of Corporate Finance, Journal of Industrial Economics, European Financial Management Journal, Oxford Review of Economic Policy, Review of Economics and Statistics.* Honorary Fellow of St. Anne's College, Oxford; Fellow of the Royal Society for the Encouragement of Arts, Manufacture and Commerce. His publications include: (with J. Kay and J. Edwards) *Economic Analysis of Accounting Profitability* (1986); (with J. Franks) *Risk, Regulation and Investor Protection* (1989); (with A. Giovannini) *European Financial Integration* (1991); (with X. Vives) *Capital Markets and Financial Intermediation* (1993); (with T. Jenkinson) *Hostile Takeovers* (1994); and articles in economic journals.

Michael Pickford held positions at the Universities of Sussex, Edinburgh and Stirling before moving to New Zealand to take up a lectureship at Massey University, later becoming a Senior Lecturer. He specialises in industrial economics, managerial economics, and the economics of competition policy.

Dr Pickford has undertaken consultancy work for the ODA in Chile, and for the World Bank in Ghana. In 1995 he was seconded to the New Zealand Commerce Commission for a year, and was then appointed as its Chief Economist, the first such appointment in the Commission.

He has published three books: *University Expansion and Finance; The Church of Scotland: An Economic Survey* (with J. N. Wolfe); and *Introduction to the Economics of Markets: A New Zealand Perspective.* A fourth volume, *The Structure of New Zealand Industry* (edited with Alan Bollard), is forthcoming in 1997. He has also written widely on industrial economics, utility regulation, and competition policy in the New Zealand context, with papers in several international journals.

Colin Robinson was educated at the University of Manchester, and then worked for 11 years as a business economist before being appointed to the Chair of Economics at the University of Surrey in 1968. He has been a member of the Electricity Supply Research Council, the Advisory Council for Research and Development in Fuel and Power (ACORD), and is currently on the electricity panel of the Monopolies and Mergers Commission. He has written widely on energy and regulation. His most recent IEA Papers are *Energy Policy: Errors, Illusions and Market Realities* (IEA Occasional Paper No. 90, October 1993); 'Gas: What to Do After the MMC Verdict', in *Regulating Utilities: The Way Forward* (IEA Readings No. 41, 1994); and 'Profit, Discovery and the Role of Entry: The Case of Electricity', in *Regulating Utilities: A Time For Change?* (IEA Readings No. 44, 1996).

Professor Robinson became a member of the IEA's Advisory Council in 1982 and was appointed its Editorial Director in 1992. He was appointed a Trustee of the Wincott Foundation in 1993. He received the British Institute of Energy Economists' award as 'Economist of the Year 1992'.

Thomas Sharpe QC, was educated at Trinity Hall, Cambridge, and, with degrees in Economics and Law, was called to the Bar in 1973. He held part-time appointments as an adviser to the Secretary of State for Trade and Industry on aspects of telecommunications, liberalisation and competition, 1981-83; Executive Director, Institute for Fiscal Studies, 1981-87; special consultant, NERA, 1984-88; 'Of Counsel' Gibson Dunn & Crutcher, London and Los Angeles, 1984-88. He entered practice at the bar in 1987, specialising in UK and EC competition law and utility regulation, and was appointed a QC in 1994. He has been involved in many MMC inquiries, has advised extensively in all aspects of EC competition law, and various Hong Kong telecommunications regulatory problems. He has also acted for British Gas, Manchester Airport, three companies in the Domestic Electrical Goods inquiries and several bus industry references.

He has contributed widely to legal journals and is a frequent lecturer on competition and regulatory topics. He is a member of COMBAR, Bar European Group and the British Institute for International and Comparative Law.

Clare Spottiswoode was appointed Director General of Gas Supply (Ofgas) on 1 November 1993, for a term of five years. She graduated in mathematics and economics at the University of Cambridge in 1975, and was awarded a Mellon Fellowship to Yale University where she took a further degree in economics. She began her career as an economist with the Treasury in 1977, leaving in 1980 to start a family and found a business which traded in gifts.

Having sold it as a growing concern, she founded Spottiswoode and Spottiswoode Ltd, a software company specialising in microcomputer software packages for the financial and corporate sectors. She sold this company in 1988, remaining as Managing Director and Chairman until 1990.

Since then she has increased her family whilst holding several part-time appointments, including being a tutor at the London Business School's Centre for Enterprise and a member of the Government's engineering deregulation task force.

John Swift QC, was appointed Rail Regulator and International Rail Regulator (Office of the Rail Regulator) in December 1993, having previously been special adviser on the railway privatisation regulatory framework to the Secretary of State for Transport from January to November 1993.

He was born in 1940 and educated at Birkenhead School and University College, Oxford, where he gained an MA with first-class honours in the School of Jurisprudence in 1963. He then gained a Diploma with Distinction at the Johns Hopkins School of Advanced International Studies at Bologna, 1963-64. He became a Barrister at Law in 1965, a QC in 1981, and a Barrister of the Inner Temple in 1992.

Geoffrey Whittington is the Price Waterhouse Professor of Financial Accounting at the University of Cambridge and a Professorial Fellow of Fitzwilliam College, and a member of the Monopolies and Mergers Commission. He is an Academic Adviser to the Accounting Standards Board. He is a Chartered Accountant and also holds a doctorate in Economics. He has previously served as a member of the Technical and Research Committees of the Institute of Chartered Accountants in England and Wales, and as a part-time economic adviser to the Office of Fair Trading.

REGULATING UTILITIES:

THE LABOUR VIEW

David Currie

London Business School

Introduction

My task is to give an appraisal of Labour's policies for regulating the utility sector. This is an important issue, and not just for the companies and employees operating in the sector.

The utilities, defined to include those sectors subject to sector-specific regulation outside the financial sector (for example, water, gas, electricity, telecoms, and parts of transportation, including rail and airports), account for around 10 per cent of the UK FTSE 100 Share Index, and somewhat under 5 per cent of GDP. Almost all consumers use the services of all the utility sectors quite regularly, and consequently their performance and efficiency have a big impact on almost everyone in the UK. Moreover, the efficient supply of energy, transport and telecoms services affects the performance of most other sectors in the economy. Effective regulation of this sector can therefore have quite appreciable benefits in terms of the productivity performance of the overall economy; and weaknesses in regulation can be costly.

This sector also matters because it has a high political profile. This is inevitable given the near-universal use of its services. As John Kay argued in last year's lecture series, a number of years after privatisation there is still a widespread view that the provision of water and energy to the home is special, and should not be subject solely to commercial considerations.[1] While most do not want to

---

[1] J. Kay, 'The Future of UK Utility Regulation', in M. E. Beesley (ed.), *Regulating Utilities: A Time For Change?*, IEA Readings No. 44, London: Institute of Economic Affairs, 1996.

see a return to state ownership, many remain critical of the way in which these industries were privatised, often giving large gains to incumbent management, to those involved in flotation, and to initial shareholders. These views have been reinforced by a number of public relations disasters by companies in these sectors: perpetrated by a small minority of firms, the fall-out has been felt by all. One aim of privatisation was to make these sectors less subject to political attention, but if anything we have seen exactly the opposite.

It is therefore not surprising that Labour Party spokespeople have devoted a lot of attention to the possible reform of the regulatory régime put in place after privatisation. Thus the industrial strategy document, *Vision for Growth*,[2] devotes a full quarter of its 60 pages to the utilities. Margaret Beckett's introduction to the document carefully states that 'it by no means represents the last stage' (of dialogue and consultation) and that 'we will continue to consult widely in government'. What I would like to do is to present my analysis of what Labour is proposing, and suggest areas where it might be improved. I should emphasise that I do this from a position of detached sympathy. Despite my recent nomination as a Labour working peer, I have not been in any way involved in the formulation of these policies, unlike many in this room who have been involved in the consultations with industry that have taken place over the past year. This enables me to say with great confidence that this lecture is not based on any inside information.

I divide my remarks into three. *First*, I consider Labour's proposals for reforming the general competition framework. This has much wider applicability than the utilities, but is of great relevance to the utilities and the framework for their regulation. *Second*, I will briefly consider the effects of competition on tariff re-balancing, before moving on to profit-sharing and the proposed windfall tax. I shall then, *third*, consider the proposed reforms to the framework for utility regulation and touch on the issue of security of supply before concluding.

---

[2] The Labour Party, *Vision For Growth*, 1996.

Competition Policy

The overall framework for competition policy plays an important role in utility regulation.[3] For a number of reasons, the utility sectors exhibit a high degree of concentration, and are likely to remain so for some considerable time. This is partly a matter of history, with the present market structure emerging from, in most cases, a single state monopoly. Furthermore, there was usually insufficient attempt to reform the structure of the industries on privatisation.[4] Economies of scale and scope in the networks also play a role in affecting concentration. A dominant company (or, in rail and power generation, companies) therefore has considerable potential to engage in anti-competitive practices that limit the scope for effective and efficient competition to develop. A weak competition framework gives scope for this potential to be realised, and therefore places greater weight on sector-specific regulation, particularly price regulation. A strong competition policy will curb the abuse of dominance and increase the range over which effective competition can emerge, thus reducing the need for price regulation. Since price regulation is typically highly imperfect, however well the regulators do their jobs, this is for the good.

This trade-off between competition policy and regulation has been seen most clearly in the recent debate between Oftel and BT. The Oftel case has been that, by putting a broad fair trading condition into telecoms licences, it can withdraw much more completely from price regulation in the telecoms market: thus its recent proposals are to set a price cap for less than one-quarter of BT's business, as compared with more than a half without the additional competition provisions. The disagreement with BT focused mainly not on the desirability of the fair trading condition itself, but on the important but separate concern by BT that incorporation into the licence gave no right of appeal against Oftel's decisions implementing the condition. It is likely that a similar trade-off between fair trading conditions will arise in gas and

---

[3] For an excellent discussion of these issues, see R. Nuttall and J. Vickers, 'Competition Policy for Regulated Utility Industries in Britain', *Regulation Initiative* Working Paper Series No. 1, London Business School, February 1996.

[4] For example, M. Armstrong, S. Cowan and J. Vickers, *Regulatory Reform*, Cambridge, Mass.: MIT Press, 1994.

3

electricity once the opening up of these sectors to competition happens in earnest.

The need for sector-specific competition provisions arises because of the relative weakness of UK competition policy. The case-by-case 'public interest' approach to competition issues instead of specific prohibitions; the formalistic approach of the Restrictive Trade Practices Act, which catches arrangements by technical form rather than economic effect; the lack of investigative powers; the absence of interim powers and the lack of penalties all act to blunt the effectiveness of current competition policy. The government has examined these issues, originally in the 1989 White Paper on restrictive trade practices and then in the 1992 Green Paper on abuse of market power, and has recognised the need for reform in the blue March 1996 DTI consultation document. However, its latest proposals go only some way to correcting the deficiencies of UK competition policy, focusing on the prohibition of anti-competitive agreements and the introduction of investigative and interim powers. In particular, vertical agreements, which are key in the utility sectors, are not subject to prohibition.[5] Many, including Sir Bryan Carsberg,[6] have called for the adoption of a prohibitions approach along the lines of Articles 85 and 86 of the Treaty of Rome.[7] This would obviate the need for sector-specific competition provisions, though it makes sense for the regulators to have concurrent powers with the Director General of Fair Trading to take advantage in such matters of their detailed knowledge of the industry.

The Labour proposals adopt this more comprehensive approach with 'a "prohibitive" approach to competition law, similar in spirit to Articles 85 and 86 of the Treaty of Rome but adapted to suit the particular needs and structure of the British economy'. What form

---

[5] However, it includes the curious proposal that the Secretary of State would have powers to introduce explicit prohibitions via secondary legislation.

[6] B. Carsberg, *Competition Regulation the British Way: Jaguar or Dinosaur?*, IEA Occasional Paper 97, Institute of Economic Affairs, 1996.

[7] Adaptation would be desirable to avoid some of the problems of EC legislation: in particular, the EC blanket prohibition on vertical agreements needs to be restricted to those agreements that have, or could have, significant adverse effect on competition. See also M. E. Beesley, 'Abuse of Monopoly Power', in M. E. Beesley (ed.), *Regulating Utilities: The Way Forward*, IEA Readings No. 41, Institute of Economic Affairs, 1994.

this 'adaptation' will take is not spelt out in detail. However, one possibility would be the adoption of the well-argued and sensible recommendations put forward by the CBI,[8] which are consistent with Labour's proposals. They envisage the application of a form of Article 85, but with guidelines to exclude agreements between companies that have no appreciable effect on competition and a *de minimis* exclusion for small companies. They also envisage a two-pronged modified version of Article 86. The first part would ban serious misconduct by dominant firms that have appreciable effects on competition, with fines introduced once experience had been gained as to how the test would be applied. The second would provide for investigation where misconduct was less clear-cut, and fines would not apply for past misconduct. Such a framework would be more closely aligned with EU law in this area, but would avoid some of the deficiencies of Articles 85 and 86. Labour may wish to be less gradualist on the introduction of fines than the CBI suggests, since the development of a body of case history will take time; but otherwise Labour and CBI thinking seem closely aligned.

Vision for Growth reasserts the case for merging the OFT and the MMC into a single Competition and Consumer Standards Office, avoiding the duplication of investigative powers inherent in the present arrangement. This would require the creation of an appeals body, perhaps along the tribunal lines of the Restrictive Practices Court, to hear appeals against competition decisions of the competition authority and appeals against the decisions on licence amendments by the utility regulators.

It is, of course, a rather new development for Labour to emphasise the virtues of competition and of an effective competition policy. What it represents is the gradual shift of Labour from a producer-oriented way of thinking to a consumer orientation, symbolised most clearly by the abandonment of Clause 4. The emphasis is not on the virtues of competition alone, since competition can sometimes be detrimental to general welfare. Rather it is on effective competition within the framework of rules provided by competition policy. The record of the Conservative government in this area shows more emphasis on competition and less on the framework of rules to ensure that competition is effective; it remains to be seen whether Labour will strike the right

---

8   CBI, *Reform of UK Competition Policy*, May 1996.

balance between these two. It is encouraging that Labour's proposals in this area make considerable sense.

Reform of competition policy is needed to provide a clearer, more consistent framework. It is also needed to make competition policy more rigorous. The evidence is that robust competition is the best way of promoting efficiency, international competitiveness and innovation,[9] and of securing the best deal for consumers. In the context of utility regulation, an effective competition policy makes it much more likely that competition will work in important parts of the telecoms, gas, electricity and transport sectors. We return later to the question of whether competition, by forcing major tariff re-balancing, will raise difficult distributional concerns for Labour about the consequences for the poorer sections of society, and if so how they are best resolved.

Vision for Growth also includes a further general proposal on merger policy that would have important implications for the utility sector. The suggestion is that, when a merger is referred, the onus of proof should be reversed, so that the bidding company must demonstrate that the proposed merger is in the public interest. This is often argued in terms of an alleged bias towards excessive merger activity.[10] But it also makes sense in terms of the asymmetry of information between the regulatory authorities and companies: since the companies have the informational advantage, it is helpful for the onus of proof to lie with them. This change could usefully be combined with the reaffirmation, proposed by the CBI, that the effect on competition should be the main criterion against which mergers are assessed.

Competition and Tariff Re-balancing

The utility sectors have historically been characterised by substantial cross-subsidies between different classes of customers. In principle, such cross-subsidies could arise from optimal pricing,

---

[9] For example, P. Geroski, *Market Structure, Corporate Performance and Innovative Activity*, Oxford: Clarendon Press, 1994, and M. E. Porter, *The Competitive Advantage of Nations*, London: Macmillan, 1990.

[10] For a recent restatement of a strong anti-merger position, see G. Stuart, D. Bailey and R. Sugden, 'Industrial Economic Policy under Labour', *Renewal*, Vol. 4, No. 4, 1996.

taking into account the need to cover costs in network industries and possible distributional concerns.[11] In practice, as Vickers observes,

> 'most of the taxes and subsidies implicit in utility prices historically are more plausibly the result of political incentives and pressures, coupled with inertia, than of rational normative calculation. Implicit taxes are less subject to legislative scrutiny and approval than explicit taxes.'[12]

The introduction of effective competition into telecoms is removing many of these cross-subsidies, and the same is in prospect in gas and electricity with the introduction of competition. Rebalancing of this kind can have important distributional consequences.[13] This issue is not addressed in *Vision for Growth*, but it could be of particular concern to a Labour Government since it is the poorer and more disadvantaged sections of society that have usually benefited in the past from hidden subsidies. If the introduction of competition led to significant price increases to these groups, there may be pressure for a Labour Government to impede the introduction of competition or to require the regulators to take distributional considerations into account in their decisions. This would be an unfortunate outcome, for two main reasons. *First*, distributional objectives are better pursued through the tax and benefit system. And, *second*, it is best if regulators have focused objectives, to avoid problems of regulatory capture, unaccountability and uncertainty.

Fortunately, it is likely that the trade-off between competition and adverse distributional impact will not be severe. Competition may well result in substantial price reductions for domestic customers. Falling average prices permit the unwinding of implicit cross-subsidies without the necessity of raising prices to those from whom the subsidy is being withdrawn; this has been the general experience in telecoms. The worst distributional consequences could result from the half-hearted pursuit of competition, which unwinds some

---

[11] For a discussion of Ramsey pricing and distributional issues, see J. Vickers, 'Regulation, Competition and the Structure of Prices', *Oxford Review of Economic Policy*, March 1997.

[12] Vickers, *ibid.*

[13] For example, R. Hancock and C. Waddams Price, 'Competition in the British Domestic Gas Market: Efficiency and Equity', *Fiscal Studies*, Vol. 16, No. 3, 1995.

cross-subsidies without giving the efficiency gains of robust competition.

Utility Regulation

The long section on utility regulation in *Vision for Growth* makes great play of the weaknesses of the current system of utility regulation. It proposes four main possible changes:

- amending RPI-x in the direction of profit-sharing;

- a windfall tax on the utilities;

- the idea of requiring the utilities to insure for consumer compensation in the case of interruption to supply; and

- institutional changes with a view to making regulators more accountable.

I consider each in turn.

Profit-Sharing

Labour's proposals for a profit-sharing arrangement in place of the current system of RPI-x has attracted recent discussion and analysis.[14] *Vision for Growth* does not endorse this proposal, but refers to it as one possibility.

It is an undoubted fact that the way the RPI-x system has been implemented has allowed a number of the regulated companies to make very substantial profits in the past (though there is considerable variation across sectors), in excess of a normal rate of profit and what was expected when price caps were first set. Much of this was due to the difficulty of setting x; that is, in judging the feasible efficiency gains that regulated companies were able to make. This was especially difficult in the early years immediately after privatisation, because, although many knew that the state-owned sectors were inefficient, few appreciated just how much. The

---

[14] For example, P. Burns, R. Turvey and T. Weyman-Jones, 'General Properties of Sliding Scale Regulation', CRI Technical Paper No. 3, 1995, and, 'Sliding Scale Regulation of Monopoly Enterprises', CRI Technical Paper No. 11, 1995; C. Mayer and J. Vickers, 'Profit Sharing Regulation: An Economic Appraisal', *Fiscal Studies*, Vol. 17, No. 1, 1996.

over-statement of investment needs ahead of the periodic review also played a role.

Advocates of RPI-x would, of course, score these unexpected efficiency gains as one of the benefits of the system: companies regulated under an RPI-x régime have strong incentives to cut costs since they keep the full benefit of larger-than-expected efficiency gains until the next periodic review. (However, this incentive is strongest just after the price cap has been set, and falls as the next periodic review approaches.) Without this incentive, for example, under a US-type régime of rate-of-return regulation, the large efficiency gains of the past might not have happened, and the consumer would now be facing higher prices. And the division of benefits between consumers and companies is not inequitable looked at on a net-present-value basis: under pure RPI-x, the large majority of the benefits go to the consumer.[15]

However, the problem with RPI-x is not so much the actual division of the gains between the regulated company (or shareholders) and consumers, but rather the timing of these gains. The benefit to the companies are front-end loaded, while benefits to customers are back-end loaded. Thus the company gets its profits up-front in the period up to the next periodic review, while the consumer gains only afterwards. This gives rise to the problem, highlighted in John Kay's lecture in last year's series,[16] that the very economic success of RPI-x in the form of large efficiency gains is transformed into political failure via embarrassingly large profits. Avoiding this problem without attenuating incentive regulation would be good for consumers, regulated companies, shareholders and regulators. Earlier sharing of the profits resulting from efficiency gains could achieve this, and, as I shall argue, need not dull incentives.

There are at least three ways in which the earlier sharing of profits could be achieved. *First*, there is the so-called error correction rule discussed as a possibility in *Vision for Growth*

---

[15] Thus with a real discount rate of 5(10) per cent, efficiency gains made immediately after a five year periodic review result in higher profits for the ensuing five years which represent, on a discounted basis, 22(38) per cent of the total discounted value of the savings. The other 78(62) per cent go to the consumer after the next five year review. For efficiency gains made two years before the periodic review, only 9(17) per cent accrue to the firm.

[16] Kay, *op. cit.*

whereby profits in any year in excess of a normal return would be shared, perhaps on a 50/50 basis, between the company and customers through lower prices.[17] *Second*, RPI-x could be modified by making the price cap conditional on variables external to the firm that influence profitability. *Third*, there is the possibility of modifying RPI-x to give the customer earlier price cuts whilst leaving unchanged the distribution of discounted benefits between companies and customers. We consider each of these options in turn.

Error correction profit-sharing maintains incentives for efficiency gains, but in an attenuated form. The suggestion is that profits above a normal level would be allowed only if prices are simultaneously cut, in accordance with an agreed formula. But the attenuation of incentives could be quite marked. If excess profits are shared on a 50/50 rule, then only a very small part of the efficiency gains would go to the firm.[18] The sharing parameter can, of course, be altered in favour of companies, but if the incentives for efficiency gains are to match those of RPI-x the customers' share parameter has to be rather low.[19] This is a serious weakness of this proposal: incentives can be maintained by giving the customer only a small early share of efficiency gains.

Error correction profit-sharing has other drawbacks. It is likely to take an asymmetric or one-sided form. This means that excess profits, not losses, will be shared, otherwise risk would be transferred from companies to customers, who are less well placed to handle it. But since profits are uncertain, this will depress average returns and the incentive to invest. It will also affect attitudes to risk: such a tax régime discourages risk-taking, or at the very least

---

[17] The term 'error correction mechanism' is drawn from the macro-econometric literature. However, as Mayer and Vickers, *op. cit.*, observe, a wrong choice of underlying assumptions on the cost of capital and asset values can be reinforced by this rule, so that it can be error reinforcing, not error correcting.

[18] Thus the 50/50 rule applied in the current year implies that only 5(8) per cent of the discounted efficiency gains accrue to the firm in extra profits. If the rule is attenuated to apply only in the following year, then this share doubles.

[19] To give companies a 22(38) per cent share of discounted gains as in RPI-x (see footnote 15 above), the customers' share parameter must be 19(13) per cent. The bulk of efficiency gains remain with the company in the early years.

promotes the combination of risky projects.[20] I would not relish a decision on Heathrow's Terminal 5 with one-sided profit-sharing, if I were on the board of BAA. Similar points apply to variants of profit-sharing which envisage a profits ceiling above which sharing starts.

There is a different view on error correction profit-sharing, but equally negative: that it will have none of these predicted economic effects because accountants will find a way round it. Certainly the arrangement would provide strong incentives to make provisions to move profits from good years to bad; and accountants have an armoury of devices for doing just that. The relevant accounts for this purpose would not be the normal tax accounts since it would be necessary to establish excess profits relative to the benchmark set by the regulator. To avoid the regulated company smoothing profits by accounting devices, the regulator would need to investigate the accounts of the company in detail, and on an annual basis, not just at periodic reviews. This has two dangers: it could easily overload the limited resources of the regulatory offices; and it could draw the regulator into excessive intervention and oversight of the company's affairs.

But perhaps the most fundamental problem with this form of profit-sharing may be that it is fighting yesterday's battle. It is very likely that the excess profits made in the past were transitional, arising from privatisation and the bedding down of the regulatory framework. Thus state assets were sold too cheaply, partly because of the speed and size of sales, and partly because they were not auctioned. The privatised companies were sold substantially under-geared, allowing gains to be made subsequently by moving to a more optimal capital structure. They were sold with an inappropriate industrial structure, far too concentrated even when broken up, as in power generation.[21] This probably induced an under-valuation of the overall business, both because of the flow-of-

---

[20] In technical terms, under such a tax régime, the company's tax liability can be thought of as a negative position in a call option. As we have learnt so graphically from the Barings crash, the value of that liability increases with volatility. The consequences for the risk-averse are clear, in contrast to Leeson. This means that firms will invest in risky projects only if the return is high enough to compensate for this additional tax effect.

[21] R. Green and D. Newbery, 'Competition in the British Electricity Spot Market', *Journal of Political Economy*, Vol. 100, No. 5, 1992.

funds consequences of large issues and because of the problem of valuing large bundles of disparate assets. Perhaps most importantly, the severe under-estimation of the inefficiencies of state ownership meant that companies could obtain very large efficiency gains that were reflected in profits, and only rather later in prices.

This combination of events will not recur. Privatisation is a one-off, at least for each sector.[22] Efficiency gains are likely to be less, and regulators have learnt to be tough. Although it can be argued that there remains some under-gearing, this is now less evident and depends on the assessment of risk in these sectors: with increased competition, some would argue that the traditional high gearing of this sector is less appropriate. With high profits less likely and efficiency gains less easy to come by, profit-sharing in a form that reduces incentives for efficiency is inappropriate.

My conclusion is that error correction profit-sharing is not desirable. However, if there is a concern to address the issue of large up-front profits, then other forms of profit-sharing are more promising. Conditioning the price cap on variables that affect profit performance could help to reduce profit fluctuations without diminishing incentives for efficiency gains.[23] This is particularly the case if it takes the form of yardstick comparisons of efficiency with comparators elsewhere in the industry, as is possible for the water companies and the RECs.

The third form of profit-sharing addresses head-on the problem that RPI-x in its present form loads at the front end the benefits to companies of efficiency gains. It would involve distributing more evenly over time the gains between firm and customer, but in such a way as to leave unchanged the overall division of benefits between customers and companies in net present value terms. This can be done through early price cuts, which are then subsequently taken into account in the next periodic review so as to leave unchanged the total benefits. A prerequisite for this is, of course, confidence that the regulator will not renege on this understanding, but that is in any case necessary for effective and efficient regulation. If that could be achieved, it would allow consumers to enjoy the early

---

[22] If it is not, in the improbable event that privatised industries are taken back into state ownership, then current regulatory institutions will in any case disappear.

[23] Mayer and Vickers, *op. cit.*

benefits of efficiency gains, whilst maintaining incentives for companies to raise efficiency.

The Windfall Tax

The language in much of *Vision for Growth* indicates that its proposals are provisional and for debate, in line with Margaret Beckett's introduction that I quoted at the beginning of this paper. That is not so in its presentation of the windfall tax, an option first voiced by John Smith in 1993. The document is categorical in saying that 'Labour will have a one-off windfall levy on the privatised utilities'. This commitment is also one of five printed on a credit-card-sized card distributed widely to all Labour Party members and others, accompanied by the words 'keep this card and see that we keep our promises'. This suggests that it would require a hugely successful lobbying campaign by the industry to deflect Labour from implementing this tax. I am sceptical of the chances of such a campaign. This policy pledge applies to taxation the principles of war: identify a clear enemy and isolate it before attacking. Because of the past public relations failures by some utility companies, this tax is unusual in having popular support, though not so much as to rival the voluntary tax that we call the National Lottery. And I do not see leading business figures outside the utility sector presenting the case against this tax.

This commitment reflects the stated view that 'excess profits in many of the utilities have been huge'. The tax is intended to pay 'over the course of a Parliament for our carefully costed new deal for young people and for the long-term unemployed'. The aim is to bring 250,000 people under 25 into work, an important economic and social objective to achieve with benefits that would flow well into the future. No figure is put in the document on the yield of the tax, but a range of £3-5 billion has been widely quoted, although there have been recent press reports of statements by an adviser close to Gordon Brown saying that the yield could be in the range up to £10 billion.[24]

There are, of course, potential obstacles to the implementation of such a tax. The scope and base of the tax need to be defined, legal

---

[24] The net yield will, of course, be less than the gross yield because of offsetting effects on other tax yields: a windfall tax will lead to lower dividend payments and less capital gains, so that tax revenues from these sources will fall somewhat.

hurdles have to be surmounted, and the Bill has to pass through Parliament. To avoid taking up valuable Parliamentary time with hybrid legislation, I guess that the architects of this tax would seek to define a class of companies to which it applies, perhaps by reference to the regulatory framework, rather than name specific companies in the Bill. I guess that they would wish to make it genuinely retrospective (that, after all, is the rationale of the tax), to prevent companies taking avoiding action, perhaps deriving the tax base from data for the period from privatisation to a cut-off date (such as 1994, when the tax first became a serious runner). This would mean that current or recent actions, in the form of large dividend pay-outs or share buy-backs, would not affect incidence.

Goldman Sachs[25] suggest that the tax may be based on current market capitalisation. This has two disadvantages: first, it is not retrospective, and is subject to influence by financial operations; second, it is a wealth levy, not a windfall tax. A more appropriate base would be to derive the base of the tax from dividend pay-outs together with the change in market valuation from the offer price at privatisation to the cut-off date (or that part in excess of the overall stock market performance); or alternatively, a measure of actual profits in excess of normal over the period since privatisation up to the cut-off date.[26] It is also likely that the regulators will be required to disregard the effects of the tax in subsequent price reviews, to prevent the windfall tax being passed straight through to consumers. Indeed, in view of the technical issues in this area, before the windfall tax is implemented, it would seem sensible for the Treasury to have an early meeting with all the regulators to discuss and agree on the details of implementation.

Retrospective taxation could, in principle, fall foul of the European Convention on Human Rights, Article 1 of Protocol 1 of which says that 'Every natural or legal person is entitled to the peaceful enjoyment of his possessions. No one shall be deprived of his possessions...' But this is not as helpful to the utilities as it might appear since it goes on to say 'except in the public interest

---

[25] Goldman Sachs, 'The Windfall Profit Tax', *Portfolio Strategy*, July 1996.

[26] Most recent press comment suggests that the second approach is the more likely. Presumably capital losses will not result in windfall rebates. For an analysis and estimates of the effects of alternative bases for the windfall tax published after this paper was written, see IFS, *Options for 1997: The Green Budget*, 1996.

and subject to the conditions provided for by law and the general principles of international law' and that 'the preceding provision shall not, however, in any way impair the right of a state to enforce such laws as it deems necessary to control the use of property in accordance with the general interest, or to secure the payment of taxes or other contributions or penalties.' Although this does give the European Court the right to review taxes, the precedents offer little basis for thinking that it might overturn a windfall tax: in 1988 it rejected the appeal of some Swedish insurance companies against a levy of 7 per cent.[27] There is also the precedent of the retrospective nature of the windfall tax imposed on the banks by the Conservative Government in 1981.[28] Moreover, the utilities would need to assess the public relations consequences of a lengthy appeal to the European Court.

An alternative legal objection may be based on the various prospectuses drawn up at privatisation and for the issue of subsequent tranches of share sales, for example in the National Power and PowerGen sales in 1995.[29] While a Labour Government would wish to argue that it cannot be bound by the decisions of its predecessors, the shareholders would press the argument that successive governments *are* legally bound by the contracts entered into by their predecessors. I am too unversed in legal matters to judge the merits of these two arguments, but enough to be sure that the argument could run for some time.

There is, of course, the possibility that companies might seek to frustrate the windfall tax in some way, as with other taxes. One option that is much talked about is that they may pay out all spare cash in the business, so that the cupboard is bare. One rationale for this, that such action would avoid liability for the tax, is likely to be flawed if, as I have suggested, the tax base is related to the past, not the present, position of the company. But another rationale would be that such actions would leave the company's finances in such a

---

[27] For further discussion, see A. Davies, 'Windfall Taxes and the Law', *The Tax Journal*, October 1995.

[28] This was a tax on the large profits that banks derive in periods of high interest rates from lending out non-interest-bearing deposits (the so-called 'endowment effect'). It was levied as a 2½ per cent tax on non-interest-bearing deposits, and raised £355 million, around £¾ billion in current prices.

[29] However, the prospectuses did include sections describing the attitude of the Opposition.

parlous state that the tax could be levied only by forcing the company to cut supplies, or in more extreme circumstances into bankruptcy. The company could then appeal to the regulator's statutory duty to maintain the viability of the business and the integrity of supply.

I think that this is a highly risky, and therefore unlikely, course of action for a regulated company to pursue. The public could well react adversely to major companies acting in this way to frustrate a clear commitment of a newly elected government. The justification that directors are required to take this course of action because it is in the best interests of shareholders is also questionable, if it undermines the company financially. The historical record shows that bankrupt or financially weak companies are easy targets for nationalisation. Despite its commitment to private ownership and markets, even a Blairite Labour government might find itself tempted to take back into state ownership companies that were in severe financial difficulty as a result of their own deliberate strategy, and if it succumbed might well find public opinion on its side. It would be tragic if privatisation, with all its benefits, was even partially reversed because of the actions of the privatised utilities themselves, but fortunately I do not expect to see this happen.

A more subtle defence available to companies is to pre-announce price cuts ahead of the windfall tax, but simultaneously announce that it will not be possible to implement them in the event that the windfall tax is imposed. There is, of course, a sense in which this is no defence at all, since the company will pay out anyway, either to the customer in price reductions or to the government in taxes. But there may be some benefit in terms of customer loyalty in passing the money to the consumer, as well as some non-pecuniary satisfaction in denying the tax man. And it would greatly reduce the popularity of the windfall tax.

There are two difficulties with this defence. To be most effective, all utility companies would need to pursue it. However, there is both a co-ordination and a free-rider problem with this: there are no obvious mechanisms to get a co-ordinated response, so possibly only a few will proceed; and some companies may well hold back, pleased to see others take the lead. Moreover, companies would have to carry out this defence ahead of knowing the basis of the tax (which companies are included, on what measure the tax would be levied, and the rate) and therefore in ignorance of their company's liability for the tax. They would be exchanging an uncertain tax liability for a certain, and possibly larger, price reduction. This probably means that, if this strategy is pursued, it will be done quite cautiously on a limited scale. But then it would be possible for the authorities to respond by setting the tax to yield a greater amount, and then to allow a tax credit against price cuts over and above those required by the regulator.

In addition to these technical, feasibility and tactical issues, there are the economic consequences of a windfall tax, both in terms of equity and efficiency. One equity issue is whether the main argument for the windfall tax, that is, the charge of past excess profits, is a valid one, or whether returns were reasonable for making unusual improvements in efficiency. Here I think that there is widespread acknowledgement that profits were unduly large, at least in some sectors, for the reasons discussed above.[30] But there is also the point that shares have changed hands since privatisation, so that current shareholders who pay the tax are not necessarily those who received the earlier benefits; this may mean some inequity, though shareholders will have discounted some of the risk. Moreover, unless all privatised companies are included in the coverage of the tax (and this has neither been proposed nor may be feasible), some gains from privatisation will be taxed while others will not.[31] In addition, there are equity considerations involved in taxing the *ex post* profits arising from *ex ante* risky investments: since privatisation, the shares of some utilities have risen while others have fallen, so that the gains of the whole utility index against the FTSE have not been spectacular.

A frequent objection to a windfall tax is that it will dull incentives for efficiency gains and increase the cost of capital for the utilities, to the detriment of the consumer in the future. If the levying of the tax leads to the expectation that windfall taxes will be levied again if profits are high, then our earlier discussion of the consequences of profit-sharing is immediately relevant: the incentives to raise

---

[30] For a view on this from someone very involved in privatisation and regulation, see C. Foster, 'The Performance of Regulation', paper presented to the British Association for the Advancement of Science, September 1996.

[31] In particular, the tax would not include many management buy-outs, the source of some of the spectacular gains that have attracted public criticism.

efficiency will be reduced and a higher return will be expected on risky investments.[32]

However, I am somewhat sceptical of these incentive effects. Labour has been explicit that the tax will not be repeated, and there will be a very strong incentive for this commitment to be honoured to avoid a sharp loss of credibility with the business community. Moreover, as I have argued above, the justification for the tax is based on conditions that will not recur. It is significant that a trawl of the literature on windfall taxes shows much written on the effects of windfall taxes on oil reserves, where the volatility of commodity prices means that gains (and losses) are endemic, but not on other applications of windfall taxes. It may be significant that, while there are papers that argue the undesirable features of the tax *ex ante* (unsurprisingly written at the time from within the banking sector), I have found no paper that shows *ex post* any detrimental effects on efficiency, incentives, or the cost of capital resulting from the 1981 windfall tax on the banks. Since academic journals are keen to publish positive results (an ambition that I have never realised is to launch the much-needed *Journal of Negative Findings*), a reasonable deduction is that any such effects were insignificant. It is not obvious why a windfall tax on utilities should be different, particularly since it is unlikely that the utility sector will once again generate the remarkable efficiency gains that we saw in the immediate post-privatisation period.[33]

Security of Supply and the Insurance Market

An important issue for regulation is to ensure that price caps do not encourage reductions in the quality, including reliability, of supply. This issue is currently handled by the regulator who sets quality standards and a schedule of rates for compensating the consumer for

---

[32] In this respect, asymmetric profit-sharing operates like a repeated windfall tax.

[33] There is the question as to whether a Labour Government can do anything to reassure the market further that the tax will not be repeated, beyond stating this categorically and presenting the tax as a correction for the policy errors around privatisation. One intriguing option would be to issue an explicit insurance policy that would refund the original windfall levy in the event that a further tax was introduced that fell in a discriminatory way on the sector. This policy would be hard to define precisely, but a clever merchant bank or consultancy could probably devise an arrangement along these lines that would bind the government. Whether politicians would wish to pursue this option is another matter.

lapses, including, in particular, the interruption of supply. A novel element in the *Vision for Growth* is the suggestion that private insurance markets may play a role in this, by taking over the policing of quality standards. Replacing regulatory enforcement by market enforcement would be a desirable development of the regulatory framework, if it can be made to work.

The suggestion is that the regulator will establish a set of guidelines on quality and continuity of supply, and a scale of financial compensation for consumers when breaches of the guidelines occur. An appropriate scale for compensation will give appropriate incentives for regulated utilities to ensure appropriate supply conditions: not gold-plated supply that guarantees supply in all conditions, however extreme, but that appropriately balances the costs of providing secure supplies against the costs of interruption of supply to the customer.[34]

The concern expressed in *Vision for Growth* is that, despite this schedule of payments, companies might cut maintenance investment to boost profits, despite the risk of supply failure and consequent fines. This is a familiar problem in the context of a fixed-term franchise arrangement. But it could also arise from a perception by the company that integrity of supply is subject to shifting standards, perhaps for political reasons; or because of other broader issues that might give rise to short-termism in corporate decision-making.

The possible option floated in *Vision for Growth* is to require utilities to insure against the need to pay customer compensation. Insurance markets would then set premia reflecting the market assessment of the company's capacity to ensure security of supply, and of other relevant factors, such as climate. This market might then provide an indicator of comparative performance between the utilities.

There are difficulties with this proposal that would need to be overcome if it were to be implemented. *First*, the insurance companies may well lack the expertise to appraise some of the technical factors required to assess integrity of supply, for example in water and electricity. *Second*, not altogether unrelated but more fundamentally, insurance markets may well not be able to cope with such risks, because of what economists call moral hazard. The

---

[34] The efficacy of this depends, of course, on whether the schedule of payments set by the regulator is appropriate.

essential point of this is that it is unwise to insure against risks over which the individual or company has control. Insurance is most feasible against those risks over which one has no control (for individuals, certain illnesses, especially if insurance is taken out when young; for companies, insurance against exchange rate uncertainty or other risks exogenous to the firm).

But insurance markets are rather unlikely to thrive when the insuree has considerable discretion, that is not easily monitored by outsiders, over the possible incidence of the risk for which insurance is sought. A few examples make this obvious. Those who engage in risky life styles are excluded from insurance markets. In personal insurance policies, there are often conditions that exclude alcohol, and other drug, abuse from the coverage of policies. Private unemployment insurance is very limited, both in scope and extent, because of the problem of ensuring that the insured do not abuse such a scheme by deliberately making themselves redundant.

The proposed scheme for insurance against utility supply failures may have the same problem. Insurance, if it arose, may well end up with those companies that observed standards compensating those that did not. Indeed, the obverse of the moral hazard problem is that insurance could reduce the incentive for firms to ensure integrity of supply. If imposed, this could mean excessive premia and the effective compensating the ineffective. Without compulsion, the insurance market may not even appear. If that is so, a Labour Government should think carefully before trying to introduce a better solution to the market. If the market does not work, it may well be because it cannot. In these circumstances, it may well be better to rely on regulatory solutions, rather than quasi-market outcomes. And the regulation of this aspect of utility performance has been receiving the benefit of greater emphasis.

Accountability of Regulators

One recurring theme in Labour Party discussions of utility regulation is the issue of the accountability of the regulators. These are often portrayed as independent operators, accountable to none. This is surely an exaggeration of the true position. Regulators are subject to the law and judicial review; they are answerable to Parliament and are required to report annually (though this line of accountability could be made more effective); and Ministers may guide their decisions.

Indeed, a close scrutiny of the legislation under which they operate reveals a surprising number of means by which Ministers could, if they chose, seek to guide, or even limit, the regulators' decisions. What is interesting is how sparingly such powers have been used. But it would be counter-productive to reintroduce, either directly or through the back door, ministerial review of regulatory decisions.[35] One of the key aims of privatisation was to distance the utilities from political intervention which became intrusive and counter-productive, increasing business uncertainty and inefficiency. Despite the high public profile of the utilities, the present regulatory framework has successfully separated politicians from the regulatory process.

Of course, there may be concern that a new Labour Government may wish to reassert more direct ministerial control over the outcomes of the regulatory process. I think that is unlikely, for three reasons. *First*, it is in the self-interest of politicians to be distanced and insulated from difficult decisions in this area, rather than assuming responsibility.[36] *Second*, over the last 20 years the cumulative effect of public sector down-sizing and of controls on civil service expenditure has been an appreciable erosion of the capacity of the civil service to make ministerial direction effective.[37] Wise ministers will limit their actions to areas where they can really make a difference, rather than second-guess well-informed regulators, and to the issue of general guidelines where appropriate.

Third, Vision for Growth does not argue for greater accountability through more ministerial intervention, but rather through enhanced openness, saying that 'the key to improving the accountability of regulators to all stakeholders in society is through greater transparency'. This emphasis is welcome. Openness in decision-making increases the range of people and interests that can engage in informed debate on regulatory issues. In the rather different area of monetary policy, we have seen the significant effects that have followed from publishing (with a month's delay) the minutes of the

---

[35] See Foster, *op. cit.*

[36] Control without responsibility is not easy to pull off, as we have seen in the case of the prison service.

[37] See C. Foster and F. Plowden, *The State Under Stress*, Open University Press, 1996, for a convincing demonstration of this point.

meetings between the Chancellor and the Governor of the Bank of England. This has introduced greater clarity and predictability into the conduct of monetary policy: the evidence for this is that City commentators now give much greater weight to the economic fundamentals, and rather less to political factors, in analysing prospective monetary policy. On the whole, the regulators have been good at revealing the basis of their thinking and promoting discussion (in this, I think the phrase 'the cult of secrecy' in *Vision for Growth* is unfair), but more can be done.

One suggestion is that each regulator would maintain individual independence and authority, but would work with a 'board of non-executive directors representative of outside interests and voices'. How workable this would be in practice depends on finding people to play this role with the time and ability to master the highly technical issues involved in regulation. It would also depend a lot on the range of interests represented and what is meant by 'representative'. Consumer interests could be represented in gas, for example, by having the head of the Gas Consumer Council as a non-executive director, but this would work less well in other sectors where consumer bodies are currently less independent of the regulator.[38] It would be sensible to have a non-executive director from other non-regulated areas of business, provided high-calibre people can be attracted. It could also make sense to have a non-executive director from cognate regulatory offices: the deputy at Ofgas serving as an non-executive director for Offer and *vice versa*.

I have more difficulty envisaging how the idea of employee representation floated at the 1996 Labour conference would work in practice: it would be awkward to choose a particular union out of several in the industry, and representation from the employees of the dominant incumbent, while easier to organise, would be unsatisfactory in neglecting the employees of other companies in the sector. But a non-executive board along these lines could play a useful role, provided that the regulator retains final executive authority. I certainly think that this is better than other proposals to merge regulators into a single board or college of regulators, which *Vision for Growth* judges to be cumbersome.

---

[38] Though this may be an argument for reform of the bodies representing consumers rather than an argument against the proposal for non-executive representation.

Conclusions

In conclusion, let me consider the different elements of the Labour Party proposals together. As I have made clear, I think there is great merit in the proposals to reform UK competition policy. The proposed reforms will have benefits throughout industry, but in the utility sectors they have the added advantage of allowing price-cap regulation to be removed to the maximum extent. The proposed reform of the institutional arrangements for utility regulation are modest and, on the whole, in the right direction. I see disadvantages in some possible forms of profit-sharing, which would reduce the incentives to make efficiency gains and increase the scope for accounting games. Instead, I would prefer to see an adjustment of the RPI-x system to allow the consumer to derive earlier benefit from efficiency gains without diminishing the incentives for companies to achieve such gains.

The windfall tax also has disadvantages, as do most taxes; but these should not include serious disincentive effects, provided that the tax is seen, as it should be, as addressing defects in the original privatisation settlements. It may also not be the worst outcome for the utilities. It is clear that a new government, of any political persuasion, is likely to adopt new policy measures towards the regulation of utilities. The current regulatory régime is starting to settle down to predictable and fairly rational outcomes. If the choice is between radical surgery on this régime on the one hand, and modest reform accompanied by the windfall tax on the other, then the latter could be the better option. Moreover, that policy combination makes sense insofar as excess profits have been due more to defects in the privatisation settlement than to weaknesses of the regulatory régime. The utilities may well prefer modest reform without the windfall tax, but that may not be a feasible political outcome given current perceptions of excess profits and other policy weaknesses in the past. The main objective should be to establish a regulatory régime that, looking forward, is efficient, fair and accountable.

Additional Reading

Burns, Philip, Ian Crawford and Andrew Dilnot (1995): 'Regulation and Redistribution in Utilities', *Fiscal Studies*, Vol. 16, No. 4, pp. 1-22.

Green, Richard C., and Eli Talmor (1985): 'The Structure and Incentive Effects of Corporate Tax Liabilities', *Journal of Finance*, Vol. 40, No. 4, pp. 1,095-1,114.

IFS (1996): *Options for 1996: The Green Budget*, October.

IFS (1996): *Options for 1997: The Green Budget*, October.

CHAIRMAN'S COMMENTS

Rt. Hon. Sir Christopher Chataway

DAVID CURRIE HAS GIVEN A MOST VALUABLE AND INTERESTING DESCRIPTION and assessment of likely Labour policies towards the utilities. He widened the focus a bit by looking initially at the general structure of competition policy. I have found Bryan Carsberg persuasive on the case for merging the MMC and OFT and for the adoption of a prohibitive approach along the lines of Articles 85 and 86 of the Treaty of Rome. Both ideas are espoused by Labour – now as David Currie said, as rather a new development emphasising the virtues of competition.

The idea of requiring a bidding company to demonstrate that a proposed merger is in the public interest sounds to me like a legacy of Old Labour. Professor Currie had a helpful phrase about the effects of competition being the main criterion nonetheless. If all that is proposed is that the bidder is asked to demonstrate that the merger is not anti-competitive then not much is changed but if one set of shareholders is going to be prevented from buying and another from selling on some subjective assessment of vague public interest notions then it will be a boon for dozy management, for lobbyists and special interest groups, and bad for efficiency.

When it came to the utilities, David Currie has, I think, been treading delicately. He has not said anything that will cause great grief to the Labour Whips in the Lords (no danger of his being cast into outer darkness with Baroness Turner). He has effectively distanced himself from the fierce criticism of the existing regulatory system and downplayed Labour's ideas for changing it. He has also – wisely in my view – sought to excuse rather than to defend the levy.

Like the Sherlock Holmes story about the dog, the most important thing surely in all this is what is not happening. This will be the first General Election in the history of the Labour Party when it is not proposing to nationalise anything. It will be the first General Election in more than 70 years when the two major parties agree that businesses belong in the private sector. That seems to me a good thing and I rejoice in it. But with a bit of caution, because I remember rejoicing at the last election when for the first time both major parties were pro-Europe. But as soon as the election was over large numbers of Conservatives began to occupy the anti-European territory vacated by the Labour Party. How long before the xenophobic tendency in the Conservative Party, cheered on by the *Sun* and the *Telegraph*, begins to attack the German ownership of merchant banks and motor car manufacturers, the French capture of British water and to call in the name of English nationalism for the public ownership of the commanding heights of the economy? But that is fanciful, I hope, and certainly a nightmare for the future.

For the present the Labour leadership has to put as good a face as possible upon one of the bigger U-turns in British political history. In the 1980s and 1990s, businesses accounting for more than 10 per cent of GDP were moved from the public sector to the private – a bigger transfer, I suppose, than that effected after 1945 in the opposite direction – and of course Labour fought it all the way, every single privatisation and usually threatening renationalisation. Now not one is to be brought back. In these circumstance, Labour clearly has to propose something supposedly to remedy what they have always said was dreadful. What is required, realistically, are not reforms of any intrinsic merit but measures which will fulfil a political purpose and not do too much damage.

Judged against that criterion, Labour's proposals for amending the RPI-x system are not too bad. Sharing of profits above a norm would, I agree, be change for the worse – a minor field day for accountants, the problem of sharing losses, some disincentive effect – but it would not be a disaster. The other two suggestions are even more modest and are to an extent employed already by regulators. The CAA has already conditioned BAA's price cap on a variable that will affect profit-performance, namely the ending, if and when it comes, of duty free. A regulator can already require earlier price cuts within the quinquennium where that is thought to be possible. BAA's last régime, for example, started with RPI-8 for two years and finished with RPI-1. But if what David Currie has in mind is that extra voluntary cuts in one quinquennium should somehow be taken into account by the regulator in the next quinquennium, I am not sure that would be in the customers' long-term interests. Because an essential feature of RPI-x, as I understand it, is that the customer from the start of each quinquennium gets the full benefit of all the productivity improvements that have been achieved and it would surely be a pity to muddy that clear water.

The big thing of course is the windfall tax. At £10 billion it would certainly dwarf the also undesirable but popular Conservative levy of 1982 upon the banks. The more carefully Professor Currie looked at it, the harder it became to justify on any respectable basis. The regulators, he says, will be told to disregard the effects of the tax in subsequent price reviews. But of course they could not. If a company is highly geared, saddled with debt as a result of the levy, x will be lower than it otherwise would have been. In part, therefore, this is a tax on the utilities' consumers, which is a rather regressive form of taxation.

The justification is said to be excessive profits. In the cases where the sale price of the asset has subsequently been shown to be low and big capital gains have resulted, Labour looks to be the principal villain of the piece. The Government, using some of the most expert investment banks in the world, has secured from a highly sophisticated market the best price that was going, but built into that price were the political uncertainties resulting from Labour threats to renationalise. Where profits have resulted from huge productivity gains, often far bigger (as David Currie said) than anybody expected, it does not do for Labour to say they ought to have been foreseen, when Labour did not think there would be any.

I am left with the feeling that any attempt to make the tax rational or fair may only make matters worse. David Currie suggests that it might be levied only upon those companies whose shareholders, since privatisation, have in dividends or capital gains beaten the market. That of course would exclude a large swathe of the sector, including BT and British Gas, and if anything like the projected sums were to be raised, would involve a large impost upon the unlucky few. This might include, for example, a well-run successful company like BAA, whose price caps have if anything been set lower than their customers asked.

The only argument for the levy is brute politics. It is the price to be paid for Labour's jettisoning public ownership. It is the least their supporters will wear. It is the last primeval thrash of Old Labour. It is the last ghastly Stag Night binge and it will not, David Currie has assured us, be repeated.

2

TELECOMMUNICATIONS REGULATION: NATIONAL, EUROPEAN AND INTERNATIONAL PERSPECTIVES

Martin Cave

Brunel University

Introduction

THIS PAPER DISCUSSES THE CURRENT STATE OF telecommunications liberalisation at the national and – more particularly – the European and international levels. A focus on the latter may require some justification as the impetus behind UK policy in telecommunications has come almost exclusively from the Department of Trade and Industry and Oftel in the UK. Later developments such as the European liberalisation programme inaugurated by the 1987 Green Paper and the WTO negotiations on telecommunications within the framework of the General Agreement on Trade in Services (GATS) have tended to follow and impose constraints on rather than to drive the process. But seen from Athens or Singapore, things would look quite different. And the significance of European and international initiatives is also huge for UK companies seeking access to overseas markets. There is thus a good case for looking at regulatory developments outside the UK at the moment – the more so because BT and Oftel have reached agreement on licence amendments which will not come into effect for 10 months, creating – subject to the outcome of BT's announced court action on the fair trading condition – a brief lull in the development of domestic regulation.

The paper is organised as follows. I first review the stages of telecommunications regulation the UK has gone through, or is projected to go through. A similar passage seems almost inevitable for followers in the deregulatory process as well, although backwardness may have some compensating advantages in the sense of shortening the birth pangs of history.

In particular, this means that the EU will over the next five or 10 years contain member-states at significantly different levels of the development of competition. In the second section I discuss the implications of this, within the context of proposals to shift the focus of regulation to the European level, through the creation of a Euro regulator, as opposed to placing more or less detailed constraints on national regulatory agencies.

The third section then considers developments within the WTO framework, where participating nations have given themselves until February 1997 to produce a new telecommunications agreement, having failed to meet the original April 1996 deadline. One of the major pay-offs to liberalisation within Europe, and more widely, is the prospect of a decline in international telecommunication charges. The fourth section outlines the well-known deficiencies of the traditional arrangements governing relations between operators in international telephony and examines the degree to which these may be undermined both by new technologies such as call-back and by the regulatory initiatives discussed earlier.

Because of the wide range of issues covered, it may be useful to clarify the structure of the argument. My interpretation of the UK experience is that it provides a pathway towards liberalisation which other European nations are likely to follow, although with varying degrees of enthusiasm. As member-states advance down this route at different speeds, they will require a variety of forms of regulation. A uniform and centralised approach is thus impracticable. Instead, in keeping with the principle of subsidiarity, it is better to have a framework of legislation embodying the degree of detail appropriate to the regulatory issue in question, sustained by effective enforcement. Broadly, the current programme of liberalisation and harmonisation seems well conceived, but doubts about enforcement remain.

Extending the benefits of liberalisation to the world level requires the application of GATS to the sector. The work of the Negotiating Group on Basic Telecommunications, now scheduled for completion in February 1997, may achieve its liberalisation objectives, but its work is complicated by the voluntary nature of countries' participation, and by the need to develop and enforce agreed principles on the regulatory framework. The prospects for success are hampered by the considerable benefits which non-liberalisers can gain at the expense of liberalisers, as a result of the historical development of the payment system for international telecommunications. These create considerable policy dilemmas for early liberalisers.

In preparing this paper I have drawn upon contributions to a workshop on competition, regulation and trade policy in telecommunications, held at the London Business School in May, within the framework of the ESRC's Research Programme on Global Economic Institutions. I cite below the relevant papers, which are published in the December 1996 issue of *Telecommunications Policy*.[1] Also to be found there is a paper by Noam and Singhali,[2] which reviews other international issues in telecommunications regulation.

UK Developments: The Road to Normalisation

I divide UK experience to date into two obvious components – the duopoly period between 1984 and 1991 and a transition period due to end in 1997, when the new price control régime agreed between Oftel and BT comes into effect and when the process of introducing the new fair trading condition (FTC) into all operators' licences begins, replacing – in the case of BT's licence in particular – a variety of more detailed restrictions. I call this third stage 'normalisation'. As noted above, the last development is subject to BT's intended challenge in the courts of the legality of the provision.[3] It is regrettable that a fundamental element in the normalisation programme, accepted – if reluctantly – by BT, might finally founder on a legal challenge: regrettable, because one of the alleged strengths of the UK regulatory system is that it is capable of

---

[1] See M. Cave and P. Crowther, 'Determining the Level of Regulation in the New Telecommunications: A Preliminary Assessment', *Telecommunications Policy*, Vol. 20, No. 10, 1996; P. Holmes *et al.*, 'Telecoms and International Competition Policy', *Telecommunications Policy*, *op. cit.*; M. Scanlan, 'Why is the International Accounting Rate System in Terminal Decline and What Might be the Consequences?', *Telecommunications Policy*, *op. cit.*

[2] See E. Noam and A. Singhali, 'Supra-National Regulation for Supra-National Telecommunications Carriers', *Telecommunications Policy*, *op. cit.*

[3] *Editor's note*: BT's action failed and the FTC was incorporated in BT's licence in early 1997.

generating outcomes based on the substance of the issues rather than upon restrictive legal interpretations.

The chief characteristics of the three stages of regulation can be summarised as follows in terms of: licensing and entry; aggregate retail price control; wholesale prices control; universal service obligations; and restrictions on the structure of prices.

Licensing and Entry

The defining characteristic of the duopoly régime is that the Government committed itself for a period of seven years from 1984 not to license any other competitor than Mercury, which itself accepted certain network roll-out obligations. In its years of grace, Mercury gained only three or four per cent of overall market share, concentrating on the more profitable parts of the market, particularly large firms with substantial international traffic. Since entry was liberalised in 1991, over 150 licences have been granted. The new licensees have in most cases entered niche or specialised markets or have exploited an economy of scope, either with another utility in the electricity industry or, most conspicuously, with cable television.

Although during the transition period the Government licensed certain operators to provide international simple resale (ISR – see below), facilities-based international competition was kept as a duopoly until 1996. The DTI is only now considering more than 40 licence applications to offer this service.

As things now stand, the most controversial restriction on entry now in place relates not to BT's competitors but to BT, which is still prohibited from supplying broadcast services under its main licence, although it is entitled to seek local delivery operator franchises, like other firms. Justified primarily as a device for promoting cable entry, and in a subsidiary way as a means of compensating for BT's inherited advantages such as the lack of number portability and equal access, this policy looks increasingly anomalous as these issues are resolved. The relevant EU body (DGIV) is currently undertaking a study of competition issues concerning the linkage between cable television and telephony throughout the EU. It will be interesting to see the study's conclusions – both on business restrictions and on joint ownership of cable television and telephony networks.

Regulating Aggregate Retail Prices

The RPI-x technique of controlling retail prices has been employed through successive, progressively tougher, price caps since 1984, and is projected to continue from 1997 for what the Director General of Telecommunications has indicated is likely to be the last four years of retail price control. The interesting variation over the period has been the coverage of the cap, which grew as a proportion of BT's revenues from less than a half in the 1980s to a peak of more than two-thirds in the early 'nineties as both private circuits and international calls were incorporated in controls. A key element of the new licence condition from 1997 is that services provided to business customers and to residential subscribers with the largest bills will be freed from control, although in some cases maximum tariffs will be linked to those included in the basket. The new control applying to services purchased by the lowest eight deciles of residential subscribers ranked by bill size will cover less than one-quarter of BT's activity. Because in the past such customers have received relatively little benefit from tariff reduction, their situation is likely to improve in consequence, despite the projected decline in the value of x from 7·5 to 4·5. The composition of the services which they buy, weighted more heavily towards quarterly rentals than is the case for the generality of customers, will also restrict BT's rebalancing possibilities. But the freeing up of prices for business customers and for a significant minority of residential customers is a major step forward.

Control of Wholesale Prices

In the duopoly period, Oftel determined, on a fully allocated historic cost basis, interconnection charges for a small number of BT's network services. After 1991, as a variety of new entrants sought interconnection, Oftel undertook a programme of unbundling interconnection services and imposed a standard price list. It also required BT to undertake accounting separation between its network and retail activities.

The key proposed changes from 1997 are that Oftel will control the price of BT's network services through a price cap arrangement, rather than through the determination of individual prices. Second, the level of the price control will be determined on the basis of the recovery of costs measured in a forward-looking incremental manner, with a mark-up to take account of common costs, rather than on historic costs. In addition, some network services, deemed to be competitive, will be excluded from the cap.

Universal Service Obligations

To date, BT has borne all the costs of the universal service obligations (USOs) imposed in its licence, except to the extent that other operators have had network roll-out obligations and limited obligations to supply. In 1997, however, Oftel may propose that the costs of such obligations should be shared by all operators in the industry through the creation of a universal service fund. This important development has been achieved in a speedy and uncontroversial manner, as the relatively small net cost of the USOs has been recognised.

Controls on Pricing Structure

Until 1991 BT was restricted from offering differentiated prices, especially quantity discounts. From 1991 these restrictions have been only gradually relaxed. Despite this, the company was able quickly to undermine Mercury's price advantage with large customers. From 1997, it is proposed that while the general prohibition on 'undue discrimination' should remain, other detailed limitations will be replaced by a single fair trading condition, under which the Director General will have the power to prohibit practices which would be considered anti-competitive within the framework of European competition law. Draft guidelines were published earlier indicating what approach would be adopted in reviewing individual practices.

These changes amount to a significant programme of deregulation. A crude quantitative index of the complexity of regulation is provided by the size of BT's licence. The inaugural licence, intended for the duopoly period, amounted to something like 70 pages. During the transition period, the licence has peaked at something like 200 pages. The bonfire of controls associated with the substitution of the FTC for many more detailed conditions will reduce it to something like its original length.

Two questions arise from this summary history and projection forward of UK experience. The first concerns the appropriateness and, more particularly, the timing of the proposed changes. The general contours of the deregulatory proposals – fully liberalised entry, withdrawal from retail price control, incentive regulation of network bottlenecks, sharing USO costs, less intervention in detailed pricing decisions – are sensible enough. But this leaves open the question of timing. BT still has a huge market share – in 1995, 95 per cent of lines, 94 per cent of local calls, 83 per cent of national calls and 70 per cent of international calls. Fortunately, however, the relative shares of BT and its competitors in terms of capacity are much more favourable to the latter, indicating greater potential for competition than current market share data show, and in particular suggesting that barriers to entry may be limited.

The second question is more directly related to the thrust of this paper. Within the European Union, some member-states have achieved levels of liberalisation at least as great as that of the United Kingdom. Others have more or less clear policies for implementation in 1998. Still others, largely but not wholly made up of countries with derogations from the 1998 deadline, are at a much earlier stage – some of them toying with the idea of a duopoly as an interim stage. Clearly countries in each of these categories require a different form of regulation, and this would render far more difficult any centralised system of detailed regulation from Brussels.

Euro Regulation

In 1994 the Bangemann Report on Europe and the Global Information Society[4] famously recommended 'the establishment at the European level of an authority whose terms of reference will require prompt attention'. In fact, however, the report only called for 'the minimum of regulation needed, at the European level, to ensure the rapid emergence of efficient European information services and structures'. It then specified that the authority would need to address

> 'the regulation of those operations which because of their community-wide nature need to be addressed at the European level and indicated that what was required was the elimination of unequal conditions of network access and the achievement of transparency and non-discrimination in interconnection charges'.

---

[4] M. Bangemann, *Europe and the Global Information Society: Recommendations to the European Council*, 1994.

Little specific about the regulatory authority has since emerged. Instead, attention has focussed on creating a regulatory and legislative basis for liberalisation and harmonisation from 1998, based upon existing institutions. However, a new high level Industry Advisory Group on the Information Society has been set up, supported by three working groups including one on the regulatory framework. Little is known about these discussions which are still at an early stage. Nonetheless, it is instructive to go back to first principles, as I now intend to do, following some joint work with Peter Crowther.[5]

Since the incorporation of subsidiarity into the Treaty on European Union in 1992, any discussion of the appropriate allocation of powers within the EC Treaty must have regard to this principle. In essence, it means that, for a task falling within concurrent powers to be allocated to the Community, two conditions must be satisfied: *first*, that the objectives cannot be sufficiently achieved by the member-states and that they can be better achieved by the Community; and *second*, connected to but analytically separate from this, is the requirement that the Community acts in a way proportional to the objectives to be achieved. This relates to the intensity or type of legislation which is issued at the Community level.

For the first part of the subsidiarity question, it is necessary to unravel the meaning of the words 'sufficiently' and 'better'. The social science literature on regulation offers some help in this regard. Accordingly, we identify a number of possible criteria against which judgements of the adequacy or superiority of all types of regulatory arrangements might be made. Essentially these come down to efficiency (substantive and procedural), accountability, and consistency with the Single Market (and other Treaty obligations).

Considerations of substantive efficiency are likely to argue in favour of centralisation where externalities such as radio interference are involved, and in favour of decentralisation where information is held locally and is difficult to communicate. Procedural efficiency also has a number of dimensions. One is that of transaction cost: if the right decision can be taken and enforced once, rather than 15 times, that is most certainly an advantage. Against this, it must be recognised that competition among

---

[5] Cave and Crowther, *op. cit.*

regulators is a discovery process. Regulators from other member-states and the Commission effectively select from alternative policies adopted at the national level. (Here we have to assume that political competition enforces good decision-making.) This is an argument in favour of multiple national solutions.

The third facet of procedural efficiency is that of regulatory capture. Is the probability of capture contingent upon the level of regulation? There are certainly arguments for believing that the form of capture, if it occurs, will vary with the level of decision-making, if only because the balance of forces and lobbying skills in a larger economic unit is likely to be different from that in each of its constituents (the same point has been made in relation to tariffs and other forms of protectionism). There is a further argument here that, in the transition to competition, the power of incumbents in individual countries will be counterbalanced by the desire of those same operators to enter other markets (assuming the effective application of competition laws to mergers and strategic alliances), thus generating a more balanced regulatory structure at a higher level. But this remains a matter for conjecture.

Individual governments and electorates will hold different views on equity, and these may bring them into conflict with a higher level European regulator on matters such as rebalancing. Vogelsang, in his study of Federal versus State Regulation in US telecommunications,[6] notes the same conflicts, which were often resolved in the US case through federal pre-emption. In view of the difficulty of discussing equity, it is better to focus upon accountability, and ask the question: to which group of electors is it appropriate for a regulator ultimately to be accountable? Here the case for national determination is strong, and is supported by the efficiency considerations given above, subject of course to the observations on externalities. It should be noted that while internalising externalities will in fact generate desirable solutions across the Union (depending on the definition of social welfare), it may conflict with national policy preoccupations.

Finally, there is the issue of consistency with other Treaty obligations, notably the Single Market. The whole *raison d'être* of the Union is the creation of a Single Market (previously termed

---

[6]   I. Vogelsang, *Federal vs. State Regulation in US Telecommunications*, WIK Discussion Paper 134, 1994.

common market, and then internal market), to which all member-states are legally committed (Article 3 EC). This may clearly preclude some forms of regulatory decisions, and provides a general yardstick by which individual policies may be judged. For our purposes, we consider the Single Market criterion to be relevant where a particular policy may have a direct or indirect, actual or potential effect on trade between member-states.

Applying these considerations to types of regulatory decision, some fall fairly readily into the centralised or decentralised category. Thus technical issues, such as spectrum allocation, standardisation of interfaces or number portability exhibit substantial externalities. Accountability arguments may suggest that issues of balance of tariffs and of choice of universal service obligations should be decentralised. A uniform approach to some regulatory issues, such as interconnection, may require a centralised approach. Others may not. Throughout, a fairly powerful argument for decentralisation can be found in the likely presence of informational economies: it is unlikely that a central regulator covering 15 or more countries will be able to dispose of information in precisely the same way as locally based regulators.

However, things are more complicated. Taking, by way of example, universal service, accountability factors would strongly suggest that some form of national regulation is most appropriate. However, 'Single Market' or Community concerns can arise due to the way in which universal service is financed. This does not, of course, provide a water-tight argument in favour of regulation at the European level. That might be the case if Europe consisted of a homogeneous group of people, all with identical preferences as to which services should be regarded as falling within a universal service obligation. However, that is not the case; neither is it true that national telecommunications networks are identical in terms of their coverage and technological qualities. Even these factors do not of themselves point unambiguously to a nationally-oriented framework. If the European regulator were perfectly informed about different political preoccupations and values in all the different member-states, then it could do the job as well as any national regulator. Of course, in the real world, the costs of obtaining such information are huge and arguably even impossible due to the spatial effects of a European regulator being located outside the country which it was seeking to regulate.

This prompts a consideration of the second arm of the subsidiarity test – that the Community act in a way proportional to the objectives to be met – which is crucial to the nature of market regulation since excluding some decisions does not necessarily imply that the locus of regulation should be at the Union level. Even if the tasks can be better achieved by the Community, the choice between national and European regulation is not a stark one. Mutual recognition (you recognise our approach and we will recognise yours), co-ordination (general policy agreements on certain directions to be taken) and harmonisation (a set of common standards and/or principles) are well-developed tools of Community policy-making, which befit the demands of subsidiarity.

What we conclude is that the proper question for the majority of regulatory functions is: what is the appropriate type of European input? Assuming that the overriding objective is to create a Single Market in telecommunications, the appropriate question to be answered is the type of regulatory framework which should be sufficient to achieve that aim in the context of all the regulatory functions identified above.

The starting point is to note that some form of basic Community input is necessary, based upon the potential negative effect on trade between member-states of failure to perform any one of the regulatory tasks given in our list above. In practice, this role is fulfilled partly by the competition provisions and partly by framework legislation. It follows that whatever the approach adopted by the member-state, it must not conflict with the aim of achieving an undistorted market for telecommunications services and infrastructure within the EU.

Although this may serve as a floor in terms of European input, the more difficult issue is to determine the functions for which European legislation should extend beyond setting a mere framework for action. In deciding the intensity of this legislation, it is clear that there is a trade-off between the amount of detail at the European level and the scope for action by national regulatory authorities (NRAs). Furthermore, an assessment of this trade-off depends critically upon the assumption made about the possibility of capture of the NRA. Finally, a distinction ought to be made between regulatory issues which are of a medium-term nature and those which can be considered permanent regulatory functions.

If this argument is accepted, then the issue becomes not one of whether regulation should be exercised by a centralised Euro Regulator, but one of how detailed should be the constraints on national decision-taking contained in European regulation.

Peter Crowther and I have attempted to indicate in general terms where upon the continuum from centralised regulation to general legislation at the Community level, the choice should fall in respect of particular regulatory functions. Thus we argue for detailed legislation at the Community level in licensing and restrictions on cross-subsidisation (for transactions costs and competition reasons), and looser regulation for such things as the balance of tariffs and universal service obligations.

It is my impression that this view is widely held and that support for a centralised and all-powerful European regulator is weak. There may, however, be a place for a better articulated system for co-ordinating national regulators. This has, for example, recently been proposed by a BT official, who argues that

> 'a Committee of National regulators, chaired by a Commissioner, meeting regularly could do an enormous amount in helping the exchange of best regulatory practice. Particularly if backed up by some form of Institute charged with advising on norms and measures of effective competition, accounting standards, cost methodology for interconnection etc – in much the same way as the European Environmental Agency in Copenhagen advises on safe SO_2 emission levels'.[7]

This is fortunate because the obstacles in the way of going beyond the existing model of liberalisation and harmonisation are considerable. In particular, the creation of an independent European regulatory authority for telecommunications would almost certainly require a Treaty amendment.

The discussion so far has concentrated on the question of how vertically to allocate regulatory functions. I have argued that framework legislation with a varying degree of detail both fits the demands of subsidiarity and is an efficient solution. It would be wrong, however, to underestimate the problems of enforcement, or

---

[7] L. Stone, *1988 – Business Reality or False Dawn?*, Abstract of Paper to the ITS Conference, Vienna, December 1996.

to deny that some member-states have an appalling record in implementing Directives.

The 'Services' Directive was implemented years late in Spain, Italy, Denmark and the Netherlands, and the Court of Justice has recently issued rulings against a number of countries including Greece for their failure to implement the 1992 ONP Directive on Leased Lines. A regulatory system is only as effective as it is enforceable, and a blind faith in the willingness of member-states to fulfil their duties under the Treaty is at worst misplaced, and at best optimistic. The compliance mechanisms at Community level are weak: a fine can be imposed by the Court of Justice only after the Commission has brought infringement proceedings against the offending country twice, and this takes years. Aggrieved 'entrants' may be able to rely on non-implemented Directives against an operator which is classified as an 'emanation of the state', although damages are not necessarily available, where these are not recognised under national law. A tightening up of compliance is highly desirable. There is also a need for a clarification of the relationship of the ONP system with the competition provisions.

To summarise: as with the arguments surrounding deregulation in the UK, choices have to be made between the competing attractions of certain but detailed regulation and less certain general provisions. The European framework approach prefers the latter, leaving considerable discretion to the national regulatory authorities, which will have to take a detailed view on the meaning of such concepts as 'non-discrimination' and 'cost orientation' when disputes occur. The costs of uncertainty about how these terms will be defined should not be underestimated. However, given the different stages of development at which the sector finds itself in the different member-states, the advantages of the framework approach appear to outweigh the disadvantages, if enforcement can be made at least adequate.

The next question is whether a similar approach can be applied at the world level. This leads us to a consideration of the role of the newly-created World Trade Organisation (WTO).

International Competition Policy and the WTO

I now turn to developments outside Europe. The creation of the World Trade Organisation (WTO) as a successor to GATT, and the extension of the coverage of trade policy from goods to services through the General Agreement on Trade and Services (GATS), have introduced a new regulator onto the scene. As Holmes *et al.* put it,[8] they effectively turn competition and anti-competitive conduct into trade issues.

Tuthill[9] summarises the role of the GATS as follows:

'As a formal legal instrument the GATS consists of two parts: the Article and Annexes which contain obligations, disciplines, exceptions and definitions and members' schedules which contain market access and national treatment commitments on specific services. The obligation not to discriminate among Members, called most-favoured nation (MFN) treatment, is, as in the GATT, the linchpin of the Agreement, giving it a truly multilateral character rather than that of a repository for bilateral arrangements. The commitments in the services schedules, like those in schedules of tariff concessions on goods, are legally bound contractual obligations of Members to guarantee specified levels of liberalization to their trading partners.'

The GATS identifies four modes of supply for services – consumption abroad, commercial presence, movement of natural persons and cross-border trade. It recognises that, for services, the chief means of cross-border transit would increasingly become telecommunications. This explains the priority given to telecommunications in implementing the GATS.

The Negotiating Group on Basic Telecommunications (NGBT) was established to deal with market opening measures for basic telecommunications, when agreement eluded the negotiators in Marrakesh in 1994. In agreeing the GATS, member-states agreed a framework of rules that would apply to the services that were to be liberalised and committed themselves to deciding what services would be liberalised at a second set of negotiations initially due to end in 1996, but extended to February 1997 for reasons discussed below.[10] The procedure operates as follows. Member-states must offer a schedule of services they propose to liberalise. They are free to offer or not offer what they wish, but once an area is

---

[8] This section draws closely on P. Holmes *et al.*, *op. cit.*

[9] L. Tuthill, 'Users' Rights? The Multilateral Rules on Access to Telecommunications', *Telecommunications Policy*, March 1996.

[10] *Editor's note*: agreement at the WTO was reached in February 1997.

scheduled and the schedule agreed, then liberalisation must be extended to all partners, regardless of their schedule, under the MFN rules.

By the original April 1996 deadline, 48 governments accounting for approximately 90 per cent of world telecoms revenue had made offers. The key issues in dispute were terms and conditions governing access to networks, safeguards against anti-competitive behaviour and foreign ownership. The United States was the key to the success of the negotiations, yet it was concerned about the possibility of asymmetric access. The Federal Communications Commission (FCC) dealt with this by introducing an 'effective competitive opportunities test'. This required that a foreign market must exhibit the potential before competition for the carrier from that market was allowed entry into the market for US international services. In the NGBT negotiations, the US framed its revised offer of February 1996 in terms of reciprocity. It offered access to all of its telecoms markets, but demanded reciprocity in the form of improved offers from other countries regarding access to markets. It also called for a 'critical mass' of offers on the question of access if the US offer were to stand. The absence of such an 'undefined' critical mass led to the agreement between the EU and the US to put the deadline back to February 1997. At the end of 1996, newspaper reports suggested that some progress towards an agreement had been made.

In the course of the earlier negotiations, the WTO prepared a reference paper setting out definitions and principles for the regulatory framework of basic telecommunication service.[11] According to Holmes *et al.*[12] this paper appears to represent a degree of consensus among the main actors. The section on interconnection requires that interconnection is provided:

a. under non-discriminatory terms, conditions (including technical standards and specifications) and rates and of a quality no less favourable than that provided for its own like services or for like services of non-affiliated service suppliers or for its subsidiaries or other affiliates;

---

[11] WTO Reference Paper, April 1996.

[12] *Op. cit.*

b. in a timely fashion, on terms, conditions (including technical standards and specifications) and cost-oriented rates that are transparent, reasonable, having regard to economic feasibility, and sufficiently unbundled so that the supplier need not pay for network components or facilities that it does not require for the service to be provided; and

c. upon request, at points in addition to the network termination offered to the majority of users, subject to charges that reflect the cost of construction of necessary additional facilities.

The reference paper also proposes that a service supplier requesting interconnection with a major supplier should have recourse to an independent domestic body to resolve disputes regarding interconnection terms. As Holmes *et al.* point out, the proposals in many ways replicate the EU's 1995 ONP Directive. However, there is no equivalent of DGIV to oversee the process, and unsatisfied entrants would have to seek recourse under the WTO disputes procedure.

International Telephone Charges and the Transition to Liberalisation

One of the major pay-offs to telecommunications liberalisation achieved through competition and trade policy is cheaper international telecommunications charges. The annual volume of international voice traffic in 1996 has been projected as 65 billion minutes. This is an area where technical progress has enormously reduced costs, yet tariffs have not come down proportionately. Scanlan estimates[13] that the excess profits on international voice traffic amounted in 1996 to US $38 billion – more than 50 cents per minute. These excess profits are, of course, typically used to subsidise domestic services. But, because demand for international telecommunications services is generally regarded as being more price elastic than demand for domestic services, the resulting welfare loss is considerable.

At the heart of the international telecommunication system lies an arrangement whereby the operator originating the call remunerates

---

[13] Scanlan, *op. cit.*

the operator terminating it. The current system started many decades ago in an era of public monopolists. Remuneration was based upon the two operators setting an accounting rate, notionally based upon the costs of a call. Those costs consisted of conveyance to the international gateway, use of the international circuit, which was often jointly owned by the operators, and termination. The originating operator would make a payment to the terminating operator, known as the settlement rate, which was almost invariably half the accounting rate. When traffic was balanced in both directions, payments cancelled out and no money changed hands. In other circumstances, the operator originating more calls would make a net payment to its partner. When the call used facilities owned by an intermediate operator, a transit fee was paid. Within Europe

TABLE 1
**Selected Accounting Rates Between US and UK and
Other Countries
(SDRs* per minute)**

	UK (BT)		US**	
	1991	1996	1991	1996
Belgium	0·41	0·30	1·0	0·4/0·6/0·8
France	0·33	0·25	1·0/0·8	0·4
Germany	0·42	0·15	1·0	0·2
Greece	0·49	0·42	1·5	0·9
Italy	0·41	0·39	—	0·4
Portugal	0·51	0·42	1·2	0·65/0·5
Spain	0·41	0·42	1·5/1	1·2/0·7
Sweden	0·41	0·23	0·5	0·1
UK	—	—	0·68/0·5	0·3
USA	—	0·25	—	—
Australia	0·07	0·59	0·7	0·4
Japan	1·40	1·00	1·0	0·6
New Zealand	—	0·60	1·4	0·3

Source: Oftel, FCC
*1·065 SDR = £1 in June 1996.
**Where two or more rates are shown, they correspond to
   different times of day.

and the Mediterranean basin a different and more cost-related procedure known as the TEUREM rate system was employed.

Accounting rates are agreed between pairs of operators, and normally not disclosed. The FCC has, however, required US operators to disclose accounting rates for many years and in 1995 Oftel first published UK rates with OECD countries, for 1991 and 1995. 1996 data (see Table 1) suggest not only that rates are high in relation to the sum of the domestic cost of call termination and half the cost of the international circuit borne by the terminating operator, but also variable in ways unlikely to be justified by cost differences. Thus the US rate with Japan is nearly twice that with New Zealand, and the UK rate with Greece and Spain twice those with Germany or Sweden. The data also show that Greece receives twice as much for terminating a call from the US as it does for terminating a call from the UK.

The data thus confirm what is universally acknowledged to be the case, that the link between accounting rates and costs is a tenuous one. Indeed, it is simple to show that negotiations over the accounting rate between two profit-maximising monopoly operators will lead to settlement rates which diverge considerably from cost, and vary from country pair to country pair.

A stylised version of how this might happen is as follows. The operators engage in a two-stage game, in the first stage of which they negotiate an accounting rate, and in the second stage they set their tariffs or collection rates. I assume that negotiations over the accounting rate are based upon the presumption that the settlement rate is half the accounting rate; this assumption requires justification,[14] but it does reflect current behaviour.

In these circumstances, each operator will have a desired optimal accounting rate. In determining this rate, the operator – if unconstrained by regulation – will strike a balance between the profits available to it from terminating a call (causing it to favour a high rate) and the desire to earn profits on outgoing calls (causing it to prefer a low settlement rate). It will take account of the fact that, in respect of potential profits from call termination, its partner will treat the settlement rate as an element of cost. Thus an operator

---

[14] See M. Cave and M. Donnelly, 'The Pricing of International Telecommunications Services by Monopoly Operators', *Information Economics and Policy*, No. 8, 1996.

with no outgoing traffic will not seek an infinite settlement rate, because that would choke off all incoming traffic. Instead, it will prefer a rate which, when factored into the partner's collection rate as an element of cost, maximises its profits on incoming calls.

These calculations made by operators of their optimal accounting rates will take account of the complexity of demand for international telecommunications services. Thus demand for calls from one country to another, as well as depending upon the conventional magnitudes, such as price and income, will also depend upon the volume of incoming calls and on the difference in the collection rates in both directions. The former effect (reciprocity) operates because a call in one direction may elicit a responding call in the other. The latter (call reversion) arises because interlocutors may agree that the call will be initiated at the end where the collection rate is lower.

Once the operators have computed – or, more realistically, approximated – their optimal accounting rates, they will then negotiate over an agreed rate. It is easy to show that, as costs fall, each will desire a lower rate. Since mutual agreement is necessary, the balance of power in the negotiation is thus likely to reside with the operator wishing to maintain the current rate, or seeking a smaller reduction in it than its partner. This will be the operator with the balance of incoming traffic. The model thus suggests that the downward trend of costs will lead to a decline in accounting rates, but with one operator (that with the balance of outgoing traffic) always seeking lower rates. That operator, or its government, may speed up the process if it can exercise leverage in the negotiations by linking them to other issues.

The system described above has transparent weaknesses. The first is that the settlement rate, a crucial element in an operator's decision about collection rates, tends to be determined at the higher of the levels desired by the pair of operators. Secondly, the process exhibits double marginalisation. The first margin arises when the operator terminating the call seeks to build in to the settlement rate a margin on the costs of call termination. That inflated rate is then taken as an input price by the originating operator in setting its collection rates. As a result of both of these considerations, collection rates are higher than they would be under a system in which rates in both directions are determined by a single end-to-end monopolist. This arrangement would eliminate the double marginalisation through vertical integration.

How might these problems be remedied? In the first place, competition at both ends of the route would bring both termination charges and collection rates into line with costs.[15] However, a country which liberalised entry itself, faced by a monopolist, would suffer. First, the monopoly operator would be able to exploit the existence of competing terminating operators to bring its termination costs down, while continuing to exploit its monopoly power to maintain a high rate for terminating calls from the liberalising country. (This is known as 'whipsawing'.) Second, the monopolist could establish its own operation in the liberalising country, and channel its outgoing calls to that operator, thus collecting for itself all the profits implicit in the settlement rate. Third, competition in the liberalising country will reduce the cost of outgoing calls, and, through call reversion, give the monopoly operator a still greater incentive to keep the accounting rate high, thus increasing its profits from call termination.

Governments or regulators in liberalising countries have responded to the first problem by introducing regulations which require 'parallel accounting', an arrangement whereby settlement rates agreed with one operator must be available to all. This prevents whipsawing. The second problem can be eliminated by requiring proportionate return, an arrangement whereby incoming traffic from any country must be allocated to competing operators in the proportions in which they originate traffic to that country. Proportionate return in a competitive environment may bring collection rates down below the settlement rate as each operator knows that more outgoing calls will entitle it to terminate more (highly profitable) incoming calls.

The third problem is, however, more intractable. Up to now, the evidence, such as it is, suggests that call reversion is not a major factor. However, the development of new services such as call-back or calling cards might make this a more serious problem in the future. These enable a subscriber in Country A to call a subscriber in Country B, but be billed by the operator in Country B, or to call a subscriber in Country C, and still be billed by the Country B

---

[15] K. L. Yun *et al.*, 'The Accounting Rate Division in International Telecommunications: Conflicts and Inefficiencies', *Information Economics and Policy*, 1997.

operator. They thus introduce competition among operators in different countries.

It is thus clear that unilateral liberalisation can cause problems for the liberalising country, and that the imposition of parallel accounting and proportionate return is not enough to solve the problem. The solution is to break the monopolistic element in the accounting rate system by somehow bypassing excessive settlement rates exacted by operators exploiting their market power.

One possible response is for an operator simply to refuse to pay the balance to its partner. This approach has been adopted in a number of instances. In one, an American operator refused to make payments to another operator. In retaliation, the latter interrupted a proportion of calls to the first operator, with a message saying that they were not being completed because of the latter's failure to pay its bills. The debt was quickly settled. In another instance, communications between two countries were cut off for a period. A third dispute has taken place between France Telecom and Telia with unclear results. The lessons of these conflicts are uncertain, but it seems to be difficult for an operator with substantial out payments simply to resolve the problem through unilateral actions.

A second approach is to exploit least accounting rate routing. This is illustrated in Figure 1, taken from Scanlan.[16] Rather than send traffic directly from A to C, the operator in A sends the call via Country B, at a charge equal to B's settlement rate with C, handing the call over to the operator in Country C for termination along with B's other traffic. The operator in A in such circumstances will pay B a transit rate, which may be different from the settlement rate for calls terminated in B. To the extent that several countries may play the intermediate role of B, there may be scope for competition to drive down the transit rate. Although under ITU rules, the operator in B should disclose the original source of the traffic, in practice that may not happen. On the contrary, many operators, and some governments, seek to establish themselves as hubs, deliberately attracting traffic from countries such as A in order to provide a relatively cheap route to higher accounting rate countries such as C.

---

[16] Scanlan, *op. cit.*

Figure 1
Least Accounting Rate Routing A to C

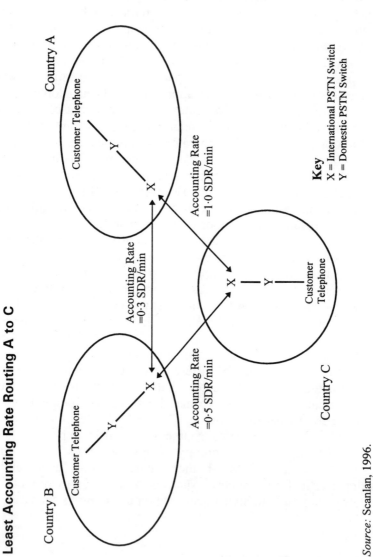

Source: Scanlan, 1996.

However, there appears to be a reluctance on the part of monopoly operators to exploit the system in this way. And it is comparatively simple for the operator in C to take counter-measures. It simply has to maintain a consistently high level of accounting rates with all partner countries, thus foreclosing alternative routes.

A variant on this approach would be for the operator in A to break out into the PSTN in B, and then pay the collection rate from B to C. This might be cheaper than the direct route to C, if competition among operators in B had driven collection rates to C down to low levels, for the reason noted above that proportionate return entitles an operator delivering more calls to C to terminate more calls from C at a highly profitable settlement rate. Taken to the limit, this competition would reduce B's welfare, demonstrating that 'hubbing' is not uniformly desirable.

A third response is to license international simple resale.[17] An ISR operator does not own facilities itself, but collects traffic at one end of an international route, conveys it to another country on an international leased circuit, and uses the facilities of another operator in that country to terminate the call. Where both domestic ends are completed on leased lines, no use is made of the PSTN, and we observe something akin to a virtual private network operating on an international scale and involving two operators. When the PSTN is used at both ends, two-end break out is said to occur. Where the PSTN is used at one end only, normally the terminating end, one-end break out occurs.

The point about the ISR is that it bypasses the accounting rate system, since the operator pays a standard 'domestic' rate to the PSTN for terminating (more rarely delivering) the call, thus bypassing the settlement rate. It is a matter of some importance whether the ISR operator can buy access to call termination services at retail or wholesale rates or whether, in the latter case, it has to pay any access deficit contribution. However, because settlement rates in many instances exceed the domestic retail tariff, ISR can be profitable, provided the price of international leased circuits is controlled.

---

[17] See M. Cave, 'The Economic Consequences of the Introduction and Regulation of International Telecommunications Services', in D. M. Lamberton (ed.), *Beyond Competition: The Future of Telecommunications*, Elsevier, 1995.

ISR is essentially an arbitrage operation, and its existence and effects are governed by the regulatory approach adopted towards them. In the UK, ISR has been permitted, but only on routes where equivalent access to the PSTN at tariff is offered at the other end. The purpose of this is to avoid one-way bypass of the accounting rate whereby Country A prohibits ISR and exacts a settlement rate on all incoming traffic from Country B, while liberalising Country B allows international traffic to enter its PSTN without payment of the settlement rate.

The existence of ISR between any two countries increases the scope for arbitrage of the accounting rate system through a practice sometimes known as 'refile' – a combination of ISR and conventional arrangements. This is illustrated in Figure 2, in which Countries A and B permit ISR traffic between them. The operator in A will then have enhanced incentives to send traffic to C via B, profiting from the combination of a low ISR rate between A and B and a relatively low collection rate for calls between B and C. To this extent, refile has the advantage of putting greater pressure on the accounting rate system through arbitrage. Moreover, the arrangement is symmetrical in that the operator in C can exploit a similar opportunity for the conveyance of traffic from C to A.

However, this symmetry is undermined if B establishes a symmetrical relationship with A, permitting ISR in both directions, but offers C the advantage of an asymmetrical relationship, in which traffic from C can pass through B to A, gaining the benefit of ISR on both links, while C forbids break-out onto the PSTN on its traffic from B, and exacts a settlement rate. In such circumstances, the operator in C benefits at the expense of the operators in A and B. In reality, A might be the US, B the UK (if it permits one-way ISR) and C France (prior to 1998).

This discussion illustrates some of the pitfalls on the way to liberalisation. It is an illustration of the 'optimal tariffs' literature of the 1950s. That literature demonstrated that while free trade normally generated higher economic welfare than universal tariffs, a single country with market power could enhance its own welfare in a world otherwise characterised by free trade by levying tariffs, ideally differentiated by each of its trade partners on the basis of cost and demand conditions. The current system of accounting rates provides a perfect illustration of the scope for such sophisticated

Figure 2
Accounting Rate By-Pass (A to B) Combined with Least Accounting Rate Routing for B to C

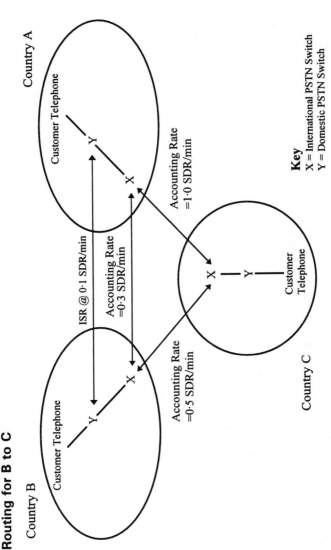

Source: Scanlan, 1996.

conduct, tempered by opportunities for arbitrage through transit and refile arrangements.

Within the EU, the euthanasia of the accounting rate system can fairly confidently be predicted from 1 January 1998, when ISR will be permitted. On the international scale, one of the pay-offs from the success of the WTO will be an equivalent liberalisation, leading to a more general collapse of the system. Unfortunately, however, hold-out countries still have scope either to decline to participate, or to delay the implementation of liberalisation. International traffic flows are so valuable that incentives to stay out, or to break the rules, are strong.

From a tactical point of view, countries have the option either of promoting the liberalisation process by unilateral action, or of insisting that any concessions are matched more widely. In any particular set of circumstances, either approach might be preferable. One of the complications of the present arrangements, however, is that one country (B in the example above) can shift the cost of some of its liberalising measures (such as permitting bypass on non-equivalent routes) to another country A. This naturally tends to exacerbate relations between the two countries. This re-emphasises the importance of the multilateral approach reflected in the EU agreement and the WTO intentions. Unfortunately, in the case of international telecommunications, the path to heaven is paved with ill intentions.

Conclusions

The conclusions of this paper are fairly optimistic and I recognise that I may be accused of adopting the role of Dr Pangloss. In the UK experience of telecommunications liberalisation I have identified a relatively disappointing period of duopoly, followed by a turbulent period of transition in which regulation became intense and highly interventionist. However, this appears to have borne fruit, in the sense that plans for 1997 involve a substantial degree of deregulation, with Oftel seeking to reconfigure itself as a competition authority rather than as a heavy-handed regulator. Doubts can be expressed about the timing of this move, but its general direction seems wholly appropriate. The prospect of abandoning retail controls entirely from 2001 is an appealing one, but the likely continuation of network price controls, even through the more decentralised mechanism of a price cap, may well prolong Oftel's life as a specialist regulator for some years thereafter.

At the European level too, I have identified a fairly sensible balance between centralisation and decentralisation of the regulatory process, consistent both with the principle of subsidiarity and with the different stages of deregulation at which various member-states find themselves. As always within the EU, however, there are serious doubts about enforcement.

I have also suggested, following Holmes *et al.*,[18] that the new player in the regulatory régime, the WTO, is seeking to adopt broadly the same kind of approach as the EU at a world level, laying down certain general rules for the definition of anti-competitive conduct. However, there are a number of problems. *First,* participation in the arrangements is essentially voluntary. *Second,* the 'rules' are still very general and under-developed. *Third,* the enforcement mechanism still has to be tested. However, the emergence of the WTO as an international competition regulator in telecommunications is an encouraging sign.

These considerations suggest that a broadly satisfactory and pro-competitive system of regulation in telecommunications is in prospect, at national, European and world levels. But the process of arriving at this Nirvana is likely to be quite difficult and painful. In particular, non-liberalising countries appear to have the capacity to take serious advantage of liberalisers in the field of international telecommunications even if all benefit from liberalisation compared with its opposite. There is a risk that this may put a brake on progress.

---

[18] Holmes *et al.*, *op. cit.*

Additional Reading

Cave, M. (1996): *The Evolution of Telecommunications Regulation in the UK,* Paper delivered at the European Economic Association 11th Annual Congress.

ITU (1995): Trade Agreements on Telecommunications: Regulatory Implications, Report of the 5th Regulatory Colloquium, 6 – 8 December.

OECD (1995): *International Telecommunication Pricing Practices and Principles: A Progress Review,* Paris: OECD.

CHAIRMAN'S COMMENTS

Sir Bryan Carsberg

THIS WAS A WIDE-RANGING AND ELOQUENTLY DELIVERED PAPER; a splendid basis for discussion. On a light-hearted note I enjoyed the characterisation of the burden of regulation in terms of the number of pages of the licence. I must confess, I also enjoyed your teasing of Jonathan Rickford for his drafting of the UK Telecommunications Act, not to mention BT's licence. No doubt he will defend himself in due course.

You began with a fascinating review of the UK scene, reminding us among other things that it has been a particularly interesting year, in which we saw the BT agreement with Oftel covering price control and the regulation of anti-competitive practices. Until the last moment, I believed that BT would not make the agreement with Oftel, because the controls on anti-competitive behaviour that Oftel were seeking in the licence seemed to me to give an extraordinary amount of power to Oftel. You might feel that the way it was settled, with the agreement that BT would undertake a legal challenge to the approach, but agree subject to that, was a clever way of resolving the issue at the end of the day. How clever it was depends on what one thinks BT's objectives and legal assessment were. It would be interesting to hear comments on that.[1]

On the UK scene, Martin Cave brought out the balance of regulation and competition. This has been the long-running controversy ever since we started with privatisation in 1984. If you are right that we are now moving to a stage where we can have more open competition (both in the sense there are many more people who are ready and able to undertake that competition and that the regulatory régime is facilitating it) by adopting a more *laissez-faire* approach, then the rather more restrictive approaches we went through were well justified. It was always my view that the end purpose was to get as much competition as possible. One interpretation of what has happened would be that it worked out

---

[1] *Editor's note*: The judgement was handed down in favour of Oftel, December 1996.

rather well. Others might think, of course, that we could have got there much sooner or much better by a different track.

Now that there have been the experiences you described, there might well be particular attention to different approaches to competition. One approach is to have competition among networks. This was part of the original UK intention: it was probably an important motivator of government policy then, although that does not imply that the government thought out very clearly how to achieve it and how much was really possible. Another approach would have been to concentrate in the early stages on liberal access to the single network that existed.   That was not followed wholeheartedly in the original developments of liberalisation of network services, as Michael Beesley, whose advice was to follow this path, will certainly remember very well.[2]

A rather restricted view of liberalisation was taken. A ban was put on simple resale which would allow third-party-voice-telephony over leased networks. I well remember the agonies with which we debated the eventual lifting of that ban in 1989, but if we had gone originally for more open access with more competition over the network, would that have inhibited the development of network competition? Would that have been a good or a bad thing? At the moment the outcome certainly looks very encouraging in that many players are interested in engaging in some form of network competition.   As Martin said, the market share of BT is still very high. The financial modelling that we did in Oftel, and in which Martin participated, makes one question just how far network competition can go.

Over the longer term, will either enough actual competition or enough potential competition allow a rather relaxed view of regulation to be taken, leaving it to basic competition policy? In my early days at Oftel, I went to the Houses of Parliament and listened to the debate on the Order following the 1984 Act. Sitting in the gallery there I heard Member after Member say that the best indication of success of this régime would be if Carsberg works himself out of a job, having generated competition to the extent that he became redundant. One of the MPs got so carried away that he said 'and I hope the Director General will take a careful note'.

---

2 M. E. Beesley, *Liberalisation of the Use of British Telecommunications' Network: An Economic Study for the Department of Industry*, HMSO, April 1981.

Feeling a need to respond to this initiative, I pulled out my pencil and made a careful note, whereupon someone rushed over to me and said 'You are not allowed to write in here, sir.' Thus were the wishes of the House frustrated.

The second main theme Martin raised was supra-national regulation, at the European and World Trade Organisation levels. I have always rather shared his scepticism about a Euro-regulator. One point not raised in the lecture was that, given the ways of Europe, a Euro-regulator would be much more subject to political control than in the UK. I do not favour political control: it seems to me to be a negative influence. In my current job of trying to bring common accounting standards to the world, there is very good agreement with the European Commission on the subject; but it is interesting to see how difficult they have found it to come to terms with the private sector standards-setting organisations, which are favoured in countries like the UK and indeed the US and others of the so-called Anglo Saxon tradition. That tradition is very much at variance with the normal way of doing things in countries like France and Germany. When I was at Oftel I noted that, whenever something European cropped up, DTI officials were not at all anxious that Oftel should carry the flag for the UK in Brussels. They always rushed to get in first. There would be a better potential for the European level of regulators if that enforced more competition.

Europe is still far short of a really homogeneous market. This makes for enormous difficulties of regulation One of the issues I had to deal with at Oftel, for example, was about privacy and itemised billing. I was in favour of itemised billing and was quite surprised to find that some people thought that it was not such a good idea because it would give information which might be used in a sinister way. I discovered that attitudes on such an apparently simple-looking question varied enormously around different European countries. In Germany, the view was that to have itemised billing would be 'over our dead bodies'. In the UK there was enough support for it to move forward. This is just one example of a number of issues of that kind making centralised regulation for Europe generally quite difficult. There is merit in the approach (which Martin Cave mentioned a BT official advocates) in bringing together a committee of the regulators from the different countries. Some modest good might come of that. That is akin to what happens in the competition policy field, in which the respective directors-general meet regularly.

At the end Martin Cave turned to the arcane subject of international accounting rates, parallel accounting and so on. If I remember correctly, in the early stages there were severe rules against transiting. These tried to limit the kind of arbitrage arrangements he was describing. In some ways the biggest motive for maintaining the *status quo* was as a disguised form of overseas aid. Typically telephone calls flowed from rich countries to poor countries because rich countries could afford to make more telephone calls so the big monthly cheques from AT & T were valuable contributions to the government budget in those poor countries. I suspect that, up to a point, the wealthier countries were tolerating that system. Presumably technology has made it more and more difficult to sustain. Certainly there must be substantial economic gains to be made from a change. I tried myself to make some modest progress in that direction.

3

COMPETITION LAW: EC AND UK

Thomas Sharpe QC

IN THE INTRODUCTION TO THE PROGRAMME PROFESSOR
Beesley refers to subjects 'which as well as being topical involve
long-standing issues needing resolution of matters of principle'.

The topic, *Competition Law: EC and UK*, is an ideal candidate: it
has been a 'long-standing' and topical issue all my working life. I
started work in the year of UK accession to the EC, which was also
the year of the passage of the Fair Trading Act. *Every* government
since 1973 has attempted to change UK competition law and the latest
technical withdrawal of the draft bill will have come as no surprise to
any of my contemporaries in the DTI.

Since 1973, of course, EC law has, in Lord Denning's memorable
phrase, come up the estuaries of England and now forms an important
element of the jurisprudence of the UK.

Indeed, competition law found in Articles 85 and 86 has gradually
moved from the position as reported in Dr Liesner's review in 1977-
78 – of one of general unfamiliarity – to one, for many companies, of
unwelcome 'over-familiarity'.

Article 85 prohibits all agreements, decisions or concerted practices
between undertakings which have as their object or effect the
prevention, restriction or distortion of competition within the common
market and which may affect trade between member-states. Article
86 prohibits all abuses of a dominant position which may affect trade
between member-states. These Articles are of direct effect in that
they create private rights which national courts and authorities are
obliged to uphold. This means that Articles 85(1) and 86 can be
pleaded in cases before English courts. Thus, the behaviour of the
Milk Marketing Board, BA, the LME, Lloyds of London, various
long-term contracts, brewery agreements, exclusive broadcasting
rights, a welter of intellectual property cases, the selective distribution
practices of leading garment manufacturers, and others, have gone
before the English courts. Many other actions have been started and
subsequently settled.

The Commission usually has parallel jurisdiction and may initiate procedures regarding suspected infringements of Articles 85(1) and 86. Some initiatives are quick and informal and may readily resolve a complaint. Other procedures can be formal, consisting of:

- a written Statement of Objections,

- with a right of reply and sight of all material on which the Commission relies;

- a chance of an oral hearing conducted by a senior independent member of the Commission;

- a role for member-states at the oral hearing and subsequently in the Advisory Committee convened to assist the Commission;

- a written Decision made by the Commission and communicated to the parties;

- a right of appeal to the Court of First Instance (CFI) and Court of Justice (ECJ) under Article 173.

The Commission has the power to take interim measures in order to avoid irreparable harm being inflicted. The Commission has published a (non-binding) Notice on Co-operation between the Commission and the courts of member-states concerning the opportunities open to a national court to seek the assistance of the Commission where uncertainties exist about the progress of Commission investigations, the likelihood of the grant of exemption and other matters.

The interaction between the public (for example, EC Commission) and private enforcement (for example, in national courts) of EC law is still being worked out. Two particular areas of doubt remain:

1. If an agreement has been exempted under Article 85(3) by the Commission, is it open to national authorities to prohibit the same agreement by virtue of the application of a different and higher national standard?

   Recent judicial statements of the Advocate General suggest that the duty, under Article 5 EC, of national courts to do nothing which would render ineffective the uniform enforcement of EC law is so high as to disable a member-state from applying a different or higher standard. In other words, exemption creates rights which national courts are bound to uphold irrespective of a different standard applying under national law.

UK law does not explicitly recognise this; indeed, the UK competition authorities would probably disagree with it as a statement of law, but it does provide a means whereby conflicts between the UK authorities, courts and the Commission can be resolved.

2. What is the status of a Decision of the Commission in the English court? If, for example, a Decision condemns a practice and, in particular, if this is upheld by the European Court of Justice, what more does a Plaintiff have to do in order to prevail in an English Court other than show the court the Decision? Or should the Plaintiff have to prove its case from scratch?

In a recent judgement involving British Plasterboard (BPB), now I believe under appeal, Laddie J. took the view that the courts should do nothing which would involve a potential conflict between the findings of the Commission and the national courts, and that any attempt on the part of a Defendant, like BPB, found by the Commission to have infringed Article 86 and which had been unsuccessful on appeal, was an abuse of the process of the Court. This places a significant premium on the value of a Decision addressed to a (potential) Defendant made by the Commission to potential Plaintiffs.

In certain circumstances, the member-state applies EC law directly. If the Commission has not made appropriate Regulations under Article 87, Article 88 provides for member-states to investigate, make and enforce decisions in respect of both agreements or anti-competitive practices. For example, no implementing EC Regulation exists in respect of air transport services between member-states and countries outside the EC or in respect of international maritime tramp vessel services. UK Regulations were made and came into force in August 1996 to provide for the Secretary of State to request the Director General of Fair Trading (DGFT) to carry out a preliminary investigation whether an agreement or practice is prohibited by Articles 85 or 86.

The Secretary of State may then do nothing or grant an exemption under Article 85(3); alternatively, the Secretary of State may refer the matter to the MMC for it to decide on the applicability of Articles 85(1)(3) or 86. Acting on the Report the Secretary of State may seek to prohibit the infringement or practice, or grant an exemption under Article 85(3). Thus, the Secretary of State and the UK authorities are, in this limited area, applying the law and standards of EC law. I should add that networking agreements between television companies are also subject to scrutiny by the DGFT and MMC using the standards of Articles 85(1) and (3): Broadcasting Act 1990, Schedule 4.

UK national competition laws are substantially unchanged since 1973, save for the advent of 'regulation' – a topic which did not then really exist as a serious academic or practical concern. The following is a brief summary:

- Agreements falling within the Restrictive Trade Practices Act 1976 come before the Restrictive Practices Court. The test of registrability is largely a legal one, capable at times of giving rise to a good deal of sophistry. However, it is probably not correct to accept the simple distinction between EC law as being 'effects' based and UK restrictive trade practices law as 'legally' based. For example, when the Restrictive Practices Court looks at informed 'arrangements' between companies – conduct giving rise to mutual expectations regarding future conduct – the relevant legal test to be adopted under UK law to identify an arrangement and under EC law to identify a 'concerted practice' is very similar in practice.

- The Restrictive Trade Practices Act excludes most vertical agreements by virtue of the requirement for at least two parties to accept restrictions (a vertical restraint can normally be imposed without the other party accepting any restrictions) or by virtue of Schedule 3, paragraph 2, excluding exclusive distribution agreements.

- Anti-competitive practices continue to be governed by the necessity to form a view, on each occasion, of whether or not any practice may be contrary to the public interest, after scrutiny by the DGFT and, possibly, the MMC. If there has been any relevant change, it has been in an acknowledgement that the procedures are lengthy and uncertain: provision is now made for more focused inquiries into specific anti-competitive practices under the Competition Act 1980, as amended, to dispense with the need for a full OFT report as a preliminary step to a reference to the MMC. Extensive provisions have been developed for companies to offer undertakings about future behaviour *in lieu* of a reference to the MMC. This involves the innovation that the DGFT himself forms a view as to the public interest, not the MMC.

- The draft Bill (of 8 August 1996) would, if enacted, have adopted a provision similar to Article 85 in respect of agreements, expanded the OFT's jurisdiction over agreements and left it to a (lay) tribunal to *rehear* any Decision by the DGFT on exemption, subject to judicial review but not appeal.

- As proposed, the Tribunal would have no original jurisdiction: it would rehear DGFT Decisions but could not hear cases privately brought by Plaintiffs for damages for any infringement of any prohibition by companies. These would be heard by the ordinary courts.

- 'Vertical' agreements would be excluded from consideration by the application of a legal test. If such agreements are thought to be problematic, they fall under the existing powers found in the Fair Trading Act 1973 and Competition Act 1980.

As for the anti-competitive practices of individual companies, the plan is to maintain the *status quo*, subject to a new interim power of relief exercisable by the DGFT. If, however, the interim relief were subsequently found to have been wrongfully granted, and the company had suffered loss, no compensation would be payable (in contrast to what would normally be the case in private litigation).

The DTI appears to have decided against the adoption of a prohibition of anti-competitive conduct and the provision of any private remedy for anti-competitive conduct. According to the DTI, there was a need to 'promote further debate'. The key concern lay in the insensitive application of a prohibition and the risk that 'genuinely competitive behaviour' might be inhibited, thus outweighing the potential benefits of greater deterrence that a prohibition system might bring. There was a fear that companies would in the words of the document, 'aim off' or act more cautiously. It was 'clearly' important that this should not take place.

In the context of regulating the utilities the roles of the respective regulators and the MMC are now established, if not immutable. Licence conditions establish the basis on which the companies may trade and, typically, licences contain specific prohibitions over particular situations: for example, Condition 17 in BT's Licence, reflecting s.8 of the Telecommunications Act 1984, prohibits undue discrimination and undue preference.

The Directors General of the respective regulatory offices usually enjoy concurrent powers with the DGFT over the exercise of the DGFT's powers under the 1973 and 1980 Acts. Note that the DGFT has sole powers over agreements: there is only one Register of Restrictive Agreements. These concurrent powers have seldom been used. Do the Directors regard these powers – which place them in the shoes of the DGFT – as adequate, that is, do they share the DTI's view that it would be premature or inappropriate to move away from a permissive system to a 'prohibition' based system? On the basis of two examples which I shall discuss, in gas and in telecommunications, the answer is probably 'no'.

It is a matter of public record that the Director General of Gas Supply wanted to have a general power over anti-competitive practices inserted into the Gas Suppliers Licence earlier this year. It is equally a matter of record that the DTI did not agree. What was inserted in Condition 13 of that Licence is an elaborate Condition which prohibits any Licensee in a dominant position from showing any undue preference or undue discrimination and prevents the setting of charges which are unduly onerous or predatory. The Director General establishes who is 'dominant' (after considering representations made to her). The Condition sets out a provision for 'meeting competition' designed to distinguish between behaviour which may be regarded as predatory and behaviour designed to respond to competitive pressure (and thus avoid the sensitivity that laws would inhibit a competitive response and encourage 'aiming off'). But the Director General does not have the last word: provision is made for a reference to the MMC seeking the removal of the Condition.

In December 1995 the Director General of Telecommunications started the formal process of introducing a general prohibition on anti-competitive practices in BT's licence, with the prospect of the same or similar terms being introduced into other licences. This was seen as a further step in the transformation of the Director General from being an industry 'regulator' to becoming a 'competition authority'. His case rests on his view that:

- existing Licence Conditions are not comprehensive;

- licence modifications follow the event but would not prevent unforeseen anti-competitive behaviour;

- it is impossible to foresee all manifestations of anti-competitive behaviour in advance;

- licence modification is slow and uncertain;

- the emergence of competition requires effective general control of anti-competitive behaviour.

As a result of the inclusion of the Condition in the Licence, the Director General has now obtained a summary power over all anti-competitive conduct, based upon a prohibition. However, unlike Articles 85 and 86, which do not require any prior Decision before a private action can be brought, private actions are not possible unless BT were subsequently to breach an Order made by the Director General.

The assumption of this power by the Director General is something less than an endorsement of the concurrent powers exercisable by the DGT under the 1973 and 1980 Acts. The MMC's role in investigating Telecommunications anti-competitive practices has been eclipsed by Condition 18A.

I note that the DTI, in the March Consultation Paper, at para. 9.13, refers to the Director General's 'vigorous arguments' in favour of the new Condition yet concludes that the

'Government is satisfied that the regulatory regime set up in the Telecommunications Act already provides the right framework for assessing the case for such an extension of powers, with scope for reference to the MMC if agreement cannot be reached ...'.

Where does all this leave us and what should be done?

There is a consensus that the present system of general control is unsatisfactory but, like surfers not venturing forward till they see the perfect wave, nothing happens. As an observer of politics, as well as a legal practitioner, I find it surprising that so much weight should be given to the (apparent) regulatory burden of effective competition laws without emphasising the benefits of effective deterrence and remedies, if only because so many policies are predicated on the existence and maintenance of effective competition.

The weakness of UK competition laws has meant that some companies have shown complete disregard for them. In sectors in which entry barriers are high, little or no import penetration is possible, or where a dominant incumbent has established a reputation for aggression, the existing laws provide:

- no deterrent;

- no firm guide to permissible conduct;

- no compensation to those who have suffered loss;

- no fast system of interim relief; and allow for

- the possibility of conflict between UK and EC outcomes.

Effective deterrence and compensation are linked. If a party feels aggrieved at an undertaking's conduct, that company, if solvent and motivated, has the best incentive to generate the necessary evidence to mount a case. If it does so successfully, and secures a remedy, it will be compensated and the Defendant company will suffer a penalty which, ordinarily, would act as a deterrent. With luck, the process of adjudication would also clarify what is or what is not lawful behaviour, adding to the educative value of the process.

If each case is viewed on its merits, with no clear, legal and economic benchmarks, the development of rules, if not impossible, is certainly inhibited.

The adoption of Articles 85 and 86 type provisions into English law, as prohibitions (which, to repeat, apply already to all cases where there is an effect on trade between member-states), would mean that companies would have to observe one set of rules rather than two. They would have to harmonise their compliance programmes with EC law. The corpus of EC law would further permit the development of UK law and it is not fanciful to anticipate that developments in UK law would also influence the development of EC law, as it has done in other areas.

As for the necessary UK institutions to ensure that these changes work, the Restrictive Practices Court is a very good model: past history suggest that specialist courts – whether in employment or patents – work extremely well in generating expertise and procedures appropriate for the subject matter. The role of lay persons in the Restrictive Practices Court should also be emphasised. A specialist competition court rather than a lay tribunal (or outdoor relief for under-employed members of the MMC), based upon this Court, hearing UK and EC cases, would materially improve the effectiveness of both UK and EC competition laws in the UK. This would assist the growth of a distinctive private competition law, stimulating remedies, deterrence and greater clarity. It would also end the virtual dependence of all complainants on the shifting priorities and benevolence of official agencies and politicians in the enforcement of competition policy.

Lastly, the MMC should retain a role in competition policy but a much less ambitious and demanding one than at present. It is clearly inappropriate to merge it with the OFT which would end the MMC's independence and detachment and add to the OFT's bureaucracy. The MMC also has an important role in utility regulation, which should be preserved on the basis that practice may make perfect. In addition, there are many examples of anti-competitive harm derived not from conscious actions by companies but from each company intelligently acting in its own interests and exploiting a particular market situation. Here, it is the *situation* which should be examined and it is right that there should be power to make sectoral inquiries and to conduct them in a non-adversarial, 'no-fault' way. The main issues lie in market failure, usually through lack of information or ability to process existing information by consumers (for example, financial services, spare parts). The remedies lie in a wider range of institutional changes, such as industry-wide disclosure, posted prices, publicity for common ownership, changes in intellectual property laws, the law of contract regarding pre-contractual disclosure, penalties and publicity – in other words, a richer menu based on a better understanding of market failure and what is required to remedy it. Existing 'complex monopoly' powers are useless and frequently abused. The conclusion is that not only the law but institutions require change.

CHAIRMAN'S COMMENTS

John Bridgeman

LET ME TAKE SOME OF THE UK AND EUROPEAN ASPECTS of competition policy first and in the reverse order to Tom Sharpe's exposition. There is no doubt that competition law in Britain is old and that it is showing signs of age. One can look back as far as the fascinating case in the 15th century when dyers were getting together to fix the cost of blue dying and relate it to some of the aspects of the law now, and think that nothing has moved on very much since. But there is a general recognition that the law will be reformed and that it will follow closely the prohibition-based system of Article 85, banning anti-competitive agreements, notwithstanding Tom Sharpe's very kind words about the Restrictive Practices Court.

The problem with restrictive trade practices law, as it is at the moment, is that whether or not an agreement has to be registered depends on its form rather than its effect and as a result a vast number of innocuous agreements between parties are caught. We have to examine all these agreements to see whether there is something in them which is anti-competitive, at considerable difficulty to the parties and expense to the tax payer. That would end with a prohibition system. No doubt a Bill will contain many provisions seen in the draft Bill of August 1996, on which work has continued to be done. As far as the abuse of market power is concerned, the explanatory document on the draft Bill of August 1996 proposed a further public debate on a prohibition-based system.

There is no doubt that we in Britain and people in Europe see things somewhat differently We think here that these matters should be kept out of the courts, and that a balance of judgement has to be made of the extent to which one emphasises exploitation of market power achieved through innovation or the extent to which one is concerned about fair reward for risks taken. The latter will include good rewards for being first, and justifiably would be called 'competition' rather than 'abuse of market power'. The courts in a number of countries have traditionally found it very difficult to balance these. Our view in Britain has been that these things are best left to practical people, for example the MMC. I suspect Tom was perhaps less than kind in some of his allusions to the MMC. It has been able to recommend some fairly powerful solutions to very complex problems. An example is vertical restraints in the beer industry. Whether you are a brewer, a pub owner, a beer drinker or a lager drinker, or whether you like 'Alcopops' or whatever, there is no doubt that British brewery companies have changed very considerably, to the benefit of competition.

The European Commission has difficulties, for example of language. There is already a seven-month backlog of material because of the problem in finding Finnish translators. And if we have a problem with the backlog in legislation because of the scarcity of Finnish translators, one can imagine the problem with simultaneous translations between Finnish and Portuguese! The current context is the expansion of the Community. In competition matters the Community is asking itself, if anything, how powers can be decentralised, not how they can be centralised, to cope with the volume of business.

Now that does not sit very well with the Commission's view that it wishes to reduce the merger threshold, in the interest of pursuing the notion of the one-stop-shop for merger issues. Trade in Europe is growing, cross-border mergers are increasing, and there is a lobby group which argues that rather than having to lodge a merger in country A, country B and country C, could there not be a one-stop-shop in which the Commission could advise on how a merger can best proceed? At the moment, because of the current threshold, the Commission handles between 40 and 50 major mergers a year. The merger threshold has been fixed for quite some time. That number could double or even treble if the merger threshold is reduced.

We also regard Article 85 as a problem, because the way it has been interpreted results in its capturing too many innocuous agreements, as does our own restrictive trade practices law. On Tom's reference to Condition 18a, I note that it is *sub judice*, so I do not intend to get involved in discussing it.[1] But perhaps I can make

---

[1] This was BT's action invoking judicial review to have declared improper the Director General of Telecommunications' actions in setting up what Tom Sharpe called a transformation 'from

Tom feel rather uncomfortable by pointing out that he has been agitating for improved remedies since he was a young don. In this particular case, he should be questioning why a regulator should not be allowed to have improved remedies available to him which one could argue is what our efforts are all about. But since it would be wrong to debate this now, I return to perceptions of where the European Commission is likely to go.

The European Commission received a large number of notified vertical arrangements. Hence, in order to deal with these with a degree of expedition, it introduced the block exemption process. The Commission is now consulting on various options by responding to criticisms that block exemptions have had a straitjacket effect and that Article 85 has been applied too widely. We might be good at legislating, and we are probably pretty good at regulating, but none of these things is useful if companies are not educated to understand how they prosecute their legitimate affairs within a transparent basis of law.

Finally, I would like to touch on the question of the national interest: the extent to which Britain is able to retrieve from Brussels matters which we believe concern us greatly. There have been two very interesting cases in the course of this year. One was the Gehe bid for Lloyds which was to be treated as a European merger. The other was the Unichem bid for Lloyds which came under the jurisdiction of the Office of Fair Trading. Purely by being considered under two different jurisdictions, there was the danger that two different processes with two different bodies of law could arrive at two rather dissimilar conclusions. In fact, the British government was successful in making a case to Europe that the Gehe bid should not be handled by the Commission but should be handled by my office.

With the powers we have taken under Article 88 of the Treaty of Rome to look at the proposed British Airways and American Airlines alliance, we have a similar situation in which we are using our own powers and our own investigatory procedures (alongside those of the Commission) to consider something which has significant implications in the UK. This is another important aspect of the way that UK and EC law works in these matters, namely,

---

industry regulator' to 'competition authority'. In December 1996, the High Court found for the Director General of Telecommunications.

ways in which people who are working in the field can talk together to ensure that we do not get nonsenses and so that competition policy can be used as the very precise instrument that it is. I say the 'very precise instrument that it is' because in the UK we think that competition policy, effectively deployed, is not a sun lamp in which British business and commerce can brown and flourish. It is a precise surgical instrument in which the authorities have the ability to intervene, to interpose themselves to correct inefficiencies or ineffectiveness in the market-place. As long as they know what to do and how to do it, they do it and they get out again quickly. As long as it is used in that precise way it is cheap and transparent.

4

UTILITY REGULATION IN NEW ZEALAND

Alan Bollard

Chairman, New Zealand Commerce Commission

and

Michael Pickford

Chief Economist, New Zealand Commerce Commission

1. Introduction

NEW ZEALAND'S APPROACH TO THE REGULATION OF UTILITIES, sometimes called 'light-handed' regulation, has attracted a lot of attention internationally. To some familiar with the costs of 'heavier' forms of regulation associated with industry-specific bodies and the compliance costs visited upon regulated firms, it may seem to offer an attractive, less economically distortionary, alternative. Others may be fearful that the approach entails regulation that is too light-handed, with the result that firms with market power operate without sufficient restraint, to the detriment of their customers and efficient production.

The New Zealand experience lies somewhere in between. The policy has had important successes for the economy. It has also encountered some still unresolved difficulties. It has been in operation for only about 10 years, and is still evolving and being refined. Success and failure also have to be measured against what practical alternatives are available, recognising that all such options are imperfect, and within the rather distinctive context of the New Zealand economy.

The purpose of this paper is to describe and analyse the policy of light-handed regulation, introduced as part of the reform of the New Zealand economy, which began in earnest in 1984. We start by looking briefly at the factors which led to poor performance of the New Zealand economy in the decade prior to 1984, at the thinking in policy-making circles which underlay the reforms then introduced, and the slow response of the economy to those reforms. Then in the following section we go on to describe the characteristics of New Zealand's approach to competition law and policy, and experience to date, because the same law is used to underpin the regulation of utilities.

In the fourth section we turn to the system of utility regulation in New Zealand: this looks at the initial reform of the utilities sector, the problems posed by utility regulation, and the light-handed approach adopted. Two key aspects of light-handed regulation – competition policy and information disclosure – are examined in more detail. The fifth section then provides brief case studies of the experience with the reform and subsequent regulation of four key utilities: telecommunications, electricity, natural gas, and ports and airports. Finally, we draw together our conclusions, necessarily tentative, on the virtue of the light-handed approach to utility regulation.

The New Zealand Context

New Zealand Economic Performance Pre-1984

For a century New Zealand developed as an agricultural economy, selling to Britain the bulk of its narrow range of produce – mainly meat, wool, and dairy products – with minimal domestic processing. Even in the early post-Second World War years between 60 and 70 per cent of New Zealand's exports, almost all agricultural products, went to Britain. This assured preferential access to the British market allowed New Zealand considerable prosperity through the exploitation of its natural comparative advantage in pasture-based primary production. By 1953 the country enjoyed what was probably the third highest standard of living in the world.

This prosperity underwrote two other key features of the economy. The first was the heavy protection provided to an inefficient manufacturing sector. Economic policy thinking was profoundly affected by the 1930s Depression, which had been 'imported' into the country. Strenuous efforts were made from 1938 to insulate the economy from international pressures, and to diversify the economic base by encouraging a range of formerly imported manufactured goods to be made locally. However, manufacturing industries remained small and orientated towards import-substitution. Secondly, prosperity encouraged the development of a generous 'cradle to the grave' state-funded welfare system, which had been initiated at an early stage (by international standards). This system made provision for universal social security, superannuation, education, housing, and health services, together with a wide range of government-run, and often subsidised, utility services, all funded out of general taxation.

The year 1973 marked a turning point in New Zealand's economic fortunes. In that year Britain joined the European Community, resulting in access for New Zealand exports becoming increasingly restricted. The country's attempts to diversify into new markets were increasingly handicapped by the EEC's distortionary Common Agricultural Policy, and by the political nature of access to US agricultural markets. At the same time the economy, in common with others, was badly affected by the large international oil price increases in 1973-74 and 1979. Trading a relatively high proportion of its GDP, and exporting a very limited range of products to a small number of markets, the economy was not well placed to weather the ensuing international recession. It was left with an inefficient manufacturing sector; a reliance on commodity production which faced difficult access, low income elasticities of demand, and volatile markets; and large terms of trade shocks combined with a structural balance-of-payments problem.

Successive governments opted to continue with interventionist policies designed to insulate the economy from overseas influences. This culminated in heavy government borrowing to finance the investment in a series of projects in the early 1980s, known as the 'Think Big' programme, aimed at reducing the country's dependence on imported oil supplies. Unfortunately, apart from the large debt incurred by this programme, some of the projects were only economic if international oil prices remained high, which they did not.

During the late 1970s and early 1980s, New Zealanders continued to demand increases in social services, to which the government responded. To finance the growing role of the government, high rates of income tax were levied, but they were not sufficient to avoid a mounting public fiscal deficit, given numerous loopholes and the narrowness of the tax base, slow growth, and ineffectual attempts to curb government spending. A lax monetary policy allowed inflation to increase significantly. There was a series of strategic currency devaluations whose competitive effects were quickly inflated away. During the decade from 1975, New Zealand public debt increased sevenfold, inflation mounted, productivity dropped, growth slowed, and overseas debt grew substantially. In the 40 years after the War, New Zealand's GDP *per capita* had dropped from 26 per cent above the OECD average to 27 per cent below it.

By the early 1980s it was clear that direct government intervention to control wages and prices, and to regulate markets, trade and investment, had been unsuccessful. There was a consensus about the need for a change in the direction of economic policy in the business community, amongst political pressure groups, and in the Treasury. Although limited and piecemeal reforms had been initiated in the late 1970s, fundamental change occurred only from 1984 with the election win of the Labour Party. The new Government assumed power in the midst of a currency crisis, and was forced immediately to devalue the New Zealand dollar to staunch the outflow of funds. Over the period 1984-87 a series of far-reaching and systematic reforms affecting all of the private, and most of the public, sectors was introduced. The reform process continued at a slower pace under subsequent governments.

In contrast to most OECD countries, the radical reform process in New Zealand was implemented very quickly,[1] mostly in the period 1984-89. This was possible because conditions in New Zealand in 1984 matched quite closely the seven required for successful economic reform identified by Williamson.[2] These are: the public perception of a crisis; implementation of extensive reforms immediately after a government takes office; the presence of a fragmented opposition; the existence of a cadre of economists in government with a common coherent view of reform; the presence of political leadership with a longer term view of history; the existence of a comprehensive programme for the transformation of the economy and a rapid timetable for its implementation; and finally, the ability to appeal directly to the public for support.

---

[1] *Editor's note*: the New Zealand reform programme is described in Donald Brash, *New Zealand's Remarkable Reforms*, IEA Occasional Paper 100, London: Institute of Economic Affairs, 1996.

[2] J. Williamson, 'In Search of a Manual for Technopols', in J. Williamson (ed.), *The Political Economy of Policy Reform*, Washington DC: Institute for International Economics, 1994.

At the time New Zealand had a relatively thin, two-party political system (with an absence of splinter groups) based on a single representative chamber, no provincial state or local government economic policies of importance, and no written constitution. The small size of the chamber combined with a tradition for large cabinets meant that a small, unified group of ministers could control both cabinet and caucus. The major potential restraint upon decisive government action was (and remains) the three-year term of office. This was addressed by adopting a 'big bang' approach, which also had the advantage of undercutting potential opposition from particular interest groups by introducing changes affecting all areas of the economy as soon as possible.

The Thinking Underlying Reform in New Zealand

In 1984 there was relatively little experience of major economic reform in other countries which might inform the New Zealand approach. The closest parallels could be drawn with the partial reforms that were in progress under Margaret Thatcher in the United Kingdom, and with the early experiments in the southern countries of South America. In addition, encouragement and some guidance for reform came from international organisations, particularly the IMF and the OECD.

The basic thrust of the reform programme was to free the market mechanism from distorting government controls and subsidies. The emphasis was on allowing the forces of enterprise, self-interest, and competition to generate efficiency and economic growth. The previous focus on distributional equity was reduced. Government participation in production was rolled back by putting its trading activities (including utilities) on a commercial footing, exposing them to competition, and in some cases, privatising them.

The underlying theoretical rationale for government economic policy in New Zealand before and after 1984 is summarised in Table 1. The justification for government micro-economic policy interventions in the production sector had been based on traditional arguments of avoiding market failure (for example, under-provision of socially desirable services), preserving equity by providing access to services at reasonable prices, and maintaining control of those services regarded as being of national importance. The poor

TABLE 1
The Changing Economic Roles of Government in New Zealand: Theory and Policy, Before and After 1984

(I) Micro-economic Role

	Funding	*Ownership*	*Provision*	*Regulation*
(i) Pre Reform Period				
Theory	Market failure	Equity and natio-nalistic arguments	Direct provision	Direct controls
Policy	Direct funding by Parliament	Widespread state ownership	Widespread public provision	Regulation of price and entry
(ii) Reform Period				
Theory	Public choice, property rights	Principal-agent	Supply-side think-ing	Contestability, light-handed regulation
Policy	Public goods and social serv-ices only	Corporatisation, privatisation	Contracting out to private sector	Commerce Act

(II) Macro-economic Role

	Fiscal	*Monetary*	*Labour*
(i) Pre Reform Period			
Theory	Eclectic Keynesian macro-economics		Social contract
Policy	'Stop-go' budgetary adjustments	Financial controls	Centralised bargaining
(ii) Reform Period			
Theory	New Classical macro-economics		Market-based bargaining
Policy	Fiscal Responsibility Act 1994 (prudent manage-ment)	Reserve Bank Act 1989 (low inflation target)	Employment Contracts Act 1991 (dereg-ulated bargaining)

performance of the economy led to the view that policies based on these arguments had failed, and encouraged a search for new frameworks in which to formulate policy. The new micro-economic models, partly derived from 'Chicago School' thinking, which offer a much reduced role for the government, found favour with New Zealand reformers.

The new view was that market failure needed to be balanced by the potential for bureaucratic failure; that a focus on equity would come at the cost of reduced efficiency; and that nationalistic ownership concerns had to be balanced against the advantages from foreign capital, technology, expertise, and overseas market access. The role of government in the ownership of trading assets was rethought, using principal-agent theory to focus on the inefficiencies arising from the incentive and monitoring problems amongst shareholders, board members, management and workers.

Whereas many utility services had been provided directly by the government in the past, supply-side and public sector crowd-out theories lent credence to a view that the private sector might prove capable and efficient. Organisational reform should be carried out in a way that allowed the Coase rule to work (with firms organising themselves so as to minimise transactions costs). A new approach to industry regulation was based on contestability theory, and on other new thinking about information asymmetries between regulators and the regulated, and the possibilities of light-handed regulation. By the early 1980s, some of these ideas were well established but they had not yet been adequately tested in real applications.

Macro-economic policy played a second-tier role in the reform period. Traditionally, New Zealand macro-economic policy had aimed at achieving a diverse range of objectives, including those relating to stabilisation and equity, but with a greater emphasis on maintaining full employment than on avoiding inflation. In this endeavour the government was limited by the scope of monetary policy by reason of the strict controls on the financial sector, and the need to finance persistent government's budget deficits. When inflation increased rapidly in the early 1980s, the government's response was to impose a price and wage freeze over the period 1982-1984. Moreover, the government propensity to intervene, and the short three-year electoral cycle, tended to generate 'boom-bust' cycles, a policy which was dignified by being called 'fine tuning'.

Labour market policy was based loosely on the notion of a social contract with strong trade unions, and a centralised wage bargaining system which made little allowance for variations between firms and across regions.

Macro-economic reform was based on new classical macro-economic thinking on rational expectations, transparency and credibility, which cast doubt on the ability of the government effectively to 'fine tune' the economy. Instead, the focus turned to giving each of fiscal, monetary, and labour market policies an achievable, specific, narrowly defined goal. At the same time, income redistribution policy by means of taxes and social welfare transfers, which had long been an important objective of the government, was downplayed. It was implicit in the emphasis on the efficiency objectives of the reform programme that the government would step back from an activist redistribution role, and that social policy would aim to adopt similar efficiency objectives to those used in industry policy. For example, there would be a greater emphasis on 'user pays', with those unable to pay receiving modest income supplements (for instance, in state housing).

The 1984 Reforms in Practice

The economic transformation of New Zealand, which began in 1984 and continued for a decade, is notable in several respects: in the pre-existing level of government intervention from which the reform process began; in the extent, consistency, and speed of the reforms undertaken; and in the degree to which the market economy has been liberalised as a result of their implementation. Today there are few areas of economic life which have been left untouched by the reforms.

The time pattern of the reforms in 12 key areas is summarised in Figure 1, in terms of the sequence in which they were initiated and the time span it took to carry them out. The reforms were generally implemented as fast as was practical without primary regard for established principles, distributional issues of gainers and losers, or sequencing matters. As indicated in the figure, most of the reforms were carried through in the period 1984-1991.

Deregulation of the factor markets took place early, particularly the three key sectors of finance, transport and energy. In the financial sector interest rate controls, and nearly all regulations on

FIGURE 1

Phasing of Economic Reforms in New Zealand from 1984

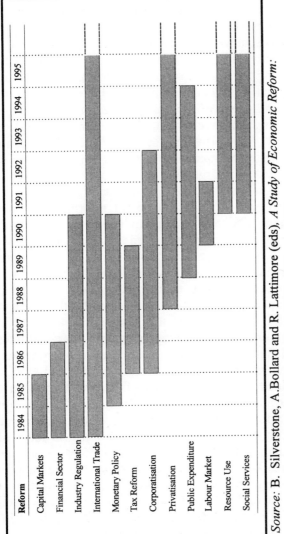

Source: B. Silverstone, A.Bollard and R. Lattimore (eds), *A Study of Economic Reform: The Case of New Zealand,* North Holland Press, 1996.

Note: This figure is conceptual in nature. Each bar represents the approximate duration of each reform (although the impact clearly took longer). The dotted lines extending the bars indicate continuing reform.

banks and other financial institutions, were removed, as were foreign exchange controls. The New Zealand dollar was devalued in 1984 to stem the foreign exchange crisis, and floated in 1985. Monetary policy was to have the principal aim of lowering inflation, a goal later enshrined in the Reserve Bank Act 1989, which established the Reserve Bank at arm's length from government and under contract to achieve price stability (currently defined as annual inflation between 0 and 3 per cent). The fiscal deficit was to be reduced, implying a redirection of stabilisation policy away from the immediate goal of full employment. Labour market reform was only partially addressed in the early stages, and it was not until 1991, with a change of government, that the Employment Contracts Act was enacted. This provided for a more flexible, decentralised approach to employer/employee bargaining arrangements, and for employees to use a bargaining agent of their choice – not necessarily a union – to bargain on their behalf.

In addition to promoting private sector reform, the government corporatised almost all of its trading departments, setting them commercial objectives, and restructured the core departments of the public service. Since then about two-thirds of the corporatised trading departments have been privatised. This, together with tight control of labour costs, has resulted ultimately in a significant reduction in expenditure. On the revenue side, the tax base was broadened with the introduction of a value-added tax; loopholes in the tax system were closed; and the income tax marginal rates were simplified and flattened, causing the top rate of income tax to be halved. When economic growth resumed in mid-1992, rising income combined with tight control of expenditure produced the first budget surpluses in many years. The Fiscal Responsibility Act 1994 lays out a framework for the full accounting and reporting of the Crown accounts, and requires the government to focus on debt reduction by running surpluses.

In product markets, the extensive system of price supports and concessional financing to the agricultural sector was abolished almost overnight in 1984, and price controls on many goods and services were eliminated (except for three items) by 1987. A general wage and price freeze was terminated immediately. Plans were established for the deregulation of many industries, ranging from eggs to cement and real estate services, and the lifting of controls on road and rail freight was completed. Quantity licensing in industries, and state regulated monopoly rights, were almost all removed. Occupational licensing was deregulated and there was a range of business law reform. To underpin the newly deregulated economy, a heavily amended and more strongly competition-focused Commerce Act 1986 was enacted.

Much of New Zealand industry had been sheltered behind a protective wall of high tariffs and import licences. From 1984 the pace of import liberalisation was accelerated, with licences being phased out in favour of tariffs, and those being reduced according to a pre-set timetable. The faster implementation of Closer Economic Relations with Australia, which eliminated most trade barriers between the two countries by 1990, added to import competition.

The Response of the New Zealand Economy

The New Zealand economy responded to these major reforms by undergoing a long restructuring recession.[3] The floating of the NZ dollar in March 1985 led it to appreciate under the influence of high interest rates, caused by the budget deficit and a tight monetary policy, which initially hurt the competitiveness and profitability of exporting industries. This, combined with growing import competition as trade barriers were progressively reduced, resulted in a significant down-turn in the traded goods sectors: manufacturing contracted by one-third, and other areas such as agriculture suffered as well. The dislocations following the 1987 share market crash, and the government's attempt to soften the impact of the recession in the late 1980s by allowing its budget deficit to widen, probably served to extend the length of the recession. During the first six years of economic reform in New Zealand, there was no overall growth in GDP *per capita*.

The year 1992 represented a watershed. From the middle of that year, as the culmination of significant improvements in efficiency, competitiveness, and the terms of trade, the economy began to grow strongly at last. Real GDP growth peaked at around 6 per cent in 1994, causing unemployment to fall from a peak of over 11 per cent to about 6 per cent. Inflation had already fallen to below 2 per cent

---

[3] For an appraisal of the rationale for, and the impact of, the reforms see: B. Silverstone, A. Bollard and R. Lattimore (eds.), *A Study of Economic Reform: The Case of New Zealand*, North Holland Press, 1996.

towards the end of 1991, and it has been contained at near 2 per cent since, albeit at the expense in the last year of a tight monetary policy which produced high real interest rates. The strong recovery and tight control of public spending pushed the fiscal balance into strong surplus. This has been used to reduce substantially the size of the public debt, and in 1996 to implement cuts in income tax. Strong growth has led to a growing trade deficit, but this appears to be the only survivor of New Zealand's historic structural and economic imbalances.

There has been considerable debate about the distribution of gains from the reforms. There is some evidence of increased inequality, particularly for the highest income category, though it is not consistent and cannot entirely be attributed to the reforms since other OECD countries with lesser reform programmes have experienced similar trends. There is also some evidence of an increasing share of income in the hands of shareholders compared to employees. Consumers, and more recently, taxpayers have undoubtedly done very well from the reform process.[4]

Competition Law And Policy In New Zealand

The New Zealand Approach

The reform process focused on strengthening the role of the market in allocating resources. Parallel to this was the revision of competition legislation, in the form of the Commerce Act 1986, which was needed to define the rules by which businesses were to operate in the newly deregulated, open economy, and to deter the possible spread of restrictive practices and mergers by firms wishing to reduce what for many would be unfamiliar competition. The Act also provided the basis for the 'light-handed' regulation of corporatised and privatised utilities with market power (see below). The reform of competition law was accompanied by reforms of other business-related legislation on consumer protection, securities, take-overs, intellectual property, and planning and environmental controls.

While the Commerce Act looked to the United States for its underlying micro-economic principles, it relied for its statutory

---

[4] For an analysis of distributional effects, see Easton in Silverstone, Bollard and Lattimore, *op. cit.*

framework on the Australian Trade Practices Act 1974. In earlier days New Zealand relied heavily on United Kingdom precedent for its interpretation of anti-trust legislation, but now legal recourse is being made increasingly to United States, Australian and European Community legal precedents.

Like other anti-trust legislation, the Commerce Act is designed to promote competition on three fronts: by ensuring that competition is not substantially lessened through arrangements or understandings between firms in competition with one another; by screening mergers and take-overs to prevent the acquisition or strengthening of a dominant position in a market; and to deter firms in a dominant position in a market from using that position for the purpose of deterring competitors.

While the Act has as its stated objective 'to promote competition in markets within New Zealand', this can be overridden in certain circumstances where efficiency advantages are considered to outweigh detriments from the loss of competition. For example, under the business acquisitions (merger) régime, companies may voluntarily apply to the Commerce Commission (the sole regulatory body) for a 'clearance' or an 'authorisation' which, if granted, protects the acquisition from further action either by the Commission or by aggrieved third parties, in the courts. A clearance is a declaration that the merger will not breach the anti-competitiveness threshold of the Act by leading to the acquiring or strengthening of a dominant position in a market. Where the clearance threshold may be breached, an authorisation can be granted if the Commission is satisfied that the acquisition would be likely to result in a benefit to the public (for example, an efficiency gain) which would outweigh any detriment from the loss of competition.

Similarly, the Act also prohibits arrangements between competitors that substantially lessen competition in the market (a lower standard of anti-competitiveness), or that exclude rivals, although such arrangements – even ones involving price-fixing – are authorisable on public benefit grounds. However, very few restrictive practices have so far been authorised.

The Act also establishes a behavioural 'code of conduct' for companies which occupy a dominant position in a market. Such companies must not use that position for the purpose of trying to restrict entry, prevent competitive conduct, or eliminate a player from a market. The Act allows for price control to be imposed in circumstances where competition is judged to be inadequate (although currently there is none in place). It is these parts of the Act which are of particular importance for the policy of 'light-handed regulation' of utilities (see below).

Competition policy reform in New Zealand was based on new industrial economic theories. Policy-makers were particularly ready to embrace contestability theory, because it seemed to offer a solution to the 'efficiency versus market power' trade-off dilemma found in many New Zealand markets, where the very few domestic firms required for efficiency might prejudice the scope for effective competition. Contestability theory reinforced the predisposition towards import liberalisation by pointing to the need to remove import protection so as to allow foreign firms to become potential entrants, thereby helping to maintain competitive markets in the interests of domestic consumers.[5] It also emphasised the importance of removing statutory and bureaucratic sources of barriers to domestic entry.

The view that large firms are likely to have achieved that position through superior efficiency also met with sympathy, especially as such firms were small by comparison with their counterparts in international markets, and yet were expected to spearhead the country's assault on export markets. In addition, the Coasian view that firms will, given the opportunity, act to minimise their transactions costs through various forms of internal and external reorganisation also found favour. These views underline New Zealand competition policy's tolerance for a wide range of intra-firm and market trade practices, which are to be judged on their behavioural outcomes rather than on pre-set prohibitions or structural thresholds.

The New Zealand Commerce Commission is established under the Act as a combined regulatory and quasi-judicial authority to administer the Act. The Commission has broad powers covering trading activities, including utilities. In New Zealand there are no statutory competition regulatory authorities specific to individual industries. The Commerce Commission's decisions may be appealed to the courts, and private rights of action are available for

---

[5] For an analysis, see M. Pickford, 'Competition Policy and Import Competition: A New Zealand Perspective', *Antitrust Bulletin*, Vol. 37, 1992.

most contraventions. While the Commission is an independent statutory authority, the government can require it to have regard to the latter's stated economic policies. The government has used this power in the past in relation to such industries as meat and dairy processing, where it favoured industry efforts at rationalisation.

Characteristics of New Zealand Competition Law

In some respects, the Commerce Act 1986 may be seen as one of the first in a new wave of competition statutes. Its characteristics are as follows:

- *Light-handed thresholds*: the threshold for merger is dominance by a single firm. The thresholds for competitive behaviour (substantial lessening of competition and misuse of a dominant position) are also relatively lighthanded. But that does not imply that enforcement is lighthanded – the thresholds are not burdensome, but are intended to be enforced.

- *Broad reach*: the Commerce Act covers almost all sectors with few exemptions (apart from export cartels, some international practices such as international shipping, and some labour market behaviour). All other markets and industries, including utilities, are included, as are all corporate forms such as co-operatives, charities and government departments if they are in trade. Common thresholds apply across this wide base.

- *A single regulator:* the Commerce Commission is the single regulator of the Commerce Act, adjudicating on business acquisitions, dominant firms, and trade practices, and enforcing compliance across the spectrum of industries, with broad scope and relatively wide powers. It treats all industries using the same competition criteria.

- *Regulatory independence:* the Commerce Commission is a quasi-judicial body at arm's length from the political and admini-strative arms of government, and making its own independent decisions.

- *Judicially-based system:* only the courts can find a breach of the Commerce Act and impose penalties. A range of injunctions, penalties, damages and (in the case of business acquisitions) divestment orders is available. However, the Commission is able to negotiate administrative settlements with companies for transgressions where it sees fit.

- *Scope for private action:* private action can be taken through the courts under most parts of the Act. The expectation is that if there is no public interest involved, enforcement action will most likely be private.

- *Behavioural not structural:* the Act does not proscribe particular industry forms or structures, nor set market share thresholds for judging potential breaches of the Act. Monopoly is not mentioned. Instead the Act focuses on how businesses behave.

- *Proscriptive, not prescriptive:* the Act and the Commerce Commission do not instruct businesses on how they should organise themselves or conduct their affairs, nor attempt to design market forms for them; rather they focus on behaviour which contravenes the Act.

- *Rule of reason based:* while there are important exceptions such as price-fixing and resale price maintenance, which are illegal *per se*, the emphasis is on a rule of reason approach to judging whether a practice breaches the Act. Most vertical and horizontal arrangements are judged according to whether they substantially lessen competition.

- *Efficiency-based:* under evolving legal precedent and government attitudes, the goal of the Act of promoting competition has come to be seen not so much as an end in itself, but as a means of generating superior outcomes in terms of productive and dynamic efficiencies. As noted above, the Act incorporates efficiency considerations explicitly through the countervailing public benefit arguments in authorisation applications.

- *Distributionally neutral:* the Commerce Commission makes no attempt to impose a distributional standard, other than to meet the requirement of the Act that the benefits should accrue to New Zealand. Thus, where monopoly pricing benefits shareholders at the expense of consumers, the dollars gained by the former may be considered to be balanced by the dollars lost by the latter, with a nil impact on economic welfare.

- *Dynamic approach:* the Commission and courts are prepared to recognise that a firm which appears to hold a dominant position in a market may be constrained by the threat of potential, as well as actual, entry. This focuses attention on the presence of possible competitors, the height of entry barriers, and in some cases, the potential for substitute products to evolve.

Competition policies across different countries may be judged by a wide range of criteria, as the above list indicates. For the purposes of illustration, Figure 2 focuses on just two dimensions: an administrative versus a judicial yardstick, and a structural versus an outcome-based approach. On the resulting four quadrants the comparative positions of certain countries are plotted. Even with this limited comparison, it is clear there are major differences, for example, between New Zealand and United Kingdom competition laws. Even though in many aspects of its law, institutions, and property rights, New Zealand has followed the United Kingdom example, the former lies squarely in the judicial/outcome-based quadrant, whereas the latter falls in the administrative/structural segment.

Experience to Date with Competition Law

Each year the Commerce Commission carries out surveillance of several hundred business acquisitions across the full range of economic activity, and deals with about 40 applications for clearance or authorisations to merge. In the last two years a substantial proportion of merger applications has been in the electricity sector, as newly deregulated local power companies have sought to gain economies of scale and of rationalisation. Business acquisition activity has also been significant in radio and television broadcasting, dairy processing, the print media, meat processing, land transport and freight, aviation, finance, waste management and fishing. A particularly large recent merger involved the acquisition by Air New Zealand of 50 per cent of the shares in the Australian airline Ansett Holdings.

FIGURE 2
Indicative Mapping of Competition Laws

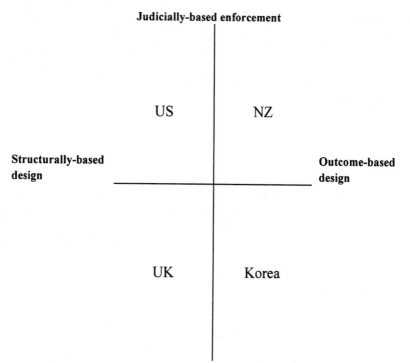

Note: The terms used in this figure are defined as follows:

• *Structurally-based design* uses market share thresholds for merger and *per se* rules for trade practices.

• *Outcome-based design* uses behavioural thresholds for merger and rules of reason for trade practices.

• *Judicially-based enforcement* involves adjudication by courts/tribunals with public/private enforcement.

• *Administratively-based enforcement* involves adjudications by departments/agencies with public enforcement.

In addition, some firms or industries have sought authorisation for particular trade practices. Recently these have been as varied as electricity wholesale market rules, financial markets rules, meat industry rationalisation, rugby union player transfer rules, and the provision of mental health services.

The Commerce Commission and private parties have taken a number of Commerce Act cases that have developed the law in the area of anti-competitive collusion, exclusion, price-fixing and resale price maintenance. Actions have included the ports, trade associations, the baking industry, the milk industry and the motor vehicle trade.

The Act prohibits in broad terms a company in a dominant position in a market from taking actions with the purpose of preventing others from competing in the market. Companies, particularly new entrants, have sought redress under this provision from alleged predatory behaviour by incumbent firms, or from denial of access to a facility owned by an incumbent regarded as 'essential' for entry into a market. Major cases to date have covered ports, airports, telecommunications, stock saleyards, yearling horse sales, and export cartels. The major cases involving utilities are covered below.

Utility Regulation In New Zealand

Reform of the Utilities Sector [6]

The term 'utility' is difficult to define precisely, but generally it is applied to the communications, energy, transport, and 'public amenities' sectors, including telecommunications, broadcasting, electricity, gas, railways, sewerage and water.[7] These industries usually exhibit two characteristics which may be shared by the ports, airports and roads. *First*, utilities provide a distribution, transmission, or transport service through a network of cables, pipes or other facilities which tend to enjoy such large-scale economies as to become natural monopolies. *Second*, since the service they provide is often regarded as an 'essential' input to other industries,

---

[6] Much of this section has been drawn from A. Bollard and M. Pickford, '"Light-Handed" Utility Regulation in New Zealand', *Agenda*, Vol. 2/4, 1995.

[7] A. Kahn, *The Economics of Regulation: Principles and Institutions*, Cambridge, Mass.: MIT Press, 1995.

the efficiency of utilities has a widespread impact on the efficiency of other firms. A further characteristic in New Zealand, and often elsewhere, is that historically the social importance of such industries, and doubts about their ability to function in competitive markets, have resulted in a history of public ownership.

Until the mid-1980s, utilities in New Zealand were generally statutory monopolies under state ownership, run by government trading departments or divisions. In the early 1980s the Treasury estimated that public sector enterprises in New Zealand, which covered but were not limited to utilities, accounted for about 12 per cent of GDP, and for some 20 per cent of investment in the economy.[8] Since they often produced 'essential' inputs used by firms in the private sector, their efficiency, price-setting and investment behaviour had a major impact on the competitiveness of the economy as a whole. However, their performance was judged by critics to have been poor:

> 'Over the twenty years to 1985/86 the government invested $5,000 million (in 1986 dollars) of taxpayers' money in the departmental trading activities of the Airways System, the Lands and Survey Department and Forest Service, the Post Office, the State Coal Mines, and the Electricity Division of the Ministry of Energy. In 1985/86 these organisations managed assets valued at over $20 billion but returned no net after tax returns to taxpayers.'[9]

Several reasons have been adduced for the inadequate performance: the conflict between various commercial and social objectives; an operating environment in which competition was usually lacking; access to funding from government sources at favourable rates of interest; lack of accountability to, and inadequate monitoring of performance by, government; and political interference.[10]

---

[8] The Treasury, *Economic Management*, Wellington: The Treasury, 1984. In 1995 the three sectors accounted for the following percentages of GDP: 'Electricity, Gas and Water', 3·4%; Transport, 6·8%; and 'Communications', 6·0%.

[9] S. Jennings and R. Cameron, 'State-Owned Enterprise Reform in New Zealand', in A. Bollard and R. Buckle (eds.), *Economic Liberalisation in New Zealand*, Allen and Unwin, 1987.

[10] See previous footnote; also J. Farrar and B. McCabe, 'Corporatisation, Corporate Governance and the Deregulation of the Public Sector Economy', *Public Law Review*, Vol. 6, No. 1, 1995.

As part of wider economic liberalisation policies, these industries were progressively reformed in the years following 1985. The most important steps were:

- the removal of nearly all statutory monopoly rights so as to expose utilities to competition;

- the corporatisation (and in some cases, privatisation) of numerous state trading departments so as to place them in a company form of organisation, with commercial objectives;

- their restructuring to isolate the natural monopoly elements from the more contestable parts of the industries;

- the abolition of social service obligations, or their explicit funding by the government, rather than, as previously, by cross-subsidisation with profits earned by the business in non-contestable markets.[11]

Under the State-Owned Enterprises Act 1986, the major government trading departments were corporatised on 1 April 1987, from which time they were required to operate as profitable and successful businesses, comparable with their private sector counterparts. Goods and services were to be marketed on a 'user pays' basis, unless an explicit subsidy was provided to finance non-commercial activities. Regulatory barriers were dismantled, thereby exposing the new corporations to private sector competition, and other forms of special assistance – such as subsidised government loans – were removed. Taxes and dividends had to be paid to the government. In short, 'competitive neutrality' was to apply.

Monitoring of performance was enhanced by the establishment of measurable targets based on profitability, although asset values were hard to assess. Departmental organisation was replaced by a company (limited liability) structure with the government as sole shareholder. Managers were given greater independence in decision-making, but were accountable to boards of directors appointed from the private sector, and ultimately to Parliament through the Minister of Finance and the responsible minister. The

---

[11] I. Duncan and A. Bollard, *Corporatisation and Privatisation: Lessons from New Zealand*, Oxford: Oxford University Press, 1992.

intention was to remove decision-making in state-owned enterprises (SOEs) from direct political interference.

While these reforms marked a major step forward, it was argued that certain problems remained with the SOE model.[12] *First*, since the ownership rights in SOEs are diverse and cannot be transferred (ownership being vested in the Crown), managers lack the incentives to perform normally provided through the share market. They face no threat of take-over, and the monitoring of performance by shareholders and investment analysts is attenuated (the free rider problem). *Second*, the incentives provided by the possibility of bankruptcy are regarded as minimal because of an implicit government guarantee. By reducing risk, this may distort the cost of capital in a downward direction. *Finally*, some claim that SOE decision-making is subject to residual government interference, since the directors are political appointees, and an annual 'statement of corporate intent' has to be approved by the government. Moreover, interest groups may pressure the government to hold inquiries into particular management decisions, as happened with the pricing of the Electricity Corporation (ECNZ) and New Zealand Post's rural mail charges in the early 1990s.

Such considerations have been argued as justifying privatisation of the SOEs, as has happened in many cases, including Telecom and New Zealand Rail.[13] Competition and other concerns have hindered moves to privatise other major utilities such as Electricity Corporation, Solid Energy (coal) Corporation, and Television New Zealand.

The Problem of Utility Regulation

In most Western countries the regulation of utilities poses more complex problems than the regulation either of non-utility SOEs, or (generally) of private sector firms through competition policy. This is partly because utilities – particularly those in the energy sector –

---

[12] New Zealand Business Roundtable, *State Owned Enterprises: Issues of Ownership and Regulation*, Wellington: NZBR, 1988.

[13] However, SOEs typically are both large and complex organisations, which would tend to make them more resistant to take-over (and bankruptcy), and more difficult for the capital market to monitor because of information asymmetries and possible managerial opportunism. Thus privatisation may not be able to solve all of the incentive problems posed by large, complex SOEs.

have intrinsic features which, by leading to small numbers of industry participants and by raising significant barriers to entry and exit, serve to attenuate competition. These features include: substantial economies of scale, sometimes to the point of natural monopoly (such as with high voltage electricity transmission lines); economies of scope (as in the provision of different telecommunication services); and large, lumpy, immobile investments in sunk assets (for example, natural gas production facilities and distribution networks; railway networks).

Further regulatory problems are raised by networks and plants (such as hydro-electric dams) typically having low marginal costs of expanding output up to full capacity, but high fixed costs associated with that capacity; by the potential for substantial externalities, especially environmental (as in coal mining and power stations); and in some cases, by inelastic demand curves (for instance, for electricity because of appliance ownership), which raise the gains from the exercise of market power.

The utility problem is most acute in those industries which provide a basic service for consumers, and where production involves the use of non-contestable or non-economically reproducible facility services owned by incumbents, to which access is required by entrants in order to compete with the same incumbent in the downstream consumer markets.

Typical examples are in local electricity supply, where independent retailers need access to the vertically integrated incumbent's local distribution lines; or in the case of a geographically isolated port, where an independent stevedoring company needs access to the wharves to be able to compete with the horizontally integrated port company's stevedoring service. It is in these sorts of areas that regulators encounter most difficulties, both with the technical, legal and economic aspects, and also frequently in coping with asymmetric information, conflicting objectives, aggressive and sophisticated incumbents, politically astute entrants, and technological change.

These problems of utility regulation are, among Western economies, probably at their most acute in New Zealand, given the small size of the economy and the difficulty of gaining the economies of scale needed for the efficient operation of many utilities. In addition, the country's geographical isolation removes any possibility of international trade in utility services with adjoining countries. Furthermore, throughout New Zealand's colonial history the state traditionally played a major role in the utilities sector, initially because the fledgling capital market was not prepared to bear the risk in major developmental projects, such as the building of the main trunk railway service. By the 1970s almost every utility service was provided by a large state trading organisation, usually operating with statutory monopoly rights, and suffering from political interference in terms of price-setting, investment planning, and other operating conditions. Deregulation was required as a first step, but this tended to generate problems for the regulator in that the industry was thrust into an initial state of disequilibrium, with incumbent and new firms both struggling to come to terms with an unfamiliar competitive environment, and sometimes with individual markets being difficult to discern after years of statutory, vertically integrated monopoly.

Left to themselves, such deregulated utilities could generate significant resource misallocation and inefficiency from their monopoly pricing, and from their potential to engage in exclusionary behaviour aimed at deterring competition from new entrants. A totally 'hands off' approach is not a viable option. At the other extreme, direct control imposed by an industry-specific regulator will be likely to generate its own inefficiencies. These could include: the costs of operating the regulatory body; the 'paper burden' or information supply costs imposed on the regulated firm; the scope for it to engage in 'opportunistic' behaviour; the compliance costs arising from the distortions caused by imperfect regulation; the losses associated with the possible corruption of the system through 'regulatory capture'; and dynamic losses associated with the control by regulators of industry structure and conduct, which may inhibit new entry, competition, investment, and innovation.

The design of a regulatory régime must therefore weigh up the potential costs and benefits involved. Success in this area is a relative concept, and has to be judged against the background of a realistic counterfactual, rather than some sort of ex-post, socially-optimal nirvana. All forms of regulation, including non-regulation, produce adverse outcomes; the relevant question is which form produces the least adverse result when assessed over a range of criteria.

Light-handed Regulation in New Zealand

Utility regulation has been approached in New Zealand in a characteristically straightforward manner, with the same set of competition principles used to regulate other industries, together with some additional light-handed elements. The concept of 'light-handed' regulation emerged from the policy debate concerning the deregulation and privatisation of telecommunications during the period 1987-90. Given the market power which a deregulated Telecom would wield, alternative regulatory régimes were evaluated. Conventional 'heavy-handed' forms of regulation were rejected in favour of a novel approach, support for which was reiterated in a policy statement by the government in December 1991:

'The Government sees competition as the best regulator of telecommunications markets. Accordingly, there will continue to be no statutory or regulatory barriers to competitive entry into (the) . . . market . . . To maintain the conditions of effective competition, the Government places primary reliance upon the operations of the Commerce Act 1986 . . . The following supplementary measures will continue to apply: (a) the Telecommunications (Disclosure) Regulations 1990; and (b) the Telecommunications (Internal Services) Regulations 1989. If it proves to be necessary, the Government will consider the introduction of other statutory measures or regulation.' [14]

The overall thrust of the policy, in common with that in other Western countries, is to encourage competition where markets are potentially contestable, and to focus regulation on the non-contestable markets controlled by incumbent utilities.

This regulation takes a number of forms:

- There is a reliance on general competition law, as expressed in the Commerce Act 1986, under s.36 of which dominant firms must not (in general terms) behave abusively towards actual or potential competitors. Contravention of s.36 exposes dominant firms to court action by private parties or by the Commerce Commission.

---

[14] Quoted in Ministry of Commerce, The Treasury, *Regulation of Access to Vertically-Integrated Natural Monopolies: A Discussion Paper*, Wellington: Ministry of Commerce, 1995, pp. 21-22.

- Information disclosure regulations, on an ascending scale of detail for telecommunications, natural gas, and electricity, require the annual disclosure of accounting and other information by incumbent operators of 'essential facilities' with market power. This is intended to encourage self-regulation through the market and to underpin the effectiveness of the Commerce Act. The regulations are administered by the Ministry of Commerce, which publishes key pricing and performance data.

- In addition to being required not to misuse their dominant position under the Commerce Act, utilities also face the standard legal requirement that they should not lessen competition through their trade practices.

- Utilities involved in business acquisitions which lead to the acquisition or strengthening of a dominant position breach the Commerce Act, although such acquisitions may be sanctioned under the standard authorisation procedure.

- Regulatory barriers to entry have been minimised through the termination of statutory monopoly rights for almost all utility areas (the reduced rights in postal services are to be eliminated in 1998), so as to encourage the entry of new competitors. Entry has occurred subsequently in the case of telecommunications, television and radio broadcasting, and domestic airlines. These industries, all formerly state-owned statutory monopolies, are thus now treated like any other industry.

- In the regulatory reform of some utilities, there has been separation of contestable and non-contestable elements of the utility's activities, either by the non-contestable business being established as a separate company (for example, the separation of Trans Power, the high voltage electricity transmission system, from the electricity generator), or by the accounting ring-fencing of the two businesses (as required of local electricity distributors who are also electricity retailers).

- In cases where there has been no such separation,[15] incumbents who refuse to provide access to natural monopoly facilities on reasonable terms may breach s.36 of the Commerce Act, which can result in punitive damages being imposed.

- A further possibility is to break up the state-owned utility into competitors, as has happened with electricity generation. A wholesale electricity market has recently been established to facilitate competition between the two generators, while allowing technical co-ordination of generation and transmission from the company's major hydro and thermal power plants.

- Competition from substitute goods and from new technologies has been encouraged. Industries which historically have been the preserve of regulated monopolists, such as long-distance transport (Tranz Rail) and parcel post (New Zealand Post), have experienced intense competition from road freight and courier services respectively. In other industries, like telecommunications, technological advances in cellular, radio and satellite-based technologies are undermining the advantages of network ownership.

- In addition to these generally light-handed forms of regulation, there is a more heavy-handed measure of last resort: the use of price control as provided for in Part IV of the Commerce Act (or potentially some other form of statutory regulation which the government may wish to introduce). The Commerce Commission can recommend to the government that it impose price control. In addition, there have been specific warnings of direct regulation for particular industries. However, there are no goods currently subject to price control, and the government has shown no great desire to re-introduce such controls into the newly deregulated environment.

- In some cases the government has retained a 'Kiwi share' to prevent changes to the Articles of Association (for instance, to

---

[15] Examples include the major gas and telecommunication utilities, which were sold complete with networks. While there may be efficiency reasons for this integration, it has complicated the entry conditions for potential new competitors (see below).

maintain a 49 per cent domestic ownership of Air New Zealand to allow the government to negotiate international bilateral access agreements). Government trading enterprises have statements of corporate intent which may also limit the scope of their operations. For example, they may be prevented from diversifying their investments.

In addition, there are other forms of regulation in New Zealand which are of a social or safety nature, rather than being a form of light-handed regulation. Some privatised enterprises are required to meet particular service obligations (such as the universal service obligation on Telecom), or social obligations agreed with the government (such as New Zealand Post's obligations which include six-day delivery and a universal service requirement).

While the emphasis is to admit and encourage competition wherever possible, New Zealand's policy of light-handed regulation clearly does not mean zero regulation, as has sometimes been asserted.

The Role of Competition Law and Information Disclosure

As indicated above, the critical elements of the policy of light-handed regulation are competition law and information disclosure. These two elements are now examined briefly in turn.

Under New Zealand's light-handed policy, owners of natural monopoly networks are likely to be in a dominant position in a market, and thus to be subject to the s.36 prohibition of the Commerce Act that they must not use that position for the purpose of limiting competition. Specifically, firms which have a dominant position in a market must not:

. . . use that position for the purpose of –

(a) Restricting the entry of any person into that or any other market; or

(b) Preventing or deterring any person from engaging in competitive conduct in that or in any other market; or

(c) Eliminating any person from that or any other market.

While section 36 prohibits dominant firms from using a dominant position for the purpose of restricting competition, it does not prohibit the dominant firm from using its market power for other than anti-competitive purposes. For instance, the charging of a 'monopoly' price in itself is not prohibited, although the inference is that monopoly profits should be competed away where entry is possible.

There has been considerable discussion in the courts about the meaning of a 'dominant position in a market', how the presence or absence of dominance may be determined, and what constitutes 'use' and 'purpose'.[16]

In the utilities area, access by Clear Communications (the new entrant) to the local telephone network of Telecom (the incumbent) has been the subject of extensive litigation, which has potentially important ramifications for other network industries. Telecom put forward the Baumol-Willig rule[17] as the way of setting the interconnection price; it states that monopolists are entitled to provide services to competitors at the same price they implicitly charge themselves, including monopoly profits. This rule was accepted by the New Zealand High Court, rejected by the Court of Appeal, and finally in 1994 sanctioned by the Privy Council, New Zealand's highest court. Critics of the rule have argued that it has undermined the effectiveness of s.36 as a mainstay of light-handed regulation.

In 1995 government officials undertook an 'analysis of the experience of telecommunications interconnection negotiations in New Zealand', produced a detailed report, and invited submissions.[18] After lengthy consideration, the Government issued a media release on 26 June 1996 in which it pledged 'to continue, for the time being, with the present regulatory regime based upon the Commerce Act'.[19] In addition, it stated that:

---

[16] An excellent review is given by McGechan J in: Commerce Commission v Port Nelson Ltd., CP NO 12/92 (NN), June 1995, pp.39-53.

[17] W. Baumol and J. Sidak, 'The Pricing of Inputs Sold to Competitors', *Yale Journal on Regulation*, Vol. 11, 1994.

[18] Ministry of Commerce / The Treasury, *op. cit.*

[19] Minister of Commerce, 1996.

'...developments since the Privy Council decision demonstrate that the major telecommunications industry players do not support the Baumol-Willig rule as a satisfactory basis for interconnection pricing. The Government considers that the...rule has the potential to lessen competition, thereby limiting the rate of introduction of new products and services and lessening the benefits to users. The Government would be concerned to see the...rule being applied in future.'

Note, however, that this statement has not yet been enshrined in statute.

Information disclosure has been developed to its greatest extent in the electricity industry. This reflects the relative lack of competition and of substitute forms of energy in electricity, and the relative slowness of technical change which might otherwise serve to undercut market power.

The Electricity (Information Disclosure) Regulations 1994 introduced the requirement to disclose information, along with the accounting separation of distribution and retailing activities. Two years' information is now available, including line charges to all consumers, prices, and other key conditions of contract; costs and revenues by load group; separate financial statements from line owners on generation, line and retailing activities; and financial and other performance measures. By facilitating comparisons of prices and performance between power companies, this information is intended to discourage monopoly pricing, excessive cross-subsidisation and uneconomic generation, and to promote competition by facilitating access to distribution lines. Any cross-subsidisation, which occurs between commercial and domestic consumers, and between urban and rural areas, will be vulnerable to price undercutting by a competitor.

Where a business in either electricity or gas combines activities which have natural monopoly characteristics and others which are potentially competitive, separate audited statements are required, in order to detect instances where market power in the latter is enhanced by the use of monopoly leverage in the former. Consumers' bills must be unbundled so as to reveal the separate line and energy components, undermining the scope for price discrimination or cross-subsidy. However, comparisons between companies will have to make allowance for the scope in the regulations for companies both to define their businesses and to allocate assets and costs between them, as well as standardising for regional variations in network density, geology, and customer profile.

So far the Commerce Commission has had to resolve three main competition issues involving utilities: business acquisitions; the price and other terms of access to network facilities; and complaints of monopoly pricing. As an example, in the local markets for the supply and distribution of electricity, the Commerce Commission has received a number of complaints alleging inability by one company to gain access to another's network, usually because of onerous terms and conditions in the 'use of system' agreements. Until recently, the Commerce Commission has taken the view that such difficulties could often be resolved by negotiation, and by further refinement to access agreements, during the 'shakedown' period of industry adjustment to developing competition; but it also acknowledges that persistently anti-competitive behaviour (whether by a network owner towards an entrant seeking access, or by arrangements between incumbent suppliers and downstream buyers) may have to be taken to court. The Commission monitors industry developments continuously, and is currently investigating some more serious cases.

Utility Case Studies

The following utility case studies, covering telecommunications, electricity, natural gas, and ports and airports are illustrative of the application of light-handed regulation. Table 2 summarises the state of ownership and regulation in these utility industries.

Telecommunications

The state telephone monopoly was corporatised as Telecom Corporation of New Zealand (Telecom) in 1987. It is New Zealand's largest company by turnover. The Telecommunications Act 1987 set out a timetable for the phasing in of competition; restrictions on the supply of all telecommunications equipment were removed by mid-1988; and Telecom's statutory monopoly right over the provision of telecommunication network services was removed on 1 April 1989. This made New Zealand the only country to liberalise its telecommunications market without establishing an independent regulatory body. Telecom was then sold in 1990 complete with the national telephone network including the local

[Cont'd on p. 108]

TABLE 2
Regulation of Utilities in New Zealand (1996)

Utility	Sector	Companies[1]	Ownership[2]
Electricity	Generation	ECNZ, Contact	SOEs
	Transmission	Trans Power	SOE
	Distribution	39 local companies	LA, trusts, private
Gas	Extraction	Petrocorp, Shell, Todd	Private
	Transmission	NGC	Private
	Distribution	NGC & 4 companies	LA, trusts, private
Telecommunications	PSTN	Telecom, Clear	Private
	Cellular	Telecom, Bell South	Private
	Distance	Telecom, Clear	Private
	International	Telecom, Clear, Telstra, Sprint	Private
Ports, airports	Ports	13 companies	LA, some private
	International airports	4 companies	LA, govt, private
	Domestic airports	Many	LA, govt, private
Water, etc	Water	Many	LA
	Sewerage	Many	LA

---

[1] Only major operators mentioned.

[2] LA = Local authority, SOE = State-owned enterprise, Govt = Central government.

TABLE 2
(Continued)

Source of Natural Monopoly[3]	Type of Natural Monopoly	Information Disclosure Required[4]	Other Regulatory Requirements[5]
-	-	Financial and operational	Price undertakings
High voltage lines	Stand alone	Financial, performance and operational	-
Low voltage lines	Vertically integrated	Financial, performance and operational	Transitional price control available
-	-	-	-
High pressure pipes	Vertically integrated	Accounting & performance	None
Low pressure pipes	Vertically integrated	Accounting & performance expected to be finalised in 1997	Price control until 1990
Local loop	Vertically integrated	Inter-connection & prescribed service terms	Universal service obligation, price undertakings
-	-	Inter-connection	-
-	-	Inter-connection & prescribed service terms	-
-	-	-	-
Some wharves	Horizontally integrated	-	-
Some runways	Horizontally integrated	Under review	Price consultation required
Some runways	Horizontally integrated	Under review	Price consultation required
Pipes	Vertically integrated	Local government requirements	Local government requirements
Pipes	Vertically integrated	Local government requirements	Local government requirements

[3] Principal areas of economic activity with some natural monopoly characteristics.
[4] In addition to normal Companies Act requirements.
[5] In addition to standard requirements of State-Owned Enterprises Acts.

loop, to a joint venture between local investors and two large US telecommunication companies, Bell Atlantic and Ameritech.

No industry-specific regulation exists, apart from limited disclosure regulations with regard to Telecom's pricing under the Telecom (Disclosure) Regulations 1990, implemented on 1 July 1990, and under the Telecommunications (International Services) Regulations 1989 (revised in 1994). The former regulation was amended in 1993 to cover prices, terms and conditions of prescribed services and all interconnect agreements reached from 1993. However, a 'Kiwi share' obligation requires Telecom to maintain free local calls for residential customers, keep the same fixed rental charge for both urban and rural customers, and prevent the rental charge from being increased faster than the rate of inflation. In addition, Telecom provided a formal undertaking to the government in 1989 'to ensure that interconnection will be provided to competitors on a fair and reasonable basis'.

Clear Communications, a joint venture between New Zealand majority investors and two large North American telecommunication companies, was incorporated in August 1990, and entered the market in April 1991 after successfully negotiating a long-distance agreement with Telecom. The company began a toll bypass service using the railways' fibre optic main trunk cable plus leased capacity on Television New Zealand's microwave radio relay, together with an international tolls service. It secured some large customers, and by 1994 the company had completed its coverage of the country. By 1995 it had 21 per cent of the domestic toll market and 24 per cent of the international calls market.[20] Clear's inroad into the market, despite its customers initially having to dial a special access code, reflected its rivalrous undercutting of Telecom's prices. In late 1991 and early 1992 this led to a tolls 'price war' which caused a sharp decline in charges.

Clear claimed its ability to compete was hindered by Telecom's insistence that its subscribers use a code for access to the Telecom network until a threshold 9 per cent market share was attained. The dispute went to arbitration, with the arbitrator ruling that Telecom had breached s.36 of the Commerce Act by delaying non-code access for four months from December 1992 to April 1993. In the international market, both companies have begun to experience

---

[20] Ministry of Commerce/The Treasury 1995, *op. cit.*

aggressive toll discounting from several new entrants using the 'call-back' system. Sprint also entered the market in May 1995, concentrating on larger corporate clients.

BellSouth launched its cellular telephone network in Auckland in 1993, and reached an interconnection agreement with Telecom at the end of that year. By the end of 1994 the company was estimated to have 5 per cent of subscribers, with Telecom having the rest. BellSouth now claims its network covers 90 per cent of the population.

Apart from the price cuts, deregulation and competition have led to a wide range of new products and services being introduced. The industry has become more customer-orientated, with a substantial improvement in service quality (for example, speed of installation of new phones, greater reliability of pay phones).

Before Clear entered the market, it negotiated and signed a general agreement with Telecom concerning local business calls and 0800 numbers as well as toll calls. While details of tolls interconnection with Telecom were established, other plans by Clear were held up in protracted legal wrangles. The process started in 1991 when Clear sought access to Telecom's local loops in order to initiate its local calls service. When negotiations broke down Clear took Telecom to court, alleging that Telecom had breached s.36 of the Commerce Act by using its dominant position to restrict or deter competition. In December 1992 the High Court found that Telecom had breached s.36 by insisting on the access code and by refusing to supply a DDI service to Clear, but no damages were awarded. The Court also considered that the Baumol-Willig rule for the pricing of interconnection did not breach s.36. Professors Baumol and Willig had argued for Telecom that an owner of a natural monopoly facility should not have to allow competitors access at a price which is lower than the price they would charge themselves, including profit forgone.[21] Clear said that it could not compete under the rule.

Both companies appealed the decision. In December 1993 the Court of Appeal upheld the dominance finding but threw out the Baumol-Willig rule on the grounds that an interconnection price could not include an element of monopoly rent. The issue was appealed to the Privy Council, New Zealand's highest court. In its 1994 decision the Privy Council largely accepted the High Court

---

[21] Baumol and Sidak, *op. cit.*

judgement, and in particular commented on the role of s.36 in preventing abuses of a dominant position, stating:

'In their Lordships' view it cannot be said that a person in a dominant market position 'uses' that position for the purposes of section 36 [if] he acts in a way which a person not in a dominant position but otherwise in the same circumstances would have acted.'

The Privy Council also said that Telecom was not breaching s.36 by insisting on an interconnection price determined under the Baumol-Willig rule, even though that price could include an element of monopoly profits. The Privy Council was of the view that s.36 would, in the long term, place some limits on monopoly profits, but that if the government wanted to control monopoly profits directly, it should use the existing price control provisions contained in Part IV of the Commerce Act.

Telecom was found to be in breach of s.36 on two separate issues – though not Baumol-Willig – in each of the three court cases, as well as in the arbitration hearing. The costs imposed on would-be entrants have been substantial. Clear and others have frequently proclaimed the need for a government-defined framework for negotiation, or for some form of independent arbitration. The industry group Telecommunications Users' Association of New Zealand said in 1992:

'Fair competition in telecommunication markets requires the co-operation of the dominant player. Telecom, being the dominant player, understands the commercial value of time, and stands to benefit if there are delays in new players entering the market.' [22]

Given the implications for access in all network industries, the government asked officials to review the Privy Council judgement and to report on policy options. A discussion paper was published in 1995 which set out a number of options for access, ranging from a continuation of the *status quo* to more detailed industry-specific pricing principles and with mandatory arbitration.[23]   Following

---

[22] Quoted in D. Russell, 'The New Zealand Experience: The Consumer Protection Lessons Australia can Learn from it', in *Passing on the Benefits: Consumers and the Reform of Australia's Utilities*, Canberra: Trade Practices Commission, 1994, p.59.

[23] Ministry of Commerce / The Treasury (1995), *op. cit.*

submissions in June 1996 the government announced that it would continue with the current policy for the time being, but did express a wish that the Baumol-Willig rule should not be used in future on competition grounds.

Following the Privy Council decision, Telecom emphasised its wish to strike a deal with Clear. Various offers and counter-offers were made, but the issue was only finally resolved when in July 1995 the government gave the parties a limited time to reach agreement or face the regulatory consequences. From that point an agreement was reached quickly, which set out prices well below Baumol-Willig rates, and provided for a move to full reciprocity in five years. Further entrants may now gain access to the Telecom network by negotiating either with Telecom or with Clear.

Electricity

Electricity reform started with the corporatisation of the electricity generation and transmission activities of the Ministry of Energy into the Electricity Corporation of New Zealand (ECNZ) in 1987, and the removal of its virtual monopoly over generation. At that stage ECNZ had about 95 per cent of national generating capacity and ownership of the national high voltage transmission grid. Following electricity shortages in 1992, the government set up a task force to examine how a wholesale electricity market could be established as a means of producing efficient pricing signals for investment in new generating capacity and to facilitate the entry of new generators.

The separation of ECNZ's high voltage transmission business into an independent state-owned enterprise (Trans Power) in July 1994 was a first step in this process. It was envisaged that the natural monopoly grid business would effectively operate as a common carrier for any generating company which wished to use it.

The next step was the splitting from ECNZ in April 1996 of a second, state-owned generating company, Contact Energy, which was given nearly 30 per cent of the country's generating capacity, leaving ECNZ with about two-thirds. The aim was to encourage competition in the generation market. In the meantime, the local electricity supply sector was reformed through the corporatisation and commercialisation of the former electric power boards, and the ending of their monopoly franchise rights. This allowed the supply companies, and new energy traders, to compete for larger customers in the retailing end of the market.

The final step came with the formation of the wholesale electricity market, which became fully operational in October 1996. Supply companies and large industrial users are now able to choose between competing, and possible new entrant, power generators – or building their own generating capacity – in order to get better deals, and the resulting prices and other information provides a better basis than ECNZ's unilateral spot prices for an entrant's investment decisions. Buyers and sellers bid against each other for electrical power in 30 minute blocks, quoted at prices relating to about 200 entry or exit points along the national grid. Bids and offers are cleared, and prices are set, through a sophisticated, computer-based trading and information system developed from the Reuters Triarch foreign exchange dealing room system used by banks around the world.

The system was established by the Electricity Marketing Company (EMCO) which was set up in 1993 by key players in the electricity industry at the behest of the government.[24] The market's rules are agreed by participants, and compliance is determined by an independent market surveillance committee, which can levy heavy fines and even exclude players if attempts are made to 'rig' the market, such as by the use of 'gaming' by generators.

There are no major regulatory barriers to entering the generation market, but an entrant may face difficulties in accessing a fuel source, and must obtain consents required by the Resource Management Act 1991. Currently there are at least 20 significant generation project proposals being considered in different parts of the country using a variety of technologies (natural gas, co-generation, wind, geothermal, hydro and others), most by electricity supply companies.

Deregulation of the local supply market was initiated in 1990. Previously the 48 local Electricity Supply Authorities, which were largely under local government control with boards elected by consumers, had been statutory, vertically integrated (distribution plus energy retailing) monopolies in franchised territories defined by their distribution networks. They were exposed to competition

---

[24] ECNZ, Trans Power, and the Electricity Supply Association of New Zealand (ESANZ) each own shares of one-third in EMCO. ESANZ is an association of the electricity supply companies.

only on their appliance retailing and electrical contracting fringes. The first step towards commercialisation occurred in 1990 when the boards were replaced by trustees under government-appointed directors.

The Authorities were corporatised from 1 April 1993 under the Energy Companies Act 1992, with the government's intention being that all 43 companies should be publicly listed. However, the issue of the ownership of the companies was not fully resolved, and in many areas there was considerable opposition to this plan. Of the 39 companies remaining in early 1996, 20 had adopted community or consumer trust structures (some of which are intended to be temporary only); 10 were wholly or majority owned by local councils or the government; and the remaining nine had given away at least some of their shares to customers, but usually continued with some form of dominant trust or council shareholding, occasionally augmented by an 'outside' shareholding. A few of the latter have sought stock exchange listing.[25]

In the first year the Act allowed the supply companies to sell to customers anywhere, up to a limit of 0·5 gigawatt-hours per customer per year. The restriction on customer size was lifted in April 1994, giving free scope for all customers to purchase electricity from any supply company, or from one of the new energy trading companies formed to take advantage of the commercial opportunities under deregulation.

There have been limited attempts by individual supply companies to connect with non-traditional customers in the former franchise areas of rival companies – in other words, to offer competition in the provision of both network and retailing services. The most attractive potential 'targets' are large industrial customers sited in close proximity to the former 'border' where connection costs are relatively low. However, border crossings are risky to the supplier because of the investment required and the need for the long-term contractual protection of those investments, and to the customer because of the reliance upon a single connecting line. Alternatively, it is sometimes possible to bypass the rival's network by connecting a customer (or new large housing sub-division) directly to the Transpower grid through an adjacent substation, although this is so

---

25 ANZ McCaughan Securities (NZ), *The New Zealand Electricity Sector*, Auckland: ANZ McCaughan, 1996.

expensive as to be viable only for the largest customers. So far very few border crossings and direct connections have been accomplished.

Apart from such bypass competition in distribution services, there is some constraint on the market power of network owners arising from various other sources, such as actual or potential competition from alternative energy sources, and the threat of price control contained in Part IV of the Commerce Act. In addition, much importance has been attached to the Electricity (Information Disclosure) Regulations 1994, which were discussed above. However, the Minister of Energy has very recently expressed reservations about the effectiveness of information disclosure.

Competition is more likely to emerge in retailing through rivals supplying electricity to new customers via each others' networks. A problem faced by such competition is the cost of the time-of-use metering usually necessary, which renders uneconomic competition for small commercial and domestic customers. However, these barriers are likely to be reduced in the next few years as technical advances lower the cost of meters and lead to the development of related equipment. [26]

The key issue since deregulation has been the terms on which a new entrant retailer or supply company can gain access to an incumbent's distribution network in order to supply a customer. The Commerce Commission has received a number of complaints alleging inability to gain access to another's network, usually because of onerous terms and conditions in the 'use of system' agreements. These include refusal to negotiate, the demanding of unreasonable reconciliation costs, and the locking in of large customers through high line charges coupled with low unit energy charges. In some cases, the incumbent has insisted on a 'conveyancing' contract, in which it retains a relationship with the consumer, rather than the new retailer, for distribution services and charges. One entrant has argued that this restricts its room for marketing initiatives. Another bone of contention is where the boundary should be drawn between distribution and retailing, with

---

[26] Households are estimated to constitute 80 per cent of electricity consumers, and to account for about 35 per cent of total sales by supply companies. The use of 'consumer profiling' as a means of overcoming metering problems, and of prototype electronic meters, have been the subject of trials this year (1997) in New Zealand.

vertically-integrated incumbents having an incentive to put most functions in the distribution business in order to restrict the area in which entrants can compete.

Nonetheless, off-network retailing, although proportionally still very small, has increased sharply, and at least two companies have achieved access to other companies' distribution networks without negotiating 'use of system' (access) agreements. This has been accomplished through the signing by the customer or the entrant retailer of the incumbent's standard customer connection agreement, and notifying the incumbent that the electricity would be purchased from another supplier.[27]

Since deregulation and corporatisation, the original supply authorities – many of them too small to be efficient – have started to investigate the scope for merger and rationalisation, mainly amongst themselves, but with the injection of some non-traditional ownership (such as the United States-based Utilicorp). This is a continuation of a trend towards rationalisation which has occurred throughout this century.

The Commerce Commission has in recent times approved a number of proposals and investigated others, although only relatively few have so far been consummated. Mergers between non-adjacent companies typically pose no competitive concerns at the moment. The same generally applies to companies whose distribution networks share a common border; since each network is to a large extent a natural monopoly, the level of market power enjoyed by a company is not likely to be significantly strengthened (and hence to breach the strengthening of a dominant position threshold) by a merger with a neighbour unless, but for the merger, significant cross-border competition would be possible.[28] Even then, likely efficiency gains (for example, from savings in administration) might offset any detriment to competition, although no purely electricity authorisation case has yet been considered by the Commission.

In the retail markets the Commission has considered that large (but not small) customers are contestable, with the market in

---

27 Ministry of Commerce/The Treasury (1995), *op. cit.*

28 Commerce Commission, *Report on Clearance Application: Mercury Energy/Power New Zealand*, Wellington: Commerce Commission, 1994.

question being national in extent. In a recent case the Commission used, as a dividing line between contestable and non-contestable consumers, an annual consumption in the range of 0·1 to 0·5 gigawatt-hours, with the smaller figure being adopted for the purposes of analysis. The Commission has found in all cases to date that competition in the retailing markets will not be significantly reduced by a merger, because of the non-contestable nature of the market for retailing to small consumers, and because of the number of actual and potential players present in the retailing-to-large consumers market. Nevertheless, the situation could change in the future if the number of independently-owned networks continues to shrink. For example, yardstick competition relies for its effectiveness on there being a reasonable number of networks against which comparisons can be made.

Natural Gas

Natural gas is produced from several fields, both onshore and offshore, in the west of the North Island. The Natural Gas Corporation (NGC) was privatised with its ownership of the extensive North Island high-pressure pipeline network intact. This transmission system delivers gas to 15 separate low pressure reticulation systems in the main population centres run by local gas utilities, as well as direct to a number of large customers. These local pipe networks are natural monopolies apart from very limited potential for entry, either through the reticulation of an area not served within an incumbent's former franchise territory, or through bypass of its network using a pipeline connected direct to the transmission line (which, as with electricity, is economic only for large customers situated close to that line). NGC is also a major retailer which, together with the other big retailer Enerco, accounts for about 80 per cent of retail sales.

The Gas Act 1992, which came into force in April 1993, abolished the franchise system of territorial monopolies for the retail supply of gas. Simultaneously, the long-standing controls on wholesale and retail gas prices were lifted. As with electricity, the extensive regulation of the industry is being replaced with a light-handed form based, in part, on information disclosure (expected to be introduced shortly) and the separation of pipeline and energy charges.

116

The existing NGC wholesale supply contracts with retailers date back to 1980, and to the era of exclusive franchising. They contain a number of restrictive provisions which, by affecting the ability of both NGC and its utility customers to compete in new markets, are likely to breach provisions of the Commerce Act. These include an arrangement for the exclusive supply of gas from NGC; considerable restrictions on NGC competing with retailers; the requirement that new delivery points for gas be mutually agreed (coupled with NGC's view that it need not deliver to points outside each utility's current distribution system); and possibly the 15-year rolling term of contracts. All the parties have agreed that the contracts are inappropriate under the new light-handed régime, and are currently re-negotiating them, with some already having entered into new contracts. The Commerce Commission is keeping a close watch on progress.

The success of the reforms will depend upon local distribution systems becoming accessible on reasonable terms to new energy traders. NGC is to provide for sales of reserved capacity on the transmission pipeline for others to use, and will have to transport gas for others at a price equal to its own internal rate to avoid breaching the Commerce Act. But so far no access agreements have been made. In 1993 the Commission considered the potential for entry was very limited in the short term because of the lack of independent sources of gas, the anticipated slow development of access to networks, the long-term contracts tying large users to existing retailers, and the view of some retailers that their supply contracts with NGC prevented them from supplying outside their existing retail areas (which would breach the Commerce Act and therefore be unenforceable).

A major case was the proposed take-over of Enerco by NGC.[29] The Commerce Commission found that the acquisition would result in a strengthening of NGC's dominant position in the transmission, wholesaling and retailing markets, and declined authorisation on the grounds that the resulting detriments would not be outweighed by the likely public benefits. The Commerce Commission thought it likely that the acquisition would lead to the failure of the government's whole deregulation initiative in the industry.

---

29 Commerce Commission, *Decision No. 270: Natural Gas Corporation/Enerco*, Wellington: Commerce Commission, 1993.

Although Enerco was dominant in its own distribution and retail markets, and had limited incentive to compete with NGC, it had acted as leader of the opponents to NGC's competitive strategies in the past. Without Enerco, the remaining smaller companies were likely to be much less effective at resisting the encroachments of NGC.

An important issue has been the extent to which other energy forms, especially electricity, are substitutable for gas, and hence may serve to constrain the market power of NGC. After extensive consideration of the matter, including econometric estimates of cross-price elasticities in New Zealand and overseas, the Commerce Commission concluded that the various forms of energy were only imperfect substitutes.

Ports and Airports

Ports and airports in New Zealand have traditionally been owned by local authorities and central government, and run by locally-elected boards, almost as an arm of local government. From 1986 onwards they were corporatised and run as stand-alone businesses, with some limited sale of shareholdings. These companies are subject to the Commerce Act.

There have been a limited number of cases in the courts where s.36 of the Commerce Act has been invoked in relation to terms and conditions for access to airport and port facilities. The first case concerned the Auckland Regional Authority (ARA), which sought a declaratory judgement in 1987 as to whether it was obliged, under the Commerce Act, to grant licences to more than the two rental car operators already holding licences at Auckland International Airport, of which it was controller (ARA *v* Mutual Rental Cars). The court found that the ARA was able to influence the relevant market, which was for rental car services at Auckland airport (rather than in the wider Auckland area), through its dominance in the market for concessions to car rental firms. Moreover, the ARA agreed that its purpose in granting concessions to only two firms was to maximise its revenue. Under the licence tendering process, the two successful firms entered higher bids when there were to be only two operators, compared to when there were to be three. The ARA was thus found to be in breach of s.36:

'Although ARA's motive may have been to maximise rent, by accepting only two rental car operators, its means of achieving this objective was the use of its dominant position to exclude competitors of the successful concessionaires.'

Barker J. also drew attention to the American concept of the 'bottleneck facility', which seemed appropriate to the case, and which 'describes a facility which is incapable of duplication and of circumvention and to which others must have access if they are to compete in a given market.' It follows that '(t)he exclusion of others by means of the bottleneck facility is anti-competitive; it should be eliminated by providing for the admission of others to the joint venture if they meet reasonable objective criteria.'

The doctrine was revisited by the High Court in Union Shipping *v* Port Nelson. Under the Port Companies Act 1988, the ports had been divided from their traditional harbour board ownership, and are run on a commercial basis by separately formed port companies. In the transfer of the commercial arm of the former Nelson Harbour Board, Port Nelson Ltd (PNL) took over the considerable number of forklifts, together with services of related personnel, needed to meet high seasonal demands. It also enjoyed a monopoly in the provision of harbour facilities in the Nelson area because there was no railway, the facilities could not be duplicated, and the nearest rival at Picton was too small and too far by road. However, the court was reluctant to incorporate the 'bottleneck (or essential facilities) theory' into New Zealand competition law for various reasons, including its derivation within a different statutory base, and its being sharply criticised by the Full Court of the Federal Court in Australia on appeal in Queensland Wire *v* BHP.

The case arose from the efforts by PNL to require the Union Shipping company to use its forklifts and drivers on the Nelson waterfront, initially through a total ban on stevedores using their own plant, and later from imposing a wharf user levy. The court found that these demands were explicable only because PNL was dominant in the market for stevedoring services in Nelson, and that it had used that position for the purpose of maintaining the optimal utilisation of its plant and manpower, to its financial advantage. But a subsidiary purpose was to inhibit others from using non-PNL plant and manpower, thereby preventing competition from others in the market, in breach of s.36. The inference was drawn not from the imposition of the levy, but from the levy exceeding what was 'commercially reasonable'. The court recommended that the dispute be resolved through an independent cost accounting analysis to produce a commercially appropriate wharf user levy, although no effort was made to define that term.

An insight into how New Zealand courts might view cross-subsidisation has recently been provided by the Court of Appeal (1996) in Port Nelson v Commerce Commission. The relevant issue was how the company should charge for its pilotage services for small ships, in competition with an independent pilotage company which was able to handle only small ships. The port company had set a $100 minimum charge for such ships, which had been found by the lower court to be below all measures of the cost of providing the service, including both avoidable (or opportunity) cost and fully allocated cost. Instead of then proceeding to calculate avoidable costs in line with the Baumol-Willig rule, the Court (p. 31) advocated a pricing policy for the port company based on fully allocated costs:

> In the circumstances of this case to fix pilotage charges according to PNL's opportunity cost of providing a pilot service for vessels under 2,500 GRT . . . while maintaining incontestable services (including for practical purposes pilotage of larger vessels) upon which all common costs then would fall would be inconsistent with the very purpose of competition law. The evidence that more directly related to the factual situation...demonstrates that an approach to costing more closely related to actual cost per vessel is appropriate.

Prior to April 1988 most airports were run as joint ventures between central government and one or more local authorities. From that date some of the joint ventures were replaced by airport companies which were to operate on a fully commercial basis, the aim being to enhance efficiency. With corporatisation, the airport companies were given the freedom to set their own charges based on the cost of providing services, subject only to the requirement under the Airport Authorities Act 1966 (amended 1986) to consult with airlines before setting charges.[30] This provision was designed

---

[30] The pricing policies of airport companies are not normally challengeable under the Commerce Act, despite the companies often being monopolies, because it is not normally possible to connect their pricing with an anti-competitive purpose. Airlines' attempts to

to offset the airports' market power derived from their natural monopoly over the provision of take-off and landing facilities. However, this constraint on the conduct of airport companies is seen as weak by airport users, and has been the subject of dispute in the courts (Air New Zealand *v* Wellington Airport).

The airport companies are also subject to general competition policy. Nonetheless, the government has stated that 'current legislation provides insufficient protection for airport users against potential abuse by airports of their monopoly power', and is currently canvassing views on proposals to strengthen the obligation on airport companies to consult with users in setting charges, and to disclose specific information to facilitate the consultation process.[31]

Summary and Conclusions

In New Zealand the corporatisation of government trading activities (including utilities) into state-owned enterprises had the goal of putting their operations into a corporate framework with commercial objectives, and in the same competitive environment as that faced by companies in the private sector. Statutory entry barriers were dismantled, some information disclosure requirements were introduced, access to networks was required, competition was encouraged, social obligations (if any) were carefully specified, and the new enterprises were subject to the prohibitions of the Commerce Act. Separating out the contestable and non-contestable parts of utilities also served the useful function of narrowing considerably the non-contestable areas upon which regulation had to be focused, compared to the situation under state ownership.

There are several industries, formerly regarded as 'utilities', such as broadcasting, whose competition outcomes nowadays pose relatively few worries, even in New Zealand's relatively small markets where economies of scale suggest small numbers of firms. For the remaining 'core' of non-contestable services, however, those factors, together with the country's geographic isolation, which

---

challenge airport pricing by judicial review on administrative law grounds of the behaviour of the statutory monopolies, by assessing the reasonableness of the asset valuations upon which prices are based, have not been successful. See Farmer, 'Transition from Protected Monopoly to Competition: The New Zealand Experiment', *Competition and Consumer Law Journal*, Vol. 1, 1993, pp. 27-29.

31 Ministry of Transport, *Review of New Zealand Airport Regulation: Proposals for Consultation*, Wellington: MOT, 1995.

eliminates any possibility of importation, render the underlying tensions between efficiencies and competition potentially as acute as anywhere in the Western world.

A key feature of New Zealand's competition law is the narrow focus on a single, well defined objective – the promotion of competition as a means of increasing efficiency, with efficiency potentially over-riding competition where the two conflict. A second key feature is the broad scope of the Commerce Act, which extends to almost all 'in trade' activities. Consistent application of the Commerce Act across the economy is encouraged by having a single body responsible for enforcement. This also reduces the likelihood of the regulator becoming captured by a specific industry; allows policy in one industry to be informed by, and to be consistent with, experience in another; and is much cheaper.

Overall, the New Zealand system of light-handed regulation has comparatively low regulatory costs incurred by the Commerce Commission and the courts, and low compliance costs incurred by businesses. On the other hand, enforcement and litigation costs can be high. For example, in April 1994 Clear claimed that since 1991 it had spent 300 days in negotiations, 56 days in mediation, 65 days in arbitration, and over $NZ7 million in litigation. However, that dispute can be seen as producing an investment in access, with socially beneficial externalities for other would-be entrants in telecommunications and beyond. Parallel cases by others, such as the Commerce Commission's prosecution of Port Nelson, have added to those benefits by extending the range of court precedent.

A key goal of utility regulation in New Zealand is that of economic efficiency in the form of productive and dynamic efficiencies. This is promoted by the encouragement of competition through new entry wherever possible. Entrants bring innovative products and processes, and stimulate former monopoly incumbents to improve the efficiency of their operations and to become more sensitive to the demands of customers. Where the market is non-contestable, the focus switches to the goal of allocative efficiency and the avoidance of monopoly pricing. Here, light-handed regulation falls back on the frequently articulated, but yet to be activated, threat of price control, with the further vague threat of some heavier form of regulation as a last resort. The credibility of this approach is likely to vary with differing industry perceptions about the readiness of successive governments to act.

Utility operators which own natural monopoly networks to which others need access if they are to compete in related markets, generally continue to enjoy incumbency advantages compared with entrants. This is partly because the legal precedents defining terms of access are as yet incomplete; partly because the slow pace of court resolutions gives scope to delay entry (especially for firms outside telecommunications whose monopoly power is local, and where the political impact is likely to be limited); and partly because the reliance on the threat of price control may lack full credibility when the policy has yet to be used.[32]

Potential entrants, on the other hand, now have a wide range of opportunities compared to the situation prior to deregulation, but still face a difficult task in entering to compete against an established incumbent (as well as other entrants, in some cases). There have been numerous complaints by entrants and user groups in various industries, particularly in telecommunications and electricity, about the light-handed regulatory system. In some cases, entrants' criticisms pre-date their entry, so it can be assumed that they knew the pitfalls of the system at the time they invested. Also, they are not averse to using the court system to their advantage wherever possible to stymie incumbents.

When the New Zealand regulatory system was designed in the 1980s, there was probably some under-assessment of the complexities of regulating utilities, especially vertically integrated natural monopolies. In addition, there was insufficient attention paid to what the new policy required from the judicial system, and whether the courts would be able to respond to the new role envisaged for them.

The reliance on a competition law approach has also posed problems. While it is often relatively straightforward to describe, from an economics perspective, what should be seen as contravening conduct, it is more difficult to capture those contraventions in a statute with the required generality and legal precision; much depends upon legal interpretation of words like

---

[32] It has recently been suggested that when firms take the price control threat seriously, their behaviour may be distorted in much the same way as occurs under more 'heavy handed' forms of rate making. See M. Pickford, 'Information Disclosure, the Baumol-Willig Rule, and the Light-handed Regulation of Utilities in New Zealand', *New Zealand Economic Papers*, Vol. 30, 1996.

'dominance', 'use', and 'purpose'. The court system has also encountered difficulties in reaching speedy conclusions in the face of logistical problems and delays caused by counsel seeking to use the system for their own strategic purposes. In addition, the courts have tended to adopt a non-economic and conservative view with regard to the imposition of injunctions, penalties, damages, and costs, thereby reducing the deterrence effect of their judgements.

Critics have argued that the law is too comfortable for incumbents and too challenging for new entrants. A number of interests – both potential entrants and customers of incumbents – have intensified lobbying for stronger s.36 penalties, for a government-determined framework for interconnection in telecommunications, and for legally binding arbitration in disputes between owners of networks and potential entrants. Such arbitration proposals have been criticised as being likely to distort investment decisions, since investors may not know in advance whether, and under what terms, they might be required to share the use of their assets with others.

It has proved difficult to specify an access rule that will necessarily prove optimal in all circumstances. As an example, the government has rejected the Baumol-Willig access pricing rule on the basis that it unduly restricts entry by setting an access price which is too high, yet this, too, could have adverse consequences. The rule is designed to solve the 'make-or-buy' issue by favouring whichever firm – the incumbent or the potential entrant – can supply the service at the lower cost. Setting an access price lower than the Baumol-Willig price has the potential to encourage the entry of firms which are less efficient than the incumbent. While this may be justified if the entrants can ultimately achieve equal efficiency through 'learning by doing', there seems to be no means of distinguishing the ultimately efficient entrants from the permanently inefficient.

Nonetheless, it is clearly important that incumbents are not protected by unduly high access prices, since the mere exposure of incumbents to the real threat of competition, even without entry actually taking place, may be sufficient to cause them to improve their efficiency. Alternatively, the promotion of inefficient entry through the adoption of other pricing rules could conceivably still be socially beneficial overall if the resulting inefficiencies were more than offset by dynamic gains from the introduction of competition in the market.

The success of light-handed regulation has to be gauged against the probability that natural monopoly is more widespread in New Zealand than in other countries, because markets are typically relatively small. Moreover, no form of regulation is able to eliminate all monopoly distortions in the economy; all operate in a 'second best' world. The costs and benefits of New Zealand's light-handed approach thus have to be compared with those likely with other imperfect, regulatory options, rather than with 'first best' outcomes in an ideal (but unreal) world.

While it is very difficult to assess what benefits other options might have brought, the current policy has made major inroads into areas of monopoly power in a relatively short time, starting from a former position of government ownership and heavy regulation. For example, New Zealand Rail's freight rates reportedly fell by 50 per cent in real terms between 1983 and 1991. Over the period 1987-1994 Telecom reduced the price in real terms of a basket of residential telephone services by 45 per cent. In comparison with some other regulatory systems (eg that of Australia), New Zealand appears to have made significant gains,[33] although fierce debate continues about New Zealand's telecommunications policy. Household and business customers alike have also benefited from large improvements in the promptness and quality of service, and in the range of options available.

New Zealand's policy is an innovative one which has attracted much international attention, but the policy is still relatively new. The reality of market entry, technical change and the development of new contractual arrangements between firms suggests that markets are dynamic, with unpredictable long term outcomes. Hence the success of the policy may only be judged by a comparison with alternatives over a longer term than is currently available.

---

[33] H. Ergas, *Telecommunications Across the Tasman: A Comparison of Regulatory Approaches and Economic Outcomes in Australia and New Zealand*, Working Paper Series, Centre for Research in Network Economics and Communications, Auckland, 1996.

Appendix: Summary Of New Zealand Competition Law (1996)

Introduction	
The Statute	Commerce Act 1996 and amendments
Objective	Promotion of competition in markets in New Zealand.
Mergers	
Threshold	Dominance
Prohibition	Acquiring or strengthening
Authorisable?	If public benefits outweigh detriments (must have regard to efficiency)
Procedure	Voluntary application for clearance, authorisation
Market Power	
Threshold	Dominance
Prohibition	Restricting entry Preventing/deterring competitive conduct Eliminating any person
Authorisable?	No
Vertical Arrangements	
Threshold	Substantial lessening of competition, exclusionary arrangements
Prohibition	Contracts, arrangements, understandings
Authorisable?	If resulting public benefits outweigh detriments

Special Provisions:	
- RPM	Presumed illegal, but authorisable
- Price discrimination	Substantial lessening of competition test, authorisable
- Third line forcing	Substantial lessening of competition test, authorisable
- Exclusive dealing, ties, etc	Substantial lessening of competition test, authorisable
Price Control	
Legislation	Part IV, Commerce Act
Procedure	Price control (currently unused)
Horizontal Agreements	
Threshold	Substantial lessening of competition
Prohibition	Contracts, arrangements, understandings
Authorisable?	If resulting public benefit
Special provisions:	
Price fixing	Presumed illegal but authorisable
Boycotts, other market arrangements	Substantial lessening of competition test, authorisable
Consumer Rights	
Legislation	Fair Trading Act
Prohibition	Misleading/deceptive conduct False representations Certain practices
Requirements	Certain product safety & consumer information requirements

Enforcement

Competition Agency	New Zealand Commerce Commission
Role	Enforcement, authorisation, adjudication
Appeals re agencies	High Court (+ lay members)
Contraventions determined by	High Court (+ lay members)
Private action	Available
Sanctions, penalties	Fines, injunctions, damages, divestitures, court orders

Jurisdiction/Exemptions

Overseas activities of citizens	Yes if affects NZ market
Domestic activities of foreigners	Yes if affects NZ market
Activities beyond borders	Yes if affects NZ market
Export cartels	Some exempted
Specific industries	International shipping and civil aviation, state pharmaceuticals exempted
Intellectual property	Generally exempt
Labour markets	Exempt

Additional Reading

Arlidge, R. (1995): 'How to Frustrate the Intent of Electricity Deregulation', *Electricity Rationalisation Conference*, Wellington, 29 – 31 March.

Auckland Regional Authority v Mutual Rental Cars (Auckland Airport) Ltd., 2 NZLR [1987] 647-681.

James, M. (1996): 'The Land of the Long White Benchmark: The New Zealand Reforms', *IPA Backgrounder*, Vol. 8/5, July.

Ministry of Commerce (1995): 'Light-handed Regulation of the New Zealand Electricity and Gas Industries', (mimeo), Wellington: Energy and Resources Division.

Pickford, M. (1985): 'A New Test for Manufacturing Industry Efficiency – An Analysis of the Results of Import Licence Tendering in New Zealand', *International Journal of Industrial Organisation*, Vol. 3, June, pp. 153-77.

Pickford, M. (1996): 'Information Disclosure, the Baumol-Willig Rule, and the Light-handed Regulation of Utilities in New Zealand', *New Zealand Economic Papers*, Vol. 30, pp. 199-218, December.

Privy Council (1994): *Telecom v. Clear*, Appeal No. 21 of 1994, Privy Council, London.

Spicer, B., R. Bowman, D. Emanuel, and A. Hunt (1991): *The Power to Manage: Restructuring the New Zealand Electricity Department as a State-Owned Enterprise*, Auckland: Oxford University Press.

Trade Practices Commission (1995): *Passing on the Benefits: Consumers and the Reform of Australia's Utilities*, Canberra: Trade Practices Commission.

Tru Tone Ltd. v Festival Records, 2 NZLR [1988] 352-364.

Union Shipping New Zealand Ltd. & Anor. v Port Nelson Ltd., 3 NZBLC [1990] 101,618-101,654.

Wellington International Airport Ltd. v Air New Zealand, 1 NZLR [1993] 671-684.

CHAIRMAN'S COMMENTS

M. E. Beesley

WE ARE ALL VERY GRATEFUL FOR THE FRANK WAY in which you have addressed the New Zealand approach. When readers pick up the lecture afterwards they will know we are also indebted to you for the mine of information provided. All this has the most useful function of beginning to correct what we think we know about the New Zealand approach.

With such a rich menu, the problem is to know where to start. I will lead, as is our custom, but because I am not a regulator whose every word has potential information content, I will not stand for long in the way of questions from the floor.

I suppose the main feeling I had in reading the paper was to wonder how far the New Zealand 'light-handed' approach was a synonym for avoiding problems which are now coming home to roost. Here are a few examples of questions which arise:

First, the big problem is trading over networks. The paper stresses the role of 'restructuring' utilities to sort out the contestable from the natural monopoly activities. Separate ownership is the key. But the paper notes continuing integration in gas and telecoms, for example. How can these situations be remedied? Must there be new legislation, always difficult to deliver? How otherwise can further separation be done?

Second, competition over networks in electricity, you say, will have to await time-of-use metering. We have recognised the likely long delay in this in the UK by introducing for 1998 customer profiles as the currency for competition. How could such a solution emerge in New Zealand? (For this question I can pass on whether profiles are desirable!)

Third, in telecoms, we would tend now to say that the 'natural monopoly' lies in the ability of the incumbent, BT, still to provide near-universal delivery of calls, not so much picking them up. I think you rightly identify the source of power still as the local loop. On your principles, it should be in separate ownership. Further, the asymmetry of delivery and pick up indicates the need for particular regulatory measures for such separated loops. What are the prospects in New Zealand for vertical separation within Telecoms *and* Clear? Could it be an analogue in New Zealand of the MMC 1993 case in Gas, on which the present separations in gas are based?

Fourth, the central interconnect deal was dealt with, as you explain, under Section 36 of the Commerce Act. Now Telecom and Clear have settled, we are agog to know what has to be done. Have you substituted a sweetheart duopoly agreement (sanctioned by the case) which will be capable of yielding very long-lasting advantages to the two companies?

Fifth, in gas competition at retail depends both on access to distributors' pipes *and* competitive supplies of gas. The paper records that no access agreements have been made. Has the Commission simply given up the ghost on both necessary conditions?

Finally, I am sad to see that in Airports, pricing policies are not normally challengeable under the Commerce Act. Private airlines' actions have failed. Perhaps there will have to be an RPI-x price control for airports after all?

All in all, I wonder whether instead of contrasting New Zealand with the rest of the world, a better thesis might be 'convergence' of regulation processes when 'regulation' means, as it always should do, both anti-trust law and specific utility regulation? If so, I will have to amend my first hypothesis to say that New Zealand's 'light hand' is a recipe for postponement of convergence, not avoidance of difficulties!

5

ELECTRICITY: COMPETITION FOR SMALL ACCOUNTS AFTER 1998

Dermot Glynn

National Economic Research Associates

Introduction

OFFER HAS RECENTLY PUBLISHED A CONSULTATION DOCUMENT[1] setting out its initial thoughts on the supply price restraints that should apply to Public Electricity Suppliers (PESs) after the introduction of full retail competition in the electricity supply market in 1998. Offer is to be complimented on much of the analysis in the report. However, the latest paper takes the need for a supply price restraint as a foregone conclusion. In my presentation today, I want to reverse this assumption. Competition has proved sufficient for larger electricity consumers; what leads us to believe that this will not also be the case for small account holders?

I want to address two main themes. I believe that there is a *prima facie* case that there will be enough competition in the market for small account holders not to warrant price controls, and I will be examining the features of the market that make this so. Second, there is a danger that continued regulatory controls could frustrate the success of competition in the electricity supply market after 1998.

The greater part of my paper will relate to the introduction of retail competition for small consumers in the electricity industry, although I will also be drawing on experience with small account holders in other utility sectors. Here, let me stress that I am focusing on the supply of electricity, not on electricity distribution, which is a natural monopoly and, as such, needs to be regulated.

---

[1] Offer, *The Competitive Electricity Market from 1998: Price Restraints*, September 1996.

Offer sees competition as a way of protecting small account holders. However, at the same time it is concerned that competition may not be 'effective' for some consumers and hence envisages the need for continued regulatory control. While placing much store in competition as the protector of small account holders, Offer appears reluctant to rely on competition alone – at least in a transitional phase following 1998. It is as though, genuinely believing in competition, but seriously enjoying regulation, they are praying to rely on competition – but not just yet.

However, there is a danger that continued regulation would distort the development of competition and undermine the benefits that competition can bring. Competition and regulation are interdependent. Regulation is justified by the presence of insufficient competition. Equally, the development of competition is very sensitive to the form of any regulatory controls adopted.

It is only when we have identified our objectives and the *specific* problems that might arise that we can judge the appropriateness or otherwise of different regulatory solutions. Offer's recent consultation document explores many different regulatory tools, in particular different forms of price restraints. Here I hope to further the discussion on the factors that might justify *any* form of regulatory control.

To justify continued controls after 1998 requires a thorough analysis of the market in order to establish that competition will not be sufficient to protect small account holders. To do this we will need:

- a definition of what counts as sufficient or 'effective' competition; and

- evidence of features of the market that prevent the achievement of effective competition.

Having discussed these questions in the context of the electricity supply market, I will address some specific aspects of Offer's current proposals which may affect the development of efficient competition in this market.

Competition in the Electricity Supply Industry

Let me first recap briefly on experience to date with the introduction of competition in electricity supply in the UK. The expansion of the competitive market has been a gradual process. Sites with a maximum annual demand of over one megawatt have been able to choose their supplier since 1990. This threshold was lowered to 100 kilowatts in April 1994. From April 1998 (or from the date of the quarterly meter reading for April – June), unless Offer accedes to the demand in some parts of the industry for a phased introduction of competition, *all* customers will be able to choose their electricity supplier.

Most of the suppliers entering the competitive ('second-tier') market to date have been generators or other PESs. It will be interesting to see whether – or rather, how far – the range of suppliers widens after 1998. Traditional retailers, in particular supermarket chains, are reported to be considering entering the market. Other utilities are also potential entrants. Indeed, British Gas has already obtained a licence to supply electricity, and may be a formidable player. A wider range of suppliers may result in fresh approaches to such matters as billing and payment methods. Competition is also anticipated to result in lower tariffs, reinforced by enhanced competition in generation as suppliers 'shop around' for cheaper power. Thus competition can be expected to exert downward pressure not only on supply costs, but also on generation costs (which account for the largest proportion of total electricity costs) as suppliers shop around.

Offer has estimated that around 5 per cent of consumers may opt for competitive supply in 1998. Significantly higher initial take-up rates of around 25 per cent were experienced in both the over 1 MW market, and the above 100kW markets in England and Wales, with the proportion of consumers taking second-tier supply rising over time. However, in Scotland only 5 per cent of eligible consumers have contracts with second-tier suppliers.

The electricity supply market is not unique in being opened to competition. The gas market is also due to become fully competitive in 1998. In the trials currently being carried out ahead of the introduction of full competition, ½ million consumers in the South West of England are already eligible to choose a competing gas supply and a further 1½ million are expected to become eligible early in 1997. Likewise, in telecoms, the entry of cable companies into the market has broadened competition for small account holders.

What is 'Effective Competition'?

With the introduction of competition in a previously monopolised sector, regulatory emphasis shifts from consumer protection to the promotion of competition, one of Offer's duties under the Electricity Act. The notion of 'effective competition' is central in Offer's approach to determining the relevant scope and duration of regulation in the electricity industry after April 1998. In Offer's consultation paper, regulation is deemed necessary for those market segments where competition is initially expected not to be 'sufficiently effective', but is intended only to be a *transitional* measure until competition does become 'effective'.

Given the central importance of this notion, it is essential to establish a clear working definition of exactly what is meant by 'effective competition', a term which is not defined in the law, nor in economic text books.

Competition is not an end in itself, but a means to an end, that of achieving greater economic efficiency. Therefore, the definition which I have always used is that to be 'effective' competition must enhance efficiency. At this series of lectures last year, John Vickers expressed this idea very succinctly:

> '...promoting economic efficiency is what effective competition is effective at doing.'[2]

The question that immediately follows from this definition is: how do we determine when competition enhances efficiency?

Competition is likely to increase efficiency if the customer has the *ability* and *incentive* to switch suppliers when, and only when, switching reduces *total* costs, including the transactions costs of appraising different suppliers, and taking expectations about future cost trends into account. Thus switching will reduce total costs when the new entrant's avoidable cost *plus* the switching costs (to the customer and the supplier) are less than the incumbent's avoidable cost. This is illustrated in the following chart:

---

[2] John Vickers, 'Competition and Regulation: The UK Experience', in *Regulating Utilities: A Time For Change?*, IEA Readings 44, London: Institute of Economic Affairs, 1996.

An Example of Inefficient Switching

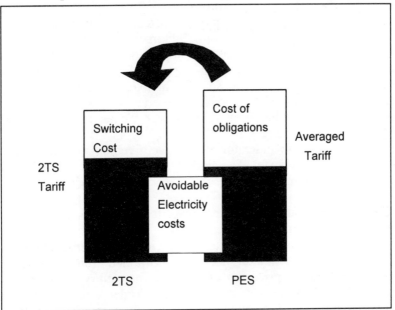

There is an important dynamic issue which needs to be considered alongside this definition. Inefficiencies in the short run, such as may arise as a consequence of measures to encourage the number of entrants into the market, *may* be necessary in order to achieve enhanced efficiency, resulting from greater competitive pressure in the long run. The cost of short-run inefficiencies therefore needs to be weighed against any anticipated benefits in the longer term. We should note that this possibility does not *in itself* justify regulatory intervention; the prospect of future efficiency gains is the basis for many investment decisions in competitive markets.

Will Competition be Effective after 1998?

The Economics of Market Power

Establishing a definition of effective competition is only the first step in justifying regulatory intervention. What is also needed is a means of identifying whether or not competition is likely to be effective, as we have defined it. That is, will consumers have the ability and the incentive to switch suppliers after 1998 when it would be efficient for them to do so?

Answering this question requires consideration of what features of the electricity supply market in 1998 may distort price signals to consumers. Given our definition, competition will be inefficient if prices do not reflect underlying costs, or if consumers are not bearing their full switching costs. To the extent that the PESs have market power after 1998 and an incentive to abuse that power, competition will not be efficient. However, we need to demonstrate that this will be the case.

There is no unique indicator of a competitive market. In order to establish to what extent a market is competitive or whether participants have market power it is necessary to look at a range of factors.

Structural measures of market power focus on market shares and the number of competitors in a market. However, taken on their own, structural measures are often a poor indicator of market power. A single firm in a market may be constrained from abusing its position and raising prices by the threat of new entry. Conversely, several firms in a market may collude in order to sustain higher prices, whether in a planned way, or as in normal oligopolistic behaviour by having regard for how their competitors may react.

The shortcomings of structural measures lead us into analysing *conduct* in order to assess the effectiveness of competition. To do this we need to define the types of behaviour which we would take as signifying an abuse of market power, such as undue price discrimination, cross-subsidy or predatory pricing. Indeed, market power is normally defined as the ability to raise or lower market price (or the quality of service provision) in relation to competitive market levels. Such price movements lead to inefficient price signals; hence, competition will not be effective.

If we define market power as an ability to charge prices which differ from those that would pertain in a competitive market, this focuses attention on the question of what is to be taken as a competitive outcome. This takes us to our third measure of market power, namely *performance* criteria. If incumbents have market power and abuse it by charging prices above competitive levels, this may be revealed by the presence of excess profits, for example, profits which are higher than those normally earned in a competitive situation with that industry's level of risk.

138

Linking market power abuse to performance is not straightforward, however. The presence of excess profits need not indicate a failure of competition, since the incumbent may (at least for a time) have a natural cost advantage over its competitors, allowing it to make high profits even if prices are set no higher than at new entrant levels. Conversely, a lack of profit does not necessarily signal an absence of market power. An incumbent with market power may prefer an easy life, with resulting high inefficiency, high costs and low profits.

An important class of conduct, which is a familiar concern in financial markets, is the ability to manipulate prices in the market. Offer's intervention in the electricity market in 1994 was prompted by concerns that the two main incumbent generators were acting together to raise the Pool price at certain times. Similarly, concern has been expressed in some quarters that the recent large increases in spot prices in the bulk gas market are not the result of market forces but are a sign that key market players may be improperly influencing prices.

All these examples show that the analysis of the extent to which a market is competitive is not straightforward. It requires detailed consideration of the features of the market. Such an analysis is crucial in supporting or rejecting assertions about the likely effectiveness of competition after 1998, and therefore in justifying any consequent intervention by the regulator. It is to that analysis that I now turn.

Definition of the Market

The first step in analysing any market is to define exactly what constitutes that market. For the electricity supply market, a key question is whether the market is local, regional (defined by the areas currently covered by each PES), or national. However, what constitutes a market can also be defined in other terms, such as load characteristics, maximum demand, or the class of consumer and his ability or willingness to pay. There is also a question as to which services are covered by the market. Is there a distinct market for electricity services, or is the market one for energy services, encompassing gas as well as electricity supply?

Oftel provides us with an example of a regulator directly addressing the issue of market definition. In its consultation paper on 1997, Oftel proposes to adopt an approach to defining distinct markets broadly similar to that used by the US anti-trust authorities, namely, that if a sole supplier of a particular product would find it profitable to increase the price, then that product or service constitutes a distinct market. This procedure is basically the same as that used by the OFT,[3] and its adoption is being contemplated by the European Commission's DGIV.

Is the Electricity Supply Market Contestable?

Once we have defined the market, the next step in the analysis is to explain what features of that market may give the PESs market power after 1998, and why they might have an incentive to abuse that power.

Some economists argue that in a *contestable* market, the incumbent will be forced by the threat of new entrants to keep prices at competitive levels. According to this view, if we are to justify regulatory intervention, we must therefore show why we do not expect the electricity supply market to be contestable after 1998.

If prices in a contestable market rise above competitive levels, new firms will enter the market, undercutting the incumbent's price and taking market share. The fundamental assumptions underlying the theory are that both entry and exit are costless, and that there are no sunk costs. Competitor firms are therefore willing to enter the market to exploit a profitable opportunity, however short-lived.

Assumptions of literally costless entry and exit are not justified in the real world. Barriers to entry and/or exit mean that entry is not costless, and the entrant will need to be in the market for a certain period to make entry worthwhile. If the incumbent has the ability to react to any entry immediately by lowering its price back to (or below) competitive levels, and is seen to be able to act in this way, this is likely to deter competitors from entering the market. Under these circumstances, the market is not contestable and the threat of entry does not prevent the incumbent from raising prices above competitive levels.

However, there is a danger in *assuming* that the electricity supply market will not be *sufficiently* contestable, rather than *demonstrating* why this is the case. It may be that contestable market theory is more applicable to the electricity supply market

---

[3] See 'Market Definition in UK Competition Policy', OFT Research Paper No. 1, NERA, March 1993.

than it is in other areas. For example, second-tier suppliers who are PESs in other regions will already have invested in some of the infrastructure and know-how needed to compete, and so may face relatively low start-up and sunk costs. And the licence conditions prohibiting undue discrimination would make it unlikely that incumbents could respond to entrants with targeted price reductions. In these circumstances, the threat of entry will do much of the job of protecting consumers that Offer wants to assign to regulation. At the very least, addressing the question of what constitutes a barrier to entry in the market, and the cost of exit, focuses discussion on the relevant features of the market which may prevent competition from being effective after 1998.

Barriers to Entry

Offer identifies several potential entry barriers, in particular economies of scale in customer service and 'first-mover advantages' arising from the PES incumbent's position. Such advantages include an established reputation and customer inertia.

It is not clear, however, that these factors necessarily constitute *material* entry barriers. For each incumbent PES, there are already 13 potential ready-made PES competitors as well as British Gas, the water companies, BT and cable companies, Direct Line, banks and supermarkets, among others. All of these companies have well-developed, consumer-focused supply businesses. The incremental costs of expanding these facilities to cover an additional market will vary from case to case, but it may well be that they are not substantial, making entry into the electricity supply business an attractive proposition, if prices are deemed to be above competitive levels. Moreover, in relation to the incumbent's supposed advantage in terms of reputation, many of the potential entrants are themselves well-respected household names, albeit in other areas or in other product markets.

Furthermore, it is likely that the ability of the incumbent PES to react to entry may be slower than in other markets. As I will explore further later, the ability of the PESs to change their prices is likely to be subject to regulatory delay in order to ensure non-discrimination, and to be hampered by political and public distrust.

For these reasons, it appears that the electricity supply market after 1998 may be highly contestable. This undermines the assumption that the PESs will have significant market power in the new competitive market from which small account holders will need to be protected.

There is one factor which has been identified as a possible barrier to entry that I would like to comment on further. There has been much discussion of a 'natural franchise' caused by customer inertia, which provides the PESs with a possible source of incumbent advantage, and acts as a barrier to entry. Proponents of this argument have pointed to the South West gas trials, where consumers have since April 1996 been able to choose a competing supplier. Few consumers switched in the Summer despite price differences of up to 20 per cent.

The observation that smaller consumers have *to date* remained with the incumbent supplier is not in itself an indication of inertia, or an inefficiency in competition which requires regulatory intervention. For larger customers, it is more likely that energy savings outweigh the costs of finding out about alternative suppliers. Therefore, these customers have an *incentive* to become knowledgeable. In contrast, for smaller consumers, the total cost of finding a cheaper supply (for example, the customer's switching cost) may well be greater than the cost savings that can be made by changing supplier. According to our definition, effective competition exists where the customer has the ability and incentive to switch suppliers only when doing so reduces *total* costs. In the case I have just outlined, it is rational and *efficient* for customers not to choose the cheaper supplier.

Moreover, it is not clear that customer inertia is a justification for specific regulation. Customers may be risk-averse: they may well wish to see whether the change of supplier works for others before themselves deciding to switch (better the devil you know...). Experience of the introduction of competition for large account holders has shown that the number of consumers taking up a competitive supply rises over time. Brand loyalty, or inertia, are features of most competitive markets, and reflect rational behaviour by consumers in the face of the cost of information and the risks of change. It is not obvious what public policy argument justifies specific intervention in the electricity sector.

Regulation and the Development of Competition

So far I have focused on the importance of establishing that competition will not be effective to justify continued regulatory intervention in the electricity supply market. However, it is also important to consider the effects of regulatory intervention on the development of competition. Regulation and competition are interdependent. The degree of competition in a market is a function of regulatory decisions, whilst the need for regulation is dependent upon the extent of competition. One determines the other.

The development of competition depends crucially on the relative costs faced by incumbent and new entry suppliers. Regulators can promote competition and the number of competitors in a market by making it easier and cheaper for consumers to switch supplier and by reducing any entry barriers faced by new entrants.

The regulator may choose to impose the costs involved with reducing switching costs on all consumers, whether they benefit from competition or not. Regulators can also tilt the playing field in favour of new entrants by shifting costs from them on to the incumbents. One of the main examples of this is the cost of social and historical obligations, which may remain disproportionately with the incumbent supplier.

For such measures to be *justified*, the long-term gains from increasing the number of competitors in the market need to outweigh any short-term costs associated with reducing entry barriers or in inefficient switching to new entrants. However, regulators do not always quantify the relative costs and benefits of entry promotion strategies and may not even admit that their policies have this effect. Instead, more competition – in the form of more competitors – is seen (or presented) as a 'good' that all should enjoy whether it is wanted or not.

Oftel's approach to number portability provides a good example of how such measures can be assessed. Allowing consumers to retain the same telephone number when they change supplier reduces their switching costs, as they no longer have to advise people that they have a new number, print new stationery, etc. The introduction of number portability was subject to an explicit cost-benefit analysis that established that the benefits of reduced switching costs were greater than the implementation costs. Oftel held a similar investigation into equal access, a facility which enables customers to access an operator of their choice without dialling additional digits. The investigation found that there was no conclusive evidence that the benefits outweighed the costs and the measure was not adopted.

In the absence of such analysis, there is a danger that measures are adopted with the vague promise of competitive benefits for all. However, we should retain some healthy scepticism about the likely level of the net benefits from greater choice. In particular:

- the threat of potential entry may have a powerful effect in constraining incumbents' behaviour; additional new entry *per se* may bring little additional benefit;

- it is difficult for the regulator to determine how much competition is 'enough'. There is therefore a real danger, at least for a period, of promoting too much competition, beyond the point where the long-run benefits outweigh the short-run costs;

- once new entrants have been granted special privileges, they will presumably lobby hard to retain them. Regulators may find it difficult to withdraw from the market in the future, resulting in the envisaged long-term benefits of such an entry-promoting policy not being realised.

Effects of Regulation on Competition in the Electricity Market

Arguably, Offer's earlier policies in the generation market have focused on the promotion of competitors rather than on the benefits of effective competition. Offer's approach to supplier contracts following the 'dash-for-gas' exemplifies this point. Offer allowed the PESs to pass through the additional costs associated with their supply contracts with new power stations as a justifiable response to the market power of National Power and PowerGen. However, it is not clear what impact this measure had on competition in the generation sector. The majority of the new stations went in as baseload. As such, the building of these stations had little impact on the duopoly in the mid-merit market.[4] The true cost of these measures is now becoming apparent as the PESs write down their investments in these new ventures.

The requirement on the two major generators (National Power and Powergen) to dispose of some of their generating capacity has also led to an increase in the number of competitors, which is

---

[4] Colin Robinson, 'Profit, Discovery and the Role of Entry: The Case of Electricity', in *Regulating Utilities: A Time For Change, op. cit.*

already quite impressive. It includes – in addition to the two main generators – generators from France and Scotland, British Energy, a large number of REC-sponsored independents and self-generation projects. Eastern Group has emerged as a large, vertically integrated market player. However, it is again not clear how far this increase in the number of competitors will translate into a corresponding increase in the effectiveness of competition, for example, in the mid-merit market (where pool prices are normally set).

This implicit preference for more competitors was reflected in Offer's initial approach to competition in the retail market after 1998. In an earlier consultation paper, Offer referred to the need:

'...to encourage a sufficient number and variety of suppliers so that customers have a meaningful choice.'[5]

A more rigorous analysis in preparing the latest consultation paper appears to have led to less emphasis being placed on the *number* of competitors. The latest paper explicitly recognises that

'...the effectiveness of competition should not be judged simply by the proportion of PES customers that decide to take second-tier supply.' (5.20)

The analysis correctly distinguishes between actual entry and the benefits of competitive pressure due to potential entry, which will lead incumbents to lower their prices. However, despite this recognition, the current proposals for 1998 do not establish a level playing field in the market for small electricity customers' accounts. Two main factors place the incumbents at a disadvantage.

Asymmetric Burden of Obligation to Supply

As a condition of their licence, the PESs have a duty to supply on request, and in setting their tariffs, cannot show any 'undue discrimination' against any person or class of persons. The proposed second-tier supply licences will include a similar condition following the liberalisation of the market in 1998. However, the Obligation to Supply is passive, whereas second-tier

---

[5] *The Competitive Electricity Market From 1998: Customer Protection, Competition and Regulation*, Section 2.9, Offer, November 1995.

suppliers *actively* market their services. In its latest consultation paper, Offer explicitly notes that second-tier suppliers can design systems that specifically target customers who are at present paying charges in excess of the costs they impose. It is also possible for second-tier suppliers to obtain a licence which effectively limits the range of customers to be supplied. For example, American Express could market electricity only to its cardholders, or only to its particularly creditworthy cardholders.

All of the above means that the incumbent PES is likely to have the *de facto* obligation to supply the customers that impose the highest costs, including those customers who cannot pay or who will not pay. In itself this is not a problem, if PESs are allowed to rebalance their tariffs to reflect closely the costs of serving individual customer classes. If charges reflect costs, consumers will switch efficiently, when the new entrant's costs plus the switching costs are below those of the incumbent.

However, in practice, regulatory, social and political constraints are likely to limit the ability of a PES to rebalance charges sufficiently. In 1993, the regional differentials in NGC's revised use of system charges were abated in response to political pressure. Similar lobbying has already started as the Pool begins to review the allocation of the costs of transmission losses. With respect to 1998, Offer has side-stepped the issue of whether higher costs justify higher prices by claiming that improved efficiency as a result of competitive pressure means that higher prices are 'not inevitable'. By building up expectations that all prices will fall after 1998, Offer is adding to the difficulties that the PESs will face in trying to rebalance prices to reflect costs sufficiently after 1998. PESs will be blamed for any attempted price increases, especially as these are likely to apply to their less advantaged consumers. In truth it is competition and failure to address the problem of social obligations square on that will be to blame.

The Settlement System

The new method of settlement is one of the key elements of the 1998 arrangements. Offer has decided that, at least initially, the cost of half-hourly metering for all consumers is prohibitive compared to the savings involved. Therefore, the Pool will use load profiles to estimate the consumption of small consumers for settlement purposes.

The use of load profiling reduces consumers' switching costs; unlike the above 100 kW market they do not need to install a half-hourly meter to change to a second-tier supplier. However, it also removes one of the main benefits of retail competition: the development of innovative pricing and metering options to meet the needs of customers with different load shapes. (With load profiles the marginal cost of consumption in any particular half-hour is the weighted average price for that load-profile group, rather than the pool price in that half-hour.) Instead, suppliers are likely to differentiate consumers according to their total consumption, the method of payment and their payment record.

The PESs are also having to develop arrangements to facilitate the new settlement system. With customers free to choose between competing suppliers, there is a need to co-ordinate billing, metering and the collection of information on consumption. Offer will allow PESs to recover the costs of developing and operating these systems from other suppliers after 1998. PESs will charge suppliers (including their own supply business) for four new services: data processing, data aggregation, metering point administration and prepayment meter systems services. Collectively these charges are to be known as the 'Competition Services Charge' (CSC).[6] Offer has proposed a limit on the total costs to be recovered, which will determine the level of the CSC.

The derivation of this 'total cost' figure appears rather arbitrary and Offer has not satisfactorily addressed the issue of whether the PESs will bear an unfair burden of these costs. The PESs also face the risk that part of the development costs will be disallowed at a later date. The CSC is due to run until 2003, but will be subject to review in 2000, when several of these services will be opened to competition and the allowed level of charges will be reassessed in conjunction with the review of distribution charges.

Both the above factors are likely to encourage inefficient switching to second-tier suppliers in the short term. If PESs cannot rebalance their tariffs sufficiently, they will be forced to charge average tariffs. Suppliers will concentrate their marketing on those consumers with costs below the average tariff and consumers may switch to a new supplier not because the new supplier is more efficient, but because its pricing freedom permits a cost-reflective

---

[6] Now referred to as the Data Management Services Charge.

tariff. In turn, the average cost of supplying those customers remaining with the PES will rise, creating yet further opportunities for 'cherry-picking'. The result could be to raise the total costs of supply to small customers despite the apparent 'success' of competition as indicated by new entry levels. Forcing the PES to bear an unfair burden of CSC costs is likely to create similar problems, since their total costs will be higher than those of their competitors. Attempts to recover the additional costs from their customers could result in inefficient switching to suppliers who bear a lower share of these costs. Furthermore, suppliers will also be allowed to pass the CSC charges on to *all* final consumers. All consumers will therefore be obliged to pay for some of the costs of the 1998 systems, whether they will benefit from competition or not.

Despite these dangers, it has still not been established that the playing field *needs* to be tilted towards new entrants. As I have already mentioned, each PES faces a large number of potential competitors, including the other PESs and other national players such as the other utility suppliers and traditional retailers. It is therefore far from clear whether the additional costs likely to result from inefficient switching would be justified in terms of the net benefits.

Gas Industry Experience

In contrast to the electricity industry, the licensing régime in the gas industry makes some attempt to establish a level playing field. In particular, the Gas Act 1995 makes provision for a social obligations levy, which shares the costs of providing certain services between all market players. The Gas Act also prohibits Ofgas from issuing 'artificial licences', for example, licences which are framed with the intention of excluding higher-cost consumers from a firm's obligation to supply. This provision is intended to limit the extent to which new entrants can 'cherry-pick' the lowest cost consumers, without also being obliged to supply more expensive consumers.

Although a move in the right direction, the above provisions suffer from many practical difficulties. For instance, it will be difficult to prove that a licence has been framed 'artificially' to exclude certain groups of customers, and Ofgas has complete discretion over the application of the levy arrangements. Ofgas's proposed cap on all of British Gas Trading's existing tariffs might further undermine the intent of this provision. Since BGT must also obtain Ofgas's approval before introducing any new tariffs, its ability to rebalance its tariffs in the face of competition might be severely constrained. Since BGT's existing tariffs reflect average costs of supply over both high- and low-cost customers, new entrants are afforded the opportunity to 'cherry-pick' lower cost consumers. Moreover, none of the measures adopted has addressed the perhaps more important question of the costs associated with BGT's historical obligations in the form of the take-or-pay gas purchase contracts.

Conclusions

There is much debate at present as to whether price controls will be necessary to protect small account holders in the newly competitive electricity market after April 1998. In closing, I would like to emphasise again what I feel to be the crux of the matter, namely the importance of having a clear definition of what will be taken as indicating the presence or absence of 'effective competition'. If they wish to justify continued regulation, Offer needs to show that the PESs will have both the ability and the incentive to act anti-competitively in the market after 1998. It is far from obvious that this is the case and the question cannot be determined without a detailed analysis of the market.

Moreover, the regulatory controls proposed by Offer may fundamentally affect the development of competition in the electricity supply market. In particular, the likely asymmetry of the obligation to supply and the Competitive Services Charge restriction are likely to tilt the playing field in favour of new entrants. Consumers may therefore be encouraged to switch supplier not because of any differences in the underlying costs of supply, but because PESs are forced to charge average tariffs which are above their costs of supplying particular consumer groups. The result will be to raise the total cost of supplying small consumers, since less efficient suppliers will be able to attract consumers.

The fundamental question to be addressed in electricity supply is the extent to which the benefits of introducing competition for small account holders in the way Offer intends outweigh the cost of these inefficiencies. That benefits exceed costs is far from obvious, and suggests the need for some basic cost-benefit analysis such as that attending the introduction of number portability in telecoms. The same type of cost-benefit analysis should also be used to justify regulatory measures intended to promote competition, which impose costs in terms of economic inefficiency.

The imposition of an explicit price restraint in the newly competitive market should be subject to similar analysis. Even if it has been established that PESs could act anti-competitively after 1998, price controls are not the only possible response. The appropriateness of any restraint needs to be judged with reference to defined objectives.

In an earlier consultation paper,[7] Offer noted that possible problems could be (at least partly) contained by the non-discrimination clause in the PESs' licences and by imposing an obligation to supply on the basis of published charges. A 'belt and braces' approach, using these methods together with the imposition of a price restraint, is unlikely to be efficient. The imposition of bad or irrelevant price controls could harm the development of competition. If prices are set too low, they will deter competitors, which may result in further inefficient measures being introduced to encourage competition. Wide-reaching tariff controls (as in the gas market), coupled with restrictions on the PESs' ability to rebalance prices, may expose the incumbents to inefficient 'cherry picking' by competitors.

It is only after it has been shown that the PESs will have the ability to act anti-competitively in a fully competitive market, and that price restraints are the correct response to this market power, that discussion of the possible form, scope and duration of the controls becomes appropriate.

---

[7] 'The Competitive Electricity Market from 1998: Consumer Protection, Competition and Regulation', *op. cit.*

CHAIRMAN'S COMMENTS

Stephen Littlechild

DERMOT GLYNN HAS PAINTED ONE SCENARIO OF 1998, one in which there is enough competition that no price controls are necessary, and indeed where the continuation of price controls could lead to less competition. I am sure that this will be an agreeable vision to many of the incumbent public electricity suppliers.

But it is not the only possible scenario. An alternative is that many potential competitors will question whether it is worthwhile to enter, given the relatively low supply margin at present and the absence of any significant scope for reduction in generation cost comparable to the recent reduction in gas prices. There are also costs of competing which need to be incurred, and a competitive supplier has to manage the generation risks. A potential entrant might wonder whether domestic customers will be interested, given the relatively limited scope for price reductions and the novelty of choosing a supplier. It is possible that PESs will have other preoccupations in 1998, and might prefer to concentrate on defending their own territories rather than attacking other territories. Other potential entrants, new to the electricity industry, might prefer to wait and see how the new market operates before getting involved.

I do not claim that this alternative scenario is more or less likely than the first, and indeed the actual outcome might well be somewhere between the two. Nonetheless, it suffices to indicate that the scenario painted by Dermot Glynn, of there being enough competition not to necessitate price controls, is one that cannot be counted on at this stage.

Given this uncertainty about how the market will develop, what is the prudent policy? Some account must surely be taken of the consequences of being wrong. If one assumes that the extent of competition may be limited, and accordingly imposes some kind of price restraint, and then competition turns out to be effective, it is relatively straightforward to remove the price restraint or reduce its scope, perhaps after a couple of years. However, if one assumes that competition will be fully effective and no price control is imposed, and then competition turns out not to be effective, customers will have suffered through unnecessary monopolistic price increases, there will be public outcry against the monopoly profits earned by the public electricity supplier, and a price control of some kind will probably have to be re-imposed. That would represent a step backwards for the cause of introducing competition in electricity supply.

In view of these alternative outcomes, it seems to me prudent to retain some kind of price restraint on that part of the market where competition is least likely to be fully effective initially. The relevant questions that we ought to focus on are not whether there should be some kind of control at all, but rather what kind of restraint it should be. Which set of customers should it cover: only domestic, or including small commercial customers as well? How long should it last: a couple of years or longer? What form should it take: pass through or a fixed price, or related to some kind of yardstick? These are the issues that I set out in my recent consultation paper, 'The Competitive Electricity Market from 1998', dated September 1996. The answers are by no means straightforward, and I should welcome any further contributions to this analysis.

6

INTRODUCING COMPETITION INTO WATER

Colin Robinson

University of Surrey and

The Institute of Economic Affairs

Introduction

IN THE EXCELLENT PAPER ABOUT WATER which he gave in last year's Regulation Lecture Series,[1] Stephen Glaister discussed 'incentives in natural monopoly'. He argued that water suffers from more severe market failures than the other utilities and so 'regulatory discipline and tax funding' have had to substitute for market disciplines.

Essentially, Stephen treated the industry from a 'public sector economics' point of view, largely accepting its natural monopoly status and saying that the present regulatory system has much to commend it. Nevertheless, he argued for a number of improvements. He pointed, for instance, to Averch-Johnson-type effects[2] which give the water companies a powerful incentive to expand their capital bases; to the funding of investment by 'direct taxes' even though there are no longer local democratic controls on the companies; and to the importance of introducing pricing mechanisms wherever possible.

He also made some very relevant observations on an issue which was topical in the aftermath of the 1995 drought and which remains so: the extent to which a big programme of investing in new capacity and repairing leaks can be justified.

---

[1] Stephen Glaister, 'Incentives in Natural Monopoly: The Case of Water', in M.E.Beesley (ed.), *Regulating Utilities: A Time For Change?*, IEA Readings 44, May 1996.

[2] H.A.Averch and L.L.Johnson, 'Behavior of the firm under regulatory constraint', *American Economic Review*, Vol. 52(5), December 1962, pp. 1,052-69.

This paper addresses different issues. In particular, it questions whether the present régime in water – set by government – attributes too much 'publicness' to the industry. Papers given in this Lecture Series in previous years have all tended to assume that the principal issue in the industry is how to regulate it:[3] questions of process and detailed regulatory matters have dominated the discussion. The question of whether there would be benefits from a greater emphasis on competition, as in the other utilities, has received little attention.

In considering this emphasis on regulation rather than competition, it is worth a reminder that only a few years ago the prevailing view was that in most of the other utilities there would be severe difficulties in introducing competition. It was claimed they had 'natural monopoly' attributes so that a single supplier (either in the country as a whole or in a region) was the natural situation. Both in gas and electricity, for example, the managements of the nationalised corporations fought long (and partly successful) battles to avoid the introduction of competition into their markets, using natural monopoly and externality arguments to reinforce their cases; they had some support from academic commentators. Water may be different from gas and electricity but the possible benefits of moving towards a more competitive market should be considered.

The first part of this paper dwells on the 'competition' part of the title and the second half discusses competitive markets and the water industry. Because water is an industry where regulation prevails – rather than one where there is incipient competition – an essential preliminary is an explanation of the advantages of competitive markets as compared with regulation. So the paper begins with general remarks, not specifically directed at water, on what is meant by a competitive market and on the related issue of whether regulation is a close substitute for competition. Then it examines the British system of utility regulation to uncover its novel features which, in some utility markets, have meant that significant liberalisation has occurred or is in prospect. Finally, the paper discusses the government's proposals, published in April 1996, for increasing

---

[3] Alan Booker in *Major Issues in Regulation*, IEA Readings 40, 1993; Colin Mayer in *Regulating Utilities: The Way Forward*, IEA Readings 41, 1994; Ian Byatt in *Utility Regulation: Challenge and Response*, IEA Readings 42, 1995; and Stephen Glaister, *op cit*. Mayer did, however, discuss briefly whether there could be actual (as distinct from yardstick) competition in the industry – for example, via franchising.

competition in water[4] and the extent to which competition is likely to emerge.

Part I: Competition and Regulation

Competition: a state of perfection?

It is necessary to deal head-on with the question of what is meant by 'competition' before we can sensibly discuss to what extent it can be introduced.[5] In particular, there is considerable confusion between the economist's ideal of 'perfect competition' and real-world competitive markets.

For non-economists I should say that a perfectly competitive market is generally assumed to be one in which there are very large numbers of small firms producing identical products, large numbers of buyers, free entry to and exit from the market and perfect knowledge.[6] Superficially, it appears an ideal market form. The force of competition is so strong that in the long run all 'excess' profits are eliminated: the only firms which remain in the industry earn just enough to pay the productive factors they employ sufficient to stop them leaving. Price is equal to marginal cost in long-run equilibrium. In this idealised equilibrium state, optimality (in the 'Pareto' sense) is attained: that is, it is impossible to find moves which will make anyone better off without someone else becoming worse off. Actually, the perfect knowledge assumption is sufficient to ensure that optimality is achieved: with perfect knowledge of present and future opportunities, any moves to optimality would be known and would presumably therefore be made.

Market failures and government policy

At least since the time of Arthur Pigou,[7] mainstream micro-economists concerned with policy in a particular market have

---

[4] *Increasing Customer Choice: Competition in the Water and Sewerage Industries: The Government's Proposals*, Department of the Environment and Welsh Office, London: HMSO, April 1996.

[5] See John Vickers, 'Concepts of Competition', *Oxford Economic Papers*, Vol. 47, 1995, for a discussion of different views of competition and of ways in which competition promotes economic efficiency.

[6] Strictly, these conditions are sufficient but not necessary. Approximations to perfectly competitive markets – for instance, markets in which firms believe they are price-takers – might be found even though some of the conditions are unfulfilled.

[7] For example, A.C. Pigou, *The Economics of Welfare*, Macmillan, 1920, 4th Edition, 1932.

proceeded to examine that market to determine whether or not it lives up to the perfectly competitive ideal. If it does not (and invariably it will not), they recommend government action to remedy the market imperfections and failures they perceive. A market may, for example, be classed as 'imperfect' because one or more companies appears to have market power. Or the market may 'fail' because of external effects: some actions by individuals and organisations may have spillover effects on others which are not fully incorporated in prices. In utility markets, for example, externalities may include effects on the environment or on security of supply.

Government remedial action can fall into one of two broad categories:

- market-improving – steps which make a market work more like a perfectly competitive market, perhaps by breaking up monopolies or by internalising external effects;

- market-displacing – measures which by-pass the market, attempting to achieve a result similar to the perfectly competitive outcome by direct government action such as imposing marginal cost pricing.

Since real-world markets will never match the perfectly competitive ideal, this approach to policy-making will appear to justify a great deal of intervention, whether directly by a government or through a system of supervision by regulators independent of direct political control.

Criticisms of the market failure approach

The approach has been criticised on a number of grounds. For example, there is the Lipsey-Lancaster 'second-best' critique[8] which points out that individual moves towards greater 'perfection' in one market (such as the imposition of marginal cost pricing), when there are constraints which prevent the conditions necessary for Pareto optimality being fulfilled elsewhere, cannot be assumed to be desirable.

Second, the usual Pareto optimality criterion is of doubtful value for policy purposes. In practice, virtually all policy moves involve

---

[8] R.G.Lipsey and K.Lancaster, 'The General Theory of Second Best', *Review of Economic Studies*, Vol. 24(1), October 1956, pp. 11-32.

losers as well as winners (if only because people judge their satisfactions relative to others), so it is rare to identify a change which makes no-one worse off.[9]

Third, there is the 'public choice' critique which argues that as well as market failure there is government failure.[10] People in the 'public' sector are neither omniscient nor altruistic, as traditional economic theory assumes them to be: government will inevitably fail to some degree when it intervenes. So, it is argued, government efforts to remedy market failures will not necessarily be beneficial.

Such devastating criticisms largely undermine 'piecemeal welfare economics' – in which the presence of imperfections and failures in a particular market is held to justify government remedial action in that market. Nevertheless, the perfectly competitive market – and its twin, the market failure approach to policy-making – have retained much of their influence in economics and they form an intellectual backing (albeit often implicit) for regulation in all its varieties. Many economists evidently retain the belief, handed down over recent generations, that there is something perfect about perfect competition. They see as entirely legitimate attempts by governments or regulators to achieve markets which are more nearly perfectly competitive or which mimic the perfectly competitive outcome.

The competitive process

But there is an even more fundamental criticism according to which, from the viewpoint of practical policy, it is misleading to see competition as a state: it should instead be regarded as a continuous process taking place over time. The distinction is of great significance when considering the role of regulation.

Economists who take this view argue that the long-run equilibrium of perfect competition is not an appropriate policy target. Indeed, it does not represent competition at all. It is an end-state in which competitive forces have been exhausted. The market is at rest,

---

[9] The problem of offsetting benefits to winners against costs to losers is circumvented, but not properly addressed, by the usual conventions of cost-benefit analysis where it is assumed that, if total gain exceeds total loss, a policy move is desirable because the gainers could compensate the losers and still be better off.

[10] For example, Gordon Tullock, *The Vote Motive*, Hobart Paperback 9, London: Institute of Economic Affairs, 1976.

whereas the essence of competition is disequilibrium characterised by continuous change.

Such views – nowadays often labelled 'Austrian' in the tradition of Hayek and others[11] – hark back to earlier 'classical' ideas about competition as a process. Perfect competition has not always been the dominant competitive paradigm; it seems to have taken over from earlier notions of competition around the time of the 'marginal revolution' in economics in the 1870s. As Mark Blaug has observed, the

> '... tendency throughout the history of economic thought to place the accent on the end-state of competitive equilibrium rather than the process of disequilibrium adjustments leading up to it...became remorseless after 1870 or thereabouts'.

Perfect competition, in Blaug's words, is '...foreign to the classical conception of competition as a process of rivalry in the search for unrealised profit opportunities.'[12]

More specifically, the ideas underlying the perfectly competitive model can be criticised as follows:

- The number of companies in a market and their sizes are irrelevant when assessing the extent of rivalry. The key to a competitive market is freedom of entry. Markets which appear concentrated and therefore 'imperfect' according to conventional measures may in practice be competitive because there is a constant threat of entry – most often, from companies with a reputation in another market which can move in if it appears profitable to do so. Thus, following Joseph Schumpeter, one can envisage a 'perennial gale of creative destruction' which sweeps away temporary monopoly power, provided market entry is possible.[13]

---

[11] F.A.Hayek, 'The Meaning of Competition', in *Individualism and Economic Order*, London: George Routledge and Sons, 1948; I.M.Kirzner, *Competition and Entrepreneurship*, University of Chicago Press, 1973, and *The Meaning of Market Process*, London: Routledge, 1992.

[12] Mark Blaug, 'Classical Economics', in Eatwell, Milgate, Newman (eds.), *The New Palgrave – A Dictionary of Economics*, Vol. 1, London: Macmillan, 1987.

[13] J.A. Schumpeter, *Capitalism, Socialism and Democracy*, London: Allen & Unwin, 5th Edition, 1976, especially Chapter VII.

- Perfect knowledge is an unhelpful assumption because, by definition, it can never exist. The knowledge everyone requires is about the future – because decisions invariably concern the future – and so it must necessarily be highly imperfect. Indeed, knowledge should not be regarded as a pool which is already in existence and which can therefore be tapped by a government or a regulator. Instead, knowledge appears as a result of the operation of rivalrous markets. Companies competing one with another are continually searching for new ways of doing things so as to satisfy consumers, and it is this competitive 'discovery' process which generates knowledge. Entrepreneurs are at the centre of such competitive markets, always looking for unrealised profit opportunities. The point is much more fundamental than the information asymmetry issue which is so often discussed in the context of regulation. It is not just that regulated industries have the information which regulators need and which has to be prised out of them. In markets which are heavily regulated rather than being subject to competitive processes, a general information deficiency is inevitable: the information which would have been provided by a rivalrous market is not produced.

- The identical products assumption of perfect competition is also foreign to economists who see competition as a process of discovery. The differentiation of product characteristics so as to satisfy consumers is one of the principal features of the process rather than evidence of 'failure'.

To summarise, a competitive market according to the older classical tradition or modern 'Austrians' would be one in which a process of competitive discovery is taking place. Companies in the market would feel the threat of actual or potential competition (because of freedom of entry) and so would bend their efforts not just to holding down costs but to finding ways of retaining existing consumers of their products and capturing new ones. Consumers have a choice of supplier and therefore have the power of exit. Discovery and knowledge-creation are the essence of the process, which is quite different from the perfectly competitive market where knowledge is assumed to be costlessly available and perfect.

Entrepreneurs, seeking profit opportunities and continually innovating, are at the centre of the market process. Israel Kirzner has captured the idea particularly well in the following passage:

> 'What keeps the market process in motion is competition – not competition in the sense of "perfect competition", in which perfect knowledge is combined with very large numbers of buyers and sellers to generate a state of perennial equilibrium – but competition as the rivalrous activities of market participants trying to win profits by offering the market better opportunities than are currently available...The competitive process occurs because equilibrium has not yet been attained.'[14]

Competitive processes and the implications for regulation

I have dwelt on these distinctions between notions of competition because they have important implications for regulation. Starting from the assumption that competition is a discovery process, driven by entrepreneurs, with markets always in *dis*equilibrium – rather than an equilibrium state in which all relevant knowledge is available to be tapped – leads to quite different conclusions for regulation.

Traditional views of the case for regulation and the scope of regulatory control arose from a preoccupation with the outcome of perfect competition. In an 'imperfect' market, there is evidently a case for regulation, either of the market-improving or market-displacing variety, to produce an outcome closer to that of the long-run equilibrium of perfect competition. Regulation is a means of achieving the results of perfect competition whilst avoiding the messy and apparently wasteful process of competition itself.[15]

Yet, if real-world markets are characterised by continous change and perpetual disequilibrium,[16] it is hard to see the value of such a view. Equilibrium can never be observed and the perfectly competitive paradigm is not helpful as a guide to action.

---

[14] 'The Perils of Regulation: A Market Process Approach', in Israel M.Kirzner, *Discovery and the Capitalist Process*, University of Chicago Press, 1985, p. 130.

[15] Colin Robinson, *Regulation as a Means of Introducing Competition*, Surrey Energy Economics Discussion Papers No. 80, Guildford, Surrey, February 1995.

[16] Markets may, of course, have equilibrium tendencies, even if permanently in disequilibrium.

Of course regulators will act. Once in office, they will make decisions which will change the market outcome because that is what they are appointed to do. But the results of action may well be unexpected and there is no reason to believe they will be an improvement on what would have happened had there been no regulatory intervention. Indeed, regulation which attempts to remove apparent 'imperfections' from the market may undermine the competitive discovery process which centres on the entrepreneur and is the prime source of innovation. For example, as Schumpeter saw, the ability of companies to retain 'excess' profits for a period is probably one of the principal driving forces of innovation. If such retention is prevented by regulators worried about market concentration, an adverse effect on innovation seems likely. Regulators have to try to preserve a fine balance in potentially competitive sectors, allowing incumbents sufficient profit to produce innovation – and to stimulate the entry which will eventually reduce those profits.

Once detached from the traditional anchor of the perfectly competitive market, the basis for regulation becomes elusive. If the outcome of a market emerges as a consequence of a discovery process, that outcome can be reproduced only by permitting the process to operate. Otherwise, the necessary knowledge is not produced. The consequences for regulation are uncomfortable. If regulators can never have the knowledge to simulate market outcomes, what then can they do except make piecemeal adjustments to deal with perceived 'failures'? The awful possibility is that, over a period of time, well-intentioned regulation will stop market processes in their tracks, making market outcomes worse rather than better. Another anchor is needed.

British-style regulation

Fortunately, in Britain this other anchor has been found – or, at least, we are groping towards it. In most of Britain's utility markets the danger that regulation will stifle innovation and entrepreneurship has been side-stepped because of the emphasis placed on pro-competition regulation. Regulators have been harnessed to the cause of stimulating competitive processes rather than hindering them.

When the early regulatory régimes were being devised, those involved were well aware of the dangers of two types of regulatory systems.[17]   One was British-style nationalisation – a form of regulation conducted behind closed doors by politicians and civil servants on ill-defined rules which removed responsibility from managements of the corporations concerned and stopped the industries from evolving. The other was US-style rate-of-return regulation, which failed to provide incentives to innovate and reduce costs and was subject to capture by producer and other interests.

Regrettably, these perceptive ideas about appropriate kinds of regulation were for a time overwhelmed by the deficiencies of the privatisation schemes. In the utility privatisations, in particular, there were many unfortunate flaws.[18] They were, in general, heavily influenced by political considerations and so concentrated on raising revenues and widening share ownership, giving only low priority to liberalising product and capital markets. Now we have a brief historical perspective on utility privatisation, we can see that in the early years of privatisation regulators have been forced to spend much of their time fighting to overcome these deficiencies (and being blamed for matters outside their control, such as the X and K factors initially set by government). It would have been much better if the government had made a cleaner separation of 'natural monopoly' areas from others at the time of privatisation and provided structures which would have permitted competition to flourish in potentially competitive areas of the industries. It would have been better also if capital markets had been allowed to operate from the beginning, placing the companies in the market for corporate control rather than protecting them with 'golden shares'.

Nevertheless, the regulatory régimes, developed since privatisation of the first tranche of British Telecom in 1984, are a considerable improvement both on nationalisation and on US regulation. The distinctive feature of British utility regulation is its emphasis on stimulating entry and promoting competition. Rather than using the stylised notions of perfect competition as a model, the underlying aim – whether conscious or not – appears to be to start competitive processes working wherever it is feasible to do so. That seems to me an entirely sensible idea which gives a strength to the regulatory

---

[17] M.E.Beesley and S.C.Littlechild, 'Privatisation: Principles, Problems and Priorities', *Lloyds Bank Review*, July 1983.

[18] Colin Robinson, 'Privatising the British Energy Industries: the lessons to be learned', *Metroeconomica*, Vol. 43, Nos. 1-2, 1992.

régime for utilities in Britain which is not found elsewhere (though it is beginning to be copied).

Advantages of the British system

More specifically, the advantages of the British system are as follows.

First is the independence of regulatory offices from direct political control. That is a very significant advance on nationalisation when there was constant interference in state-owned corporations, generally for short-term political reasons, and managerial incentives to be entrepreneurial were sadly lacking. Although there are complaints that regulation is not as open as it should be, it is a far cry from the old régime of backdoor arm-twisting of senior executives which meant that some of the industries (such as electricity) were largely instruments of state policy.[19] Of course, Ministers still try to intervene, but it is now more difficult for them to do so. A necessary condition for competitive markets to develop was removal of the old form of political control.

Second, price cap regulation is more closely consistent with competitive markets than rate-of-return regulation and is a vast improvement on price control under nationalisation. Under state ownership, there was blatant interference with nationalised industry pricing. Despite occasional attempts, such as in the 1967 White Paper,[20] to introduce some economic principles into pricing, governments were never willing to give up interfering with the prices of commodities prominent in the retail price index.[21] Compared with rate-of-return regulation, price caps have advantages, though there is a tendency to revert to rate of return which has to be resisted: the tendency exists because regulators often look at profits and rates of return in setting X and because of the pressures on regulators to review controls frequently. A price cap régime is to some extent arbitrary, as is all regulatory price control, but if reviews are relatively infrequent (say, every five years), it has a very desirable charac-

---

[19] Colin Robinson, 'Profit, Discovery and the Role of Entry: The Case of Electricity', in M.E.Beesley (ed.), *Regulating Utilities: A Time For Change?*, IEA Readings 44, Institute of Economic Affairs, 1996.

[20] *Nationalised Industries: A Review of Economic and Financial Objectives*, Cmnd. 3437, London: HMSO, 1967.

[21] David Heald, 'The Economic and Financial Control of UK Nationalised Industries', *The Economic Journal*, Vol. 90, No. 358, June 1980.

teristic. Because it allows the regulated companies to retain unanticipated cost savings between reviews, therefore giving them an incentive to improve efficiency, it is the regulatory equivalent of Schumpeterian competition. Instead of Schumpeter's 'gale' extinguishing profits, that task is performed by the next regulatory review.[22]

The third feature of British regulation which is innovative and an improvement on most other regulatory systems is the pro-competition duty which, in one form or another, the utility regulators have. I am not claiming that the government gave them this duty in full awareness of its significance. Indeed, as I have explained elsewhere, there was an accidental element in its imposition in gas.[23] It can also be argued that it has proved so significant mainly because of the deficiencies of the privatisation schemes: had markets been liberalised more at privatisation there would have been correspondingly less need for liberalising action by regulators.

But, whether or not the government realised what it was doing, the pro-competition duty has become a key feature of the British system. The emphasis on stimulating entry and starting competitive processes outside natural monopoly sectors has not only permitted regulators to take the initiative in promoting entry to a market in very unpromising circumstances (as Sir James McKinnon did in the early days of gas privatisation). It has also changed the incentives of regulators so that capture by producers or other groups is not the issue here that it has been in the United States. When one of the principal duties of a regulator is to promote or facilitate competition, the interests of consumers must be to the fore and the chances of his or her succumbing to the lobbying of producers is much diminished.

These key features of British utility regulation – independent regulatory offices, price caps and the competition promotion duty – have avoided the worst pitfalls of regulation. Taken together, they have provided a regulatory emphasis on market entry and liberalisation and there is a good chance that the scale and scope of regulation will decline over time as it is displaced by competition. If you accept my view about the importance of setting competitive

---

[22] M.E.Beesley, 'RPI-x: Principles and Their Application to Gas', in M.E.Beesley (ed.), *Regulating Utilities: A Time For Change?*, *op. cit.*

[23] Colin Robinson, 'Gas: What to do after the MMC Verdict', in M.E.Beesley (ed.), *Regulating Utilities: The Way Forward*, IEA Readings 41, London: Institute of Economic Affairs, 1994.

processes to work, this emphasis is extremely important. It is a big improvement on a traditional regulatory system which does not explicitly promote competition and has no built-in tendency to wither away over time: rather, such a system tends to breed more regulation because of empire-building tendencies and the influence of pressure groups.

Pro-competition regulation and large consumers

Furthermore, the pro-competition emphasis in the utilities has had another effect which was not generally predicted – and which has not been widely remarked. That is the tendency for large consumers of goods and services provided by utilities to be enlisted to the cause of competition. It is usually (and correctly) argued that government policies are dominated by producer interests. Consumers, it is claimed, are not well-organised and have little influence when policies are being formulated. Producer groups, however, are organised and have strong incentives to lobby for policy moves which favour their members. Investment in lobbying is expected to yield high returns because any gains are concentrated on members whereas the costs are dispersed over the population as a whole. Vote-seeking politicians have an incentive to yield to such lobbying because organised groups, which are often the main sources of information on a subject, can provide convincing cases in support of their demands and usually appear able to deliver blocks of votes.

What has been revealed by utility privatisation and subsequent regulation, however, is that large companies – acting in their consumer roles – can be powerful forces for liberalisation.[24] Both in gas (where large consumers stimulated an MMC reference within a year of privatisation) and electricity, large companies which felt short-changed by relatively illiberal privatisation schemes have put pressure on regulators to promote competition in the utility concerned to bring down prices and improve service. Acceding to such demands, where feasible, has suited the regulators because of their pro-competition duties. Thus there has been a happy combination of consumer pressure and regulatory incentive to introduce competition to most utility markets, albeit mainly for the benefit of large consumers so far. Small consumers remain unorganised and unable to exert significant

---

[24] Robinson, *Metroeconomica, op. cit.*

pressure, but the demonstration of what competition can do for larger consumers has helped the regulators in pressing ahead with schemes (such as '1998' in gas and electricity) which give households freedom to choose supplier.

Part II: The Water Industry and Competition

Utility regulation and the water industry

My conclusion about British utility regulation in general is that, partly by accident and partly by design, the régime which has emerged places a most useful emphasis on stimulating competitive processes. In some utilities – gas, electricity and telecoms – markets, despite being regulated, are being liberalised, companies are becoming more entrepreneurial and markets are evolving in ways which would have been impossible under state ownership. It seems a fair prediction that, provided markets are allowed to continue evolving without political interference,[25] despite the inevitable transitional problems, in all these markets privatisation and subsequent regulation will a few years from now be judged a success.

Water does, however, stand outside the general régime I have been discussing. It has been beneficial to have an independent regulator and to have price cap regulation and it is fair to say that regulation of the industry is regarded as a model of openness.[26] But competition-promotion in the product market has been in the background compared with other utilities. The market for corporate control has begun to operate as take-overs have occurred. However, the capital market may be distorted by the lack of product market competition: would-be entrants may feel that a bid for an existing company is the only way in.

There is a continuing tendency, carried over from pre-privatisation days, to rely on exhortation – whether consumers are being told they should not 'waste' water or companies are being told they should reduce leakage rates – which suggests market-place incentives are lacking. There is also some reliance on statutory duties – such as the

---

[25] Robinson, 'Profit, Discovery and the Role of Entry', *op. cit.*

[26] For an explanation of regulatory processes in water, see Ian Byatt, 'Water: The Periodic Review Process', in *Utility Regulation: Challenge and Response, op. cit.*

companies' duty to promote the efficient use of water by consumers[27] – in place of economic incentives.

Yardstick competition is another feature of the industry: many of Ofwat's publications compare performance across the 29 companies. In the early days when privatisation was being discussed, there were hopes that competition by comparison would prove useful in stimulating backward companies to emulate those which were performing better. But it is extremely difficult to standardise sufficiently to make useful cross-company comparisons: the chances of stimulating competitive behaviour via comparisons with others seem remote. An emphasis on yardstick competition also imparts a regulatory bias against mergers between water companies, because they reduce the number of comparators, and towards cross-utility mergers (between, say, water and electricity companies).[28]

Only recently have ideas about stimulating competition in water begun to stir, evidently as a result of a joint initiative by the regulator and the government. When water was privatised, the emergence of significant competition was apparently regarded as most unlikely. Indeed, as explained below, there are respects in which establishing competition is more difficult than in the other utilities.

Nevertheless, if you accept my view that regulation can never be a close substitute for competitive processes, it is a matter for concern that such a major industry is as yet so little touched by those processes. As much of the industry as possible surely needs to be brought within the general framework of regulatory action which applies to other utilities and which has, at its heart, the promotion of competition in all potentially competitive areas. Then the water companies would be in a rivalrous market where they would feel pressure to seek better ways of serving consumers and they would have incentives to solve the industry's problems rather than having to be exhorted or instructed to do so. Regulation would be reduced in scale and in scope, concentrating on activities which, given present technology, can be classed as natural monopolies (such as the network of pipes).

---

[27] 'Water companies told to prepare water efficiency strategies', *Ofwat Press Release*, 14 June 1996.

[28] 'UK water', *Financial Times*, the LEX column, 2 October 1996.

Introducing competition into water

In principle, the water and sewerage industries appear much the same as other network utilities. Like electricity and gas, for example, production takes place at a variety of locations. For producers to supply consumers, a transport system is required which efficiency considerations suggest is best provided as a common network of pipes or wires. Provided there is open access to the network, and it is possible to measure inputs by producers into the system and consumption by individual consumers, competition in production and in supply to consumers can be established. Thus a competitive process can be instituted, even though there is a 'natural monopoly' element (the network) embedded in the industry which has to be regulated (or conceivably could be franchised). Both in electricity and gas, some success is now being achieved with this sort of competition across a network.

In water, it might be claimed there are more serious obstacles to introducing competition than there are in other utilities. *First*, there are probably greater difficulties in bringing into production new sources of supply in water, because of public objections, than in electricity and gas. *Second*, there is no integrated network in water and sewerage as there is in gas and electricity and water transport costs are higher. It is sometimes claimed that high transport costs are the main reason why, at the time of privatisation, the government envisaged little competition in the industry.[29]

Third, water varies significantly from source to source and its quality is strictly regulated so that, it is argued, mixing in a common network becomes difficult. There are, however, similar difficulties in introducing gas from new entrants into a gas network (because of variations in calorific value and other characteristics), and electricity from entrants into an electricity system (because the technical integrity of the network might be compromised).

But a *fourth* problem, related to the third – the division of regulatory functions between Ofwat, responsible for 'economic' regulation, and 'social' regulators, together with the strong influence of Brussels in environmental and quality matters – clearly complicates

---

[29] See, for instance, 'Increasing Competition in the Water Industry', Ofwat Information Note No.10, April 1992 (revised April 1996), para. 2.

the whole regulatory issue in water.[30] At the time of privatisation, a big investment programme was instituted, designed to improve the quality of water and sewerage services so as to make up for a period of apparent neglect and to meet EC standards. Other British utilities have had to invest because of EU directives (such as the restrictions on sulphur emissions which have affected fuel choice in electricity generation). But, in the case of water, the major factor driving up consumer bills since privatisation has been the cost of improving quality, mainly to comply with EU directives. More costs are to come. The Urban Waste Water Treatment Directive will increase prices in the next few years and there are proposals to revise Directives on drinking water and bathing water and to introduce an Ecological Quality of Water Directive:[31] all are likely, other things equal, to increase charges.[32] I will return to the problem of 'social' regulation at the end of this paper.

Fifth, gas and electricity consumers are used to being metered whereas water metering is rare for smaller consumers. Most smaller water consumers pay flat rate charges still based on rateable values which, apart from giving them no incentives to economise on their use, place an obstacle in the way of a competitive system: consumers do not receive proper price signals and their consumption cannot be precisely calculated. Only 8 per cent of households at present have meters,[33] though the percentage is increasing. Problems of a similar kind – if to a lesser degree – exist in other utilities. For example, in electricity, it seems likely that standardised profiles will be substituted for sophisticated half-hourly metering when domestic market competition arrives.[34]

---

[30] Mayer, *op. cit.*, pp. 23-24. There is a good discussion of the interaction between 'economic' and 'environmental' regulation in the early days of water privatisation in Dieter Helm and Najma Rajah, 'Water Regulation: The Periodic Review', *Fiscal Studies*, Vol. 15, No.2, May 1994.

[31] Ofwat National Consumer Council Annual Report 1995-96, July 1996, p. 8.

[32] On 15 October 1996, Ofwat announced its next review of price limits would be in 1999. The DGWS said that 'Customers have seen prices rising for too long' and that efficiency savings should be passed on to consumers. (Ofwat News Release 41/96, 15 October 1996.)

[33] Ofwat National Consumer Council Annual Report, *op. cit.*, p. 13.

[34] Half-hourly meters (to give detailed load profiles) and associated communications links are at present too expensive for smaller consumers of electricity so a set of load profiles is expected to

None of the problems just mentioned is insuperable – and they might indeed be resolved within a genuine market – but starting from where we are they clearly create difficulties.

The government's proposals

Despite such difficulties, the government decided in the Spring of 1996 to put forward proposals to increase competition in the water and sewerage industries.[35] At about the same time, Ofwat published a consultation paper on one of the crucial issues – regulating common carriage arrangements.[36] The opening paragraphs of the government paper include a fine statement of principle about the virtues of competition and the need to limit regulation:

'The Government's policy is...to restrict the ambit of regulated monopoly to the essential minimum. Wherever possible, it wants to introduce effective market competition as the best guarantee of the customer's interest in the short and long term.

'Competition amongst suppliers provides the best assurance for customers that they receive value for money for the service that they purchase. It gives opportunities for customers to choose combinations of price and service which best meet their particular needs. Where such combinations are not at present available, it provides the opportunity for existing operators or new entrants to develop them where they believe that it would be profitable to do so.

'Competition gives scope for new and existing providers to develop innovative and economic approaches to meeting customers' needs. It also encourages operators and prospective operators to provide services more efficiently and cheaply and to improve standards.'

The general aim appears to be a gradual approach which proceeds by '...building on experience with initially limited numbers and types of cases'. The paper points out the opportunities which already exist

---

be introduced. (See Offer, 'The Competitive Electricity Market from 1998: Price Restraints', September 1996, p. 21.)

[35] 'Water: Increasing Customer Choice', *op. cit.* The government's proposals are summarised in 'Increasing Competition in the Water Industry', *Ofwat Information Note No. 10, op. cit.*

[36] Ofwat, *The regulation of common carriage agreements in England and Wales: a consultation paper*, April 1996.

for non-statutory water and sewerage operators which are not regulated by Ofwat (though water supplies are subject to drinking water standards). As regards changes in policy, it proposes that two of the already available means of introducing limited competition – 'inset appointments' and cross-border supplies – should be extended. Another move designed to promote competition is the removal of water undertakers' monopolies on main connections. Potentially most important, the government's proposals include provision for common carriage arrangements supervised by the regulator.

Inset appointments

Under the original privatisation scheme, a new water or sewerage 'undertaker' could penetrate the area of an existing undertaker via an 'inset appointment'. The opportunity was limited. Only 'qualifying sites' were eligible: they were sites not connected to the existing undertaker's main or sewer and situated 30 metres or more away from that main or sewer.

The potential for inset appointments was increased in 1992, under the Competition and Service (Utilities) Act which removed the 30-metre rule for sites not connected to the existing undertaker's main or sewer; permitted insets for premises receiving water or sewerage services from an undertaker provided the supply was 250 megalitres a year or more; and allowed applicants for inset appointments to apply for a bulk water supply from or a main connection to the sewerage system of an existing undertaker.

According to the government, rivalry caused by the threat of inset appointments has had the effect of reducing prices to large-quantity users (though in some cases, tariff rebalancing has resulted in 'marginally higher' tariffs for households).[37] However, the procedures necessary to determine whether or not inset appointments should be made have been time-consuming and rather cumbersome, involving the applicant, the incumbent, the customer and Ofwat.

To encourage inset appointments, the government paper proposes the following steps.[38] *First*, the 250 megalitres a year test – which restricts insets to only a few hundred very large consumers – should

---

[37] *Water: Increasing Customer Choice, op. cit.*, paras. 3.1 to 3.3. The first inset appointment under which a commercial customer changed supplier was Buxted Chicken's move from Essex and East Suffolk Water to Anglian in May 1997.

[38] *Ibid.*, paras. 4.1 to 4.6.

be widened to incorporate more premises. In water, as in other utilities (such as electricity) where competition thresholds have been set, arguments inevitably arise over premises which are in common ownership but where there is some physical separation. The proposal is that the test should in future apply not to individual premises but to premises in common ownership which are separated by roads, railways or watercourses.

Second, the Director General of Water Services (DGWS) will be able to depart from the present onerous arrangement for inset appointees which makes them statutory water undertakers in the inset area with consequent obligations to supply water or sewerage services to anyone who wants those services. These obligations last until the appointee is replaced. The new proposal is that the DGWS can make inset appointments for limited terms (say, 5 or 10 years) instead of in perpetuity. In making the appointment, he will have power to nominate the successor to the inset appointee if the latter does not wish to continue.

Third, it is proposed to speed up the procedure for granting inset appointments which depend on a bulk water supply or a sewerage connection. Incumbents will be placed under an obligation to offer terms for an agreement on bulk water supply or a sewerage connection agreement.

Cross-border competition

Under the present régime, a water undertaker can supply across a border to customers in another area without an inset appointment. Little use has been made of this provision, which is very restrictive because it applies only to domestic consumers (where the costs of pipe-laying are likely to be large relative to the size of expected revenues from small consumers). The new proposals would lift the prohibition on non-domestic cross-border supplies so that industrial, commercial and agricultural consumers can be included, possibly leading to supplies to domestic consumers also through the same pipes.

Connection agreements

A constraint on competition which operates in water – and has parallels in other utilities – is the undertaker's monopoly of making connections to the water main. The same restriction does not apply in the case of connections to sewers where customers have the right to make the connection.

Customers can lay pipes up to the water mains but the undertaker can recoup 'reasonable expenses' for making the connection and so has no incentive to keep costs down. Another disincentive for consumers to carry out work themselves is that pipes laid to the main are not the responsibility of the undertaker unless he specifically agrees. Disputes about charges have necessarily resulted: according to the government, in 53 of 62 cases referred to the DGWS for determination, charges have been found to be excessive and refunds have been made.[39]

To provide improved incentives to keep down costs, the government's proposal[40] is that customers should be given the right to make connections to the water main and that the pipe to the main should automatically become the responsibility of the undertaker.

Common carriage

Potentially the most important proposal in the April 1996 paper relates to the shared use of pipes through common carriage arrangements for large users. Large users are, for this purpose, defined, as for inset appointments, as those taking 250 megalitres or more a year (about 600 consumers) or disposing of a similar amount of sewage.[41] However, the government is considering whether a lower limit would be possible so as to include more users.

The problem which the government's common carriage proposals attempt to address arises because, as in other utilities, the privatisation scheme for water established vertically integrated companies each of which had a natural monopoly network at one of the stages of integration. Although customers do not have to take their water from their local licensed water undertaker, because there is potential competition in supply, that undertaker has a big advantage

---

[39] *Ibid.*, para. 4.10.

[40] *Ibid.*, para. 4.13.

[41] *Ibid.*, para. 4.25, and *The Regulation of Common Carriage Agreements in England and Wales, op. cit.*, p. 1. The government's proposals are primarily concerned with common carriage of clean water, but para. 4.46 states that there will be similar provisions for common carriage of waste water.

stemming from ownership and control of the network of pipes.[42] An arrangement which removes the incumbent's exclusive rights to use the network, permitting any supplier to use it on payment of a charge, is therefore in principle capable of significantly extending competition.

Under the proposed common carriage arrangements, a potential supplier to an area (with a suitable source of supply and prospective customers) would negotiate terms with the incumbent to use its network. The incumbent would have a duty to provide a prospective entrant, on request, with details of the terms on which it would permit use of its pipes. If terms could not be agreed, the Director would be able to determine them.

Entrants which are existing water undertakers would be given a statutory right to use another undertaker's network on terms agreed or, if agreement could not be reached, imposed by the DGWS. A supplier which is not already a statutory undertaker would be issued by the DGWS with a direct supply licence entitling it to use the relevant network; it would be able to lay pipes to connect to the network for common carriage purposes and to connect customers to that network. Entrants would not have the full obligations of a statutory undertaker: in particular, they would not be obliged to supply all consumers in a given area.

A number of potential difficulties are identified in the government's paper. For example, there is the problem of mixing. Customers of an entrant would be unlikely to receive water supplied direct by that entrant. The entrant would agree to supply a quantity of clean water to a customer and then agree to put the appropriate amount of treated water into the incumbent's network so that sufficient supplies would be available for all consumers. Given the quality regulations, provisions would be required to ensure that the entrant met those requirements and also did not compromise the incumbent's ability to meet them. It is proposed that both the entrant and the incumbent should have duties to provide water which is 'fit and wholesome'. The entrant would be subject to regulation by the Drinking Water Inspectorate and the Environment Agency in the

---

[42] The absence of common carriage arrangements may have been one of the reasons why an attempt by South Staffordshire Water Company to supply households in Wolverhampton (in the Severn-Trent region) did not succeed. (See 'Government urged to open up water market', *Financial Times*, 13 January 1996.)

same way as the incumbent. The DGWS would have the power to stop common carriage agreements from proceeding or terminate existing agreements if, on advice from the Drinking Water Inspectorate, he believed that water quality might be compromised. He could also prevent agreements which increased the risk of supply disruptions.

Another issue is whether existing customers would suffer from the incomer's entry to the market (for example, because the entrant is cross-subsidising or because the incumbent increases prices to its remaining customers). To deal with this, the government proposes a series of checks to ensure that charges paid by entrants for network usage reflect costs, that there is no undue discrimination among customers, that artificially low pricing to discourage entry is avoided, and that water companies are not allowed to rebalance tariffs when they lose customers to competitors. If there would be adverse effects on other customers, the DGWS would have the power to stop the common carriage arrangement. He is also examining the idea of separating the market into tariff and non-tariff segments, thus circumventing the rebalancing problem. As in the other utilities, it makes no sense to regulate prices of companies which operate in a competitive market.[43]

Benefits of the proposals?

The government claims that its proposals will gradually extend competition to the benefit of consumers[44] because:

- competition in connections will reduce costs;

- more premises will qualify for inset appointments as the 250 megalitre test is modified and limited period inset appointments are possible;

- non-domestic users will gain from being allowed to take cross-border supplies;

---

[43] According to Ofwat's 1995-96 *Report on Tariff Structure and Charges*, the tariff basket is being reviewed to limit the scope for rebalancing tariffs between groups of consumers and to determine whether '...competition for large users would enable their charges to be removed from the tariff basket, because they are part of a more competitive market not requiring the same degree of regulation.'

[44] *Water: Increasing Customer Choice, op. cit.*, para.5.1.

- domestic consumers may benefit because, if they are close to an inset appointment or a cross-border supply, changing supplier may become economic;

- large consumers will benefit from the common carriage arrangements (and the threshold may be lowered to include consumers below the 250-megalitre threshold).

No doubt there will be gains to consumers as competition is enhanced at the margin and the government is to be congratulated for putting forward positive proposals to stimulate competition in this regulated industry. But I think there must be doubts whether the overall impact will be large. There appear to be two principal problems.

Incumbent advantage and the network of pipes

One difficulty which will afflict attempts to bring competition into water is the incumbent advantage which will continue because of ownership and control of the pipes and possession of the information which goes with ownership. As experience elsewhere has shown, incumbent ownership of the network is bound to make life difficult for would-be entrants. Indeed, wider experience in Britain suggests that any régime which gives incumbents a significant voice in whether or not entrants are admitted is, not surprisingly, likely to hinder entry.

To take an example outside the network utilities, under nationalisation there was a provision for British Coal Corporation (and its predecessor, the National Coal Board) to permit entry to coal mining through a licensing system run by the Corporation.[45] The terms of licensing were restrictive – only very small operations were allowed and royalties had to be paid to the Corporation. Obviously, the nationalised corporation had no incentive to allow the entry even of small competitors and the 'licensed mining' sector remained very small.

An example closer to water is gas, where many of the problems which have arisen in liberalising the market stem from the initial decision in 1986 to leave ownership of the pipeline network in the

---

[45] Colin Robinson and Eileen Marshall, *Can Coal be Saved?*, Hobart Paper No. 105, Institute of Economic Affairs, 1985, pp. 36-39.

vertically integrated British Gas.[46] That was one of the principal reasons entry to the industry was difficult and why competition was slow to develop. From the early days of privatisation the regulatory authorities tried to find ways to overcome this problem which the government had bequeathed them. The first Monopolies and Mergers Commission (MMC) report into the industry[47] proposed that BGC should publish rates at which it would be willing to transport other suppliers' gas through the pipeline network.

But this proposal was generally thought inadequate. An OFT report in 1991 recommended a more radical solution – the separation of the pipeline system from the rest of BGC. The 1993 MMC report,[48] which also recommended separation (but of trading), encapsulated the issue rather neatly in the following passage about British Gas which, it claimed, is:

'...both a seller of gas, and owner of the transportation system which its competitors have no alternative to use. In our view, this dual role gives rise to an inherent conflict of interest which makes it impossible to provide the necessary conditions for self-sustaining competition.'[49]

Eventually, British Gas itself reached the conclusion that its activities should be divided and that Transco should in 1997 become a separate organisation (though including some upstream activities as well as pipelines).

Similar problems affected electricity when attempts were made, while it was still nationalised, to promote entry. Before privatisation, the Energy Act of 1983 – which, *inter alia*, required the nationalised industry to allow private producers to use its transmission and distribution system at published charges – proved ineffective as a means of stimulating entry into the industry.[50]

When electricity privatisation was conceived, the government learned from British Gas privatisation to the extent that it separated

---

[46] Robinson, 'Gas: What to do after the MMC Verdict', *op. cit.*

[47] Monopolies and Mergers Commission, *Gas*, Cm. 500, London: HMSO, 1988.

[48] Monopolies and Mergers Commission, *Gas and British Gas plc, op. cit.*

[49] *Ibid.*, Vol. 1, para. 1.6.

[50] Elizabeth Hammond, Dieter Helm and David Thompson, 'Competition in Electricity Supply: Has the Energy Act Failed?', in D.Helm, J.Kay and D.Thompson, *The Market for Energy*, Oxford: Clarendon Press, 1989.

transmission from generation. Nevertheless, the distribution network was left in the hands of the RECs, with only accounting separation. Regulatory problems are much enhanced if the regulator has to try to supervise organisations where natural monopoly networks are combined with potentially competitive areas of business. Stephen Littlechild has pointed to the '...wide range of concerns associated with the lack of separation'of the RECs' distribution businesses.[51] In his view, '...clearer separation between monopoly networks and potentially competitive activities is more conducive to effective competition and full protection of customers'.[52]

Experience in other British utility markets seems to indicate that, so long as water companies are both suppliers of water and sewerage services and at the same time owners of the pipes which entrants would have to use to compete with them, entry will remain very limited. No matter how assiduous the regulator in trying to facilitate competition via common carriage arrangements, the proposed régime seems likely to produce numerous disputes and long delays given that incumbents have every incentive to claim that entry will have adverse spillover effects. Indeed, the government's proposals list for the incumbents several claims they can make – that entry will cause supply disruptions or that water quality will be compromised or that customers other than those of the entrant will suffer. There is obviously a large subjective element in evaluating such claims and, as explained below, the involvement of regulators other than Ofwat is likely to favour the incumbents.

A separate network?

In the end, if the government is serious about its aim of restricting '...the ambit of regulated monopoly to the essential minimum', instead introducing 'effective market competition', it will probably have to consider separation of water pipes from the rest of the industry. Even though there is no national water grid, my understanding is that most of the major companies have their own reasonably interconnected grid systems. These transport networks – which are the conduits for actual and potential suppliers to reach consumers – would be better in the hands of one or more organisations with no incentive to exclude

---

[51] Stephen Littlechild, 'Competition in Electricity: Retrospect and Prospect', in *Utility Regulation: Challenge and Response*, *op. cit.*, p. 113.

[52] *Ibid.*, p. 114.

newcomers. Otherwise, the volume of entry is unlikely to be sufficient to start a competitive market process in the water industry.

With a separate network, it should in the course of time be possible to allow competition to reach even domestic consumers – who, once they have choice of gas and electricity suppliers, may want to know why they cannot have a similar choice in water. Entry from outside the present water industry seems likely to be limited under the present régime because an entrant would have to construct assets (including pipes) at present-day prices whereas the water companies were sold for much less than the replacement cost of their assets.[53] But, with a separate network, there would be a much improved prospect of entry to compete in supply (as in the other utilities).

The problem of regulators other than Ofwat

A related problem which would not, in itself, be solved by a separate network of pipes is one which raises much wider issues than regulation of the water industry – the involvement of health, safety and environmental regulators ('social' regulators, for short), both in Britain and the EU, and the incentives which they have. In all the utilities – indeed, across most of British industry and commerce – regulators deal with health and safety matters and environmental protection. As I shall explain, regulation of this sort can be extremely costly. But, in water, the problems of 'social' regulation are particularly serious because of the explicit involvement of quality and environmental regulators (the Drinking Water Inspectorate and the Environment Agency) as well as Ofwat. When common carriage proposals are considered, for example, these other agencies have specified roles.[54] But, whereas Ofwat has a duty to facilitate competition, the other regulators do not. That is an important difference because the pro-competition duty is both a built-in constraint on the imposition of additional costs on consumers and a defence against regulatory capture.

Even though the relevant competition duty of the DGWS is expressed in more passive terms in the legislation than similar duties of other utility regulators (to 'facilitate' rather than to 'promote'

---

[53] John Kay, 'An idea full of leaks', *Financial Times*, 12 April 1996.

[54] Helm and Rajah, *op. cit.*

competition),[55] the DGWS knows that the extent to which he succeeds in increasing competition is a significant element in how his performance is judged. But assessment of the performance of the other water regulators presumably places no weight on any contribution they make to market liberalisation.

The incentives of these other regulators are particularly important. Because of scientific uncertainty, it would be naïve to assume that 'social' regulators can readily perceive what is in the 'public interest' and it would also be naïve to assume that, even if the public interest were clear, regulators would invariably be altruistic enough to pursue it. We may all be in favour of being healthy and safe and having a clean environment, but it does not follow that regulators charged with providing such desirable features of life are wise and disinterested servants of the public good.

So, what incentives do they have? First, consider what is not likely to attract them. It is not plausible to believe that the Drinking Water Inspectorate, the Environment Agency and their counterparts in Brussels have any particular interest in increasing competition in the water industry. On the contrary, they appear to have powerful incentives to play safe, reducing the risks they run by pushing companies towards the technical limits of what can be achieved in the provision of 'pure' water and avoiding circumstances in which there is even a low probability the regulators might attract blame. There seems no obvious limit to the regulations which might be imposed, from within Britain or from Brussels, to 'improve' the qualities of clean and waste water, whether or not consumers are willing to pay for such changes. Incumbent water companies are not likely to resist fiercely given the attractiveness to them of expanding their capital bases[56] and the likelihood that increasing regulation will make entry to the industry more difficult.

A public choice view of this kind of regulation would regard the 'social' regulators as pursuers of their own interests, largely unconstrained by cost considerations (even if under a formal

---

[55] The main duty of the DGWS is to ensure that water and sewerage companies can carry out and finance the functions specified in the Water Industry Act 1991. Secondary duties are to protect the interests of consumers, promote efficiency and economy and facilitate competition. His various duties are set out in Section 2 of the Act and are summarised in 'The Role of the Regulator', Ofwat Information Note No. 26, March 1994 (revised February 1996).

[56] Stephen Glaister, 'Incentives in Natural Monopoly: The Case of Water', *op.cit.*

obligation to carry out cost-benefit analyses of proposed regulations). The costs of recommended actions lie in the future and are very uncertain; in any case, they fall on others and so are not of great significance in the utility functions of regulators. Indeed, what are costs to others may be benefits to regulators: insistence on stringent standards has advantages for them, in terms of their public images, the furtherance of careers and the building of empires (since the scale and perceived importance of the regulatory operation depend on how active the regulator is in setting and monitoring standards).

Even if one allows for a measure of 'public-spiritedness' in regulatory decisions, it is hard to see what attraction the introduction of competition can hold for regulators other than Ofwat. In general, they seem unlikely supporters of radical economic change, if they foresee even a slight prospect of ensuing complaints about quality or environmental damage. They are particularly likely to be wary in the face of claims by the incumbent – probably frequent in common carriage applications – that health and safety might be compromised by the entry of newcomers.

Earlier I identified one of the major strengths of the British utility regulation régime as its pro-competition emphasis. But, with such explicit involvement in water of regulators with no incentive to facilitate competition, there is a danger that this key feature of the régime will be undermined.

Of course, the issue I have raised goes far beyond the water industry and the utilities in general. There is a rising tide of 'social' regulation. Many companies now find that regulators insist on setting standards with very high compliance costs. They find also that appeal against the regulators' decisions is difficult and costly, particularly for smaller organisations. Larger firms, as explained earlier, may welcome regulation as a barrier to entry: they may also see it as establishing an influential organisation they can hope to capture.

An insidious expansion of 'social' regulation in various forms appears now to be proceeding and, as a consequence, some markets are being severely constrained.[57] Moreover, without the pro-competition duties which restrict utility regulators, 'social' regulation

---

[57] One estimate of the annual cost of federal government regulation in the United States is over $670 billion – equivalent to over one-third of federal government spending. (See Clyde Wayne Crews Jr., *Ten Thousand Commandments: A Policymaker's Snapshot of the Federal Regulatory State*, Washington DC: Competitive Enterprise Institute, September 1996.)

seems likely to continue to grow under its own momentum. The consequences for the economy and society have not been properly considered since there is a widespread, if misguided belief that this form of regulation is always and everywhere no more than a benign means of internalising externalities. In fact, any intellectual respectability it appears to have rests on the market failure model which, I argued earlier, is of little help in practical policy-making. This is not the place to discuss these wider issues, but it does seem that, in the course of time, the expansion of 'social' regulation could result in a society with rigidities similar to those which used to afflict centrally planned economies. Market processes will be obstructed and so entrepreneurship and innovation will be inhibited.[58]

Dealing with 'social' regulation

It is not easy to deal with the problem of self-generating and self-perpetuating regulation where over-zealous regulators take actions whose invisible victims are consumers (because market processes are prevented from working). There are at least two broad approaches.

First, the existing régime could be retained but with the incentives of the regulators altered. For example, a clear burden of proof might be placed on them to demonstrate that their actions are likely to be beneficial to consumers. Regrettably, I doubt whether it is possible to make such a system work satisfactorily since the costs and the benefits of those actions are in the future and, given the pervasiveness of uncertainty on scientific issues, clear-cut judgements will invariably be hard to make. Another way of changing incentives might be to make appeal against regulators' decisions easier, though if consumers (rather than entrants) are the likely appellants there will be the usual problem of deterrence through high transactions costs.

A more radical (and more promising) approach would be to change the régime to one which greatly reduced the influence of the 'social' regulators. There could, for example, be a less interventionist system which switched the emphasis away from detailed standard-setting to one in which companies were left to formulate their own programmes for health, safety and environmental protection. Regulators, freed from detailed standard setting and less numerous

---

[58] Norman Barry, 'The Market, Liberty and the Regulatory State', *Economic Affairs*, Vol. 14, No.4, June 1994.

than now, could be given the task of monitoring whether these programmes are being achieved (as they do now with offshore oil platform safety).

Or there could be a more decisive move away from detailed regulation on health, safety and environmental protection grounds. Companies which inflicted damage on others, despite the programmes they had formulated, would be subject to penalties (pre-set or under normal legal processes). Such a system in water would probably lead the water companies to insure against possible claims which, in turn, would induce insurance companies to investigate means of assessing company programmes, setting premiums and monitoring company performance.

It is possible that an insurance-based system could substitute to some degree for public bureaucracies in regulation. In some industries – such as lifts and hoists, steam boilers and 'transportable gas containers' – safety regulation has to some extent migrated to the private sector. Briefly, the system under present legislation is that inspection of the relevant activity is required by a 'competent person' who provides safety certification. Insurance companies have naturally taken on the inspection function as well as insurance to provide them with the information they require to assess risks. Provided the usual problems of adverse selection and moral hazard can be avoided – so that insurance companies can make a reasonable *ex ante* assessment of the risks and can monitor *ex post* whether companies are shirking on their duties – either a compulsory or a voluntary system of insurance might help overcome some of the problems of the present régime. At least the idea seems worth consideration because of the serious difficulties to which the present system – regulation with no obvious bounds – is likely to lead over a period of years.[59]

Conclusions

I would conclude that, compared with the other utilities, water is as yet little touched by the forces of competition. That would not matter if regulation could be a close substitute for such forces. But I have argued that a competitive process is required if companies are to be entrepreneurial and innovative and if consumers are to be protected

---

[59] The idea of giving a greater role to insurance in regulation is discussed in a forthcoming IEA paper by Richard North, with a commentary by Martin Ricketts.

adequately. Regulation should be very much a last resort, reserved for 'natural monopoly' activities and for transitional periods when competition is being stimulated. Otherwise, it ought to be withering away.

There are obstacles to introducing a competitive process in water. Government proposals to overcome these obstacles, both by making existing methods of entry easier and by introducing common carriage, are well-meaning. However, their impact will be marginal unless two further steps are taken. The first is separation of the network of pipes so they are in the ownership (or at least control) of independent organisations with no incentive to exclude prospective newcomers. The second is to find a means of reducing the influence of regulators other than Ofwat who, no matter how well-intentioned they may be, are all too likely to undermine efforts to enhance competition in the industry.

CHAIRMAN'S COMMENTS

Ian Byatt

COLIN ROBINSON ARGUES FOR MORE COMPETITION IN THE WATER INDUSTRY – presumably in the collection of sewage as well as the supply of water. He approves of the proposals in the Government's consultation paper, but wants to go further, in particular:

- to separate the network of pipes (and sewers?) from other parts of the water companies; and

- to find a way of reducing the influence of regulators other than Ofwat.

It should be noted that you do not need to be licensed as a water or sewerage undertaker to provide these services. There are private water suppliers. Businesses can – and do – treat their own trade effluent. Individuals can connect to sewers (but not yet water mains). The charging policies of undertakers, for example, for trade effluent, affect the scale of this activity.

Network separation is only one solution. There are other things that could be done first. In particular, I would like to see:

- legislation to require water companies to provide common carriage and to specify (subject to challenge by the regulator) terms and conditions of use, for large users;

- liberalisation of inset appointments so that they could be limited in time – say, five years – in order to relax the safeguards required for a permanent new appointee, and to ensure future contestability. The original supplier would have the obligation of supplier should no one contest the market after a time-limited appointment lapsed.

There is much to be done in order to ensure that such arrangements work well. The engineering and quality aspects of transporting electricity and gas are well understood and considerable practical experience already exists – which is being built upon to develop competition further in the electricity and gas markets. In water we need first to learn how to walk.

While I welcome moves to ensure that quality regulators are constrained in their enthusiasm for new and better regulations – and here I speak more of the EC Commission and political procedures in Brussels than of the DWI or the Environment Agency – I hope it will prove possible to introduce competition on the basis of whatever quality standards are in place at the time. There are indeed arguments for greater self-regulation and less prescriptive standard setting, but these are best pursued in their own right. (The effect on competition, however, strengthens the argument for something which would be sensible for other reasons.)

The Environment Agency believes in water conservation in order to avoid dry rivers and loss of wetlands. These laudable aims point to the greater use of meters and reducing leakage – both of which I approve. But competition is more likely to thrive if producers or potential producers have reasonable access to the raw material – water. This raises the issue of transferable abstraction licences and a market in rights to abstract.

Colin Robinson draws attention to the cost of transporting water and to the advantageous cost position of existing undertakers. The situation on costs is unfavourable to the development of common carriage on a large scale. The replacement costs of the assets of existing undertakers are much greater than their regulatory value (about 10 times). This suggests that, contrary to the situation – which often arises in other utilities – where existing undertakers are handicapped by stranded assets whose economic value is less than their original cost, the incumbent has an inevitable financial advantage.

The main effect of competition so far, through inset appointments, has been to realign prices of bulk (wholesale) and retail water. This should improve resource allocation – and is a more effective route than the no undue discrimination or preference rules. Competition opens up the prospect of further unbundling of prices, perhaps geographically.

For the economist, it may be no bad thing to have such pressures in the pricing arrangements. Water prices are averaged over the area of a company and are therefore subject to big changes at the frontier of a company's territory. But geographical de-averaging would have its own political awkwardness, whatever its economic merits. So I would advocate caution in moving the 250 megalitres threshold downward – although on competition grounds this could be very sensible. In particular, I think there would be difficulties in living with rural/urban differences in price – although there are clear rural/urban differences in cost.

Finally, I was very interested in Colin Robinson's characterisation of competition as a process of rivalry and discovery rather than market structure. His conclusion, if I understand it correctly, is that regulators should not seek to reproduce what would be expected to happen in a structurally competitive market – for example, follow the rules so elegantly set out in Abba Lerner's *Economics of Control*, and in subsequent work on public utility pricing – but to encourage rivalry and entry.

I rather agree with this, which seems to me as much Chicago as Vienna, and wanted to finish by applying it to comparative competition. Comparative competition, in my view, goes well beyond 'useful cross-company comparisons' and the technicalities of adjusting data for differences in operating environment. The existence of comparators provides a framework within which companies are pushed – by customers, politicians and the financial markets – to reduce costs and improve customer service. I remain unrepentant in my support for this situation and my reluctance to see it eroded by internal mergers.

The econometrics may be difficult. But our analysis shows clear evidence that companies who have performed badly do bounce back. You need look no further than Northumbrian or South West Water. This effect on behaviour is very powerful and goes way beyond what could ever be achieved by a regulator collecting and analysing data.

7

TRADING AND COMPETITION IN GAS:

MARKET DEVELOPMENTS AND NEEDS

Stephen Glaister[1]

London School of Economics

THIS PAPER IS ABOUT THE *STRUCTURE* OF GAS
CHARGES, how that affects domestic consumers, and how the
structure might affect, and be affected by, the development of
competition in the industry. In the first part I discuss pricing and
competition in the transmission network. In the second part I
analyse the domestic gas market and discuss the impacts that
competition may have there.

I argue that since privatisation British Gas[2] has followed a policy
of moving towards uniformity and averaging in its charges. This
conflicts with the agreed, and stated, objective of long-run marginal
cost pricing. As with uniform postal rates, averaging creates
opportunities for competitive entry and 'bypass' of the existing
transmission system. I discuss some of the ways this could occur. It
also needlessly raises the price of gas to many domestic consumers
much of the time and fails to provide incentives to use gas
parsimoniously at peak times. Finally, I analyse the nature of
competition in the domestic consumer market and explore the
geographical location of opportunities for competitive gas suppliers.

---

[1] Paper prepared for the third lecture in the LBS/IEA Regulation Lecture Series delivered on
15 October 1996 at the Royal Society of Arts. I am most grateful for assistance and
comments from Michael Beesley, Simon Griew, David Kennedy, Robin Holland, Ed
Mineman, Andrew Waters, the Library of Ofgas and others. Dan Graham has provided able
research assistance in producing the mapping analysis.

[2] At the time of writing British Gas plc was a single enterprise with internal division between
trading and transport. In early 1997 the trading (Centrica) and transport (TransCo) activities
were legally separated.

The Abundance of Natural Gas

Natural gas is now an abundant commodity. Figure 1 shows how the discovery of new reserves has outstripped the cumulative consumption of gas. Together with the fall in oil prices this has led to a fall in the spot price of UK Continental Shelf gas from about 16 pence a therm in the early 1980s to close to 10 pence per therm.

There now seems to be no hesitation about exploiting this resource. Current policy statements to be found in the DTI *Energy Report* are self-congratulatory about the level of investment and the rate of growth of output in the industry. In 1998 the Interconnector will open in order to allow export of gas from Bacton to Belgium.

Figure 2 shows the growth in consumption of gas, and how it has replaced other energy sources in non-transport uses. The growth has been particularly important for domestic users.[3] The average domestic gas bill was about £325 a year in 1995.[4] Heating accounted for 88 per cent of the domestic load, and cooking and other uses for 12 per cent.

For domestic consumers gas accounts for about two-thirds of energy used. It is now supplied to some 18 million out of 22 million UK households. About 56 per cent of gas by volume and 71 per cent by revenue is sold to domestic consumers.[5] Provided that the industry is managed in such a way that the gas is delivered in a cheap and efficient manner, natural gas offers a major source of economic well-being for the general population. Competition to supply gas is now open for all customers in the South West, including the smallest domestic ones. The rest of the country is to be progressively opened up to competition.

For the purpose of constructing tariffs British Gas defines three kinds of cost:

- *commodity costs*: those costs which vary in relation to the volume of gas;

---

[3] See Monopolies and Mergers Commission, *British Gas plc*, 1993, p.24.

[4] Ofgas, *1997 Price Control Review*, June 1996, p.11.

[5] Monopolies and Mergers Commission, *op. cit.*

Figure 1: Natural Gas Reserves and Cumulative Production: UK 1980 to 1995

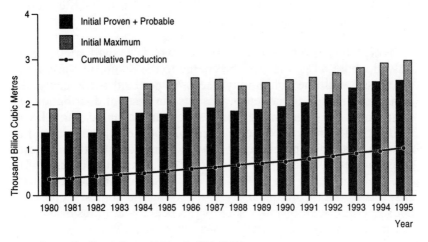

Source: *The Energy Report, Volume 2, 1996, HMSO.*

Figure 2: Final energy use by fuel in the domestic sector, 1970 to 1991 (therms)

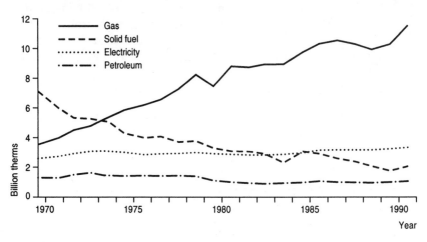

Source: *Monopolies and Mergers Commission, 1993, Vol. 2, p.24.*

191

- *capacity costs*: those costs which are related to the ability to supply or transport gas to customers on the peak day to satisfy the maximum demand for gas; and

- *customer costs*: those costs which are related to each customer, for example the meter and service.

Under the current pricing régime, which I shall argue to be flawed, about 43 per cent of the charge to the domestic consumer is associated with the commodity itself, 43 per cent is the charge for transmission and 10 per cent represents the costs of distribution and retailing.[6] The remaining cost is gas unaccounted for. Having landed at the beach at between 10 and 20 pence a therm (depending on the particular purchase contract), it is sold to the domestic consumer at 40 to 50 pence a therm plus a standing charge. The important point for our purpose is that a significant portion of the *cost* (as distinct from the *charge*) of serving the domestic consumer does not vary with quantity supplied, especially at times of the year when the physical infrastructure has spare capacity.

The Geographical Flows

Map 1 shows that most gas arrives at terminals on the east and far north east coasts, with one landing point on the north west. It is distributed by the pipe system shown. The map also shows the major compression (pumping) and storage facilities.

The geography implies that the distances gas has to be moved to serve customers varies enormously. It moves both from north to south and from east to west. To serve the south west it must move considerable distances. (Bacton to Land's End is about 450 miles, over 700 km.)

A basic technical relationship in gas transmission is:[7]

$$(\text{pressure out})^2 \text{ is proportional to } (\text{pressure in})^2 - (\text{pipe length}) \times (\text{flow})^2 / (\text{diameter})^5.$$

---

[6] Ofgas, *op. cit.*

[7] TransCo, 1996, p.12.

Map 1

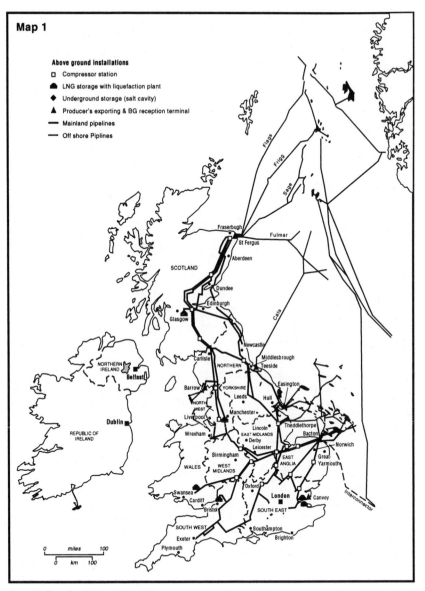

Above ground installations

☐ Compressor station

⬛ LNG storage with liquefaction plant

◆ Underground storage (salt cavity)

▲ Producer's exporting & BG reception terminal

━━ Mainland pipelines

── Off shore Piplines

Source: The Energy Report, Volume 2 1996, HMSO.

193

This shows that, for a given pipe size and flow rate the costs of transmission rise with pipe length. Obviously, construction and maintenance costs of a given type of pipe increase strongly with length. Incidentally, since costs of laying and maintaining pipes rise less than proportionately with diameter, there is considerable scope for optimising pipe diameter for a given flow and distance.

The Peaked Nature of the Demand for Gas

The demand for gas on the maximum demand day is of the order of four times the demand during the summer and about twice the annual average daily demand. This excludes demand for interruptible gas which may not be met at the winter peaks.

Demand will be higher than normal in a severe winter. British Gas plans and operates the supply and transmission system to meet the volume of firm winter demand which is expected to be exceeded in not more than one year in 50. This dictates the amount of long-term storage necessary to compensate for the shortfall of gas taken from the suppliers over the course of the Winter.

Figure 3 shows the gas load distribution curve, in which the demand in the busiest day is plotted first, the demand in the second busiest day plotted second, and so on. If the demand were even this would be a horizontal straight line. In fact, the diagram shows that demand is heavily peaked. The load duration curve shows that the tariff sector (most of which is the domestic consumer) imposes much more severe peak demands on the system than the contract market.

This is the long-term average, but there will always be significant random variation, mainly associated with the weather. Since it takes time to call on long-term storage there must be provision to deal with daily peaks when the weather is unexpectedly cold. So there is a second planning standard which is the volume of demand from firm customers in a period of 24 hours which would not be expected to be exceeded in more than one year in 20.

A depleted gas field at Rough provides a large, if slow to respond, storage facility. Salt cavities at Hornsea, East Yorkshire, have less capacity but can respond more quickly. Gas can be liquefied under pressure and stored in tanks. This is expensive and it provides relatively low capacity. But it can be sited more flexibly and it can respond more quickly to unexpected demands. Gas can also be

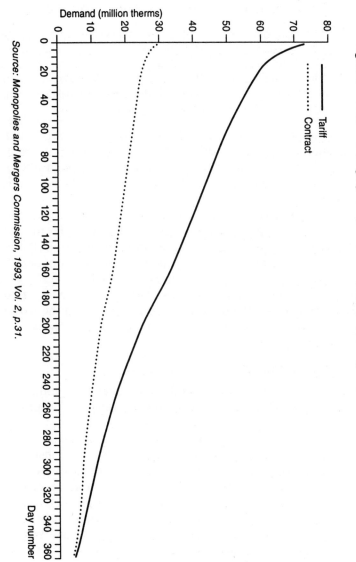

Figure 3: 1990/91 average year load duration curve showing tariff and contract load

Source: *Monopolies and Mergers Commission, 1993, Vol. 2, p.31.*

195

stored in the pipes themselves by increasing the pressure, providing sufficient capacity to meet the diurnal peaks in demand on the National Transmission System. Local distribution networks make use of gasometers.

There are around 50 compressors on the system:

> 'Compressors are a relatively expensive part of the National Transmission System (NTS) both in capital and operating terms. Currently compressors use 70 million therms of gas [of the order of one third of one per cent of total national consumption] as an operating fuel in an average year. Minimising the use (and cost) of compressors is a major operational objective of the NTS.'[8]

It is important for what follows to note that before natural gas was available in large quantities from the North Sea it was imported in liquefied form, by ship, from Algeria through the terminal at Canvey Island. Canvey Island terminal was decommissioned in 1995.

To summarise, natural gas at the beach is a cheap commodity in abundant supply. A large part of the cost to the consumer is associated with charges for delivering the gas from the beach to the consumer. The domestic consumer is the most important part of the market and gas is the most important, and cheapest, fuel for most domestic consumers. There are variations in transport cost because of distance and the degree of spare capacity on the particular route. Domestic consumers present a particularly peaked pattern of demand.

Marginal Cost Pricing and Competition

There appears to be general assent that the guiding principle in setting prices is that they should be related to long-run marginal cost.

The standard 'economic efficiency' case for this is as follows. The price of an extra therm of gas is what the consumer sees when deciding whether to increase his or her consumption at the expense of consumption of something else. It therefore represents the value of gas to the consumer. The long-run marginal cost is the cost to the industry of supplying the extra therm, taking full account of any need to adjust the infrastructure to achieve delivery. If price is

---

[8]   Monopolies and Mergers Commission, Vol. 2, para 2.40.

substantially above long-run marginal cost then some gas is withheld even though its value to consumers is higher than the cost of supply. If price is lower than long-run marginal cost then gas is consumed even though its value is below the cost of provision.

Marginal cost pricing helps to give correct locational signals for entry to the system and also for site location, particularly for power stations and other large users; it encourages efficient development of the transmission system and of storage; and it gives the correct signal for shippers and producers in deciding between use of the system and other onshore or offshore systems. Prices convey the correct information to both producers and consumers about what is and is not worth doing, providing correct incentives.

The efficiency case for marginal cost pricing rests on an assumption that the consumer does indeed trade gas against other commodities: then different gas prices relative to other commodity prices correspond to different quantities the consumer would like to consume ('the demand curve slopes downward'). But if consumers did not respond to price changes then the same quantity would be purchased whatever the price ('the demand curve would be vertical'). Then, as far as economic efficiency is concerned, any price is as good as any other: the case in favour of long-run marginal cost pricing evaporates. Differences in charges would only cause differences in the distribution of who bears the recovery of cost.

In their public statements of their objectives British Gas state this argument very clearly (see below).

Cost Allocation

The correct logic is: understand the cost structure; understand long-run marginal cost; derive an appropriate price structure. Allocation of costs has little part to play in proper long-run marginal cost pricing.

Marginal cost pricing will often yield insufficient revenue to cover total costs, because of the presence of fixed costs or some other form of increasing returns to scale. The question then arises as to how the residual costs should be *recovered* (or over-recovered in order to give a return on capital and/or a profit). Generally, one wants to avoid distorting the relationship between marginal cost and marginal benefit (price) as far as possible. It is unlikely to be sensible simply to scale all marginal costs in direct proportions to produce the required total. A well known solution, known as Ramsey pricing, involves adopting a degree of price discrimination: increasing prices more in inelastic markets. This has the effect of distorting *quantities* away from the efficient situation by similar amounts.

Standing charges

One method of cost recovery is by means of the two-part tariff. Users are charged marginal cost for the commodity and a fixed standing charge. The standing charge covers those costs which are not recovered by marginal cost pricing – in particular, costs of making and administering the connection to the network. Essentially, this scheme maximises the benefits to consumers – the consumer surplus – by allowing them to consume on the margin at the true marginal cost, and then abstracts some of that surplus by means of a lump sum tax. This scheme works well provided that the standing charge does not cause some consumers to drop out of the market. In practice they will drop out and so it is necessary to compromise the ideal system by reducing standing charges and raising commodity charges above marginal costs. A balance has to be struck between excluding too many people from the market and raising commodity charges too much above marginal cost.[9]

Monopolistic pricing

Even if a monopolist is free to adopt discriminatory, fully commercial pricing, marginal cost is the guiding rule: marginal revenue will be equated to it and, as a consequence, the wedge between price and marginal cost will depend on the relevant price elasticity. Both efficient prices and fully commercial prices are tied to long-run marginal cost. Pricing at average cost will achieve neither economic efficiency nor profit maximisation.

Competition

There is a second, rather different, reason for using long-run marginal cost as a bench mark. There has been a general acceptance that the industry should move away from its old, monolithic state-owned structure towards a more competitive structure. If the

---

[9] For a detailed exposition, see M. Armstrong *et al.*, *Regulatory Reform*, Cambridge, Mass.: MIT Press, 1994.

industry were to be truly competitive, with no fixed costs to be recovered, no barriers to entry, and in long-run equilibrium, then a price above long-run marginal cost could not be sustained because it would precipitate profitable competitive entry. In particular, if long-run marginal costs varied greatly in differing markets and if uniform average cost pricing were adopted in an industry which is not making overall losses, then competitive entry would be likely in the more profitable markets. This is essentially the reason for statutory monopoly protection of mail services from competition in order to sustain costly services which have to be cross-subsidised by monopoly profits earned on the cheap ones. In the gas industry, by analogy, this has become known as 'postalisation' of rates.

The Characteristics of the Ideal Pricing System

We can now relate the earlier observations about the nature of the industry to the notion of marginal cost pricing.

It costs more to supply gas to a remote location than to a near one, first because of the extra pumping that is required and second because more physical equipment – such as pipes, pumps and land – is required. This equipment has to be maintained and it has to be replaced. Here the margin is distance, and one would expect prices to reflect increasing distance of transport.

Second, we observed the phenomenon of the seasonal peak. To identify long-run marginal costs correctly it is necessary to distinguish the peak period from the rest. It is the period during which capacity of the system is fully used: to carry an extra therm requires 'reinforcement' of the system. This is unlike the off-peak, when there is spare capacity: then delivering more gas only means more pumping activity, but not more investment in physical infrastructure.

The implication is that all costs associated with capacity should be borne by the peak users. Off-peak users cause no additional capacity to be provided so they should not be charged for capacity. Note that capacity is measured as the ability to shift units of volume per unit time over a defined distance. The capacity charge for any one therm of peak gas should depend on how long the peak lasts: the longer it lasts the more therms can be shifted during the peak and so the more therms there are to bear the costs of the physical infrastructure. If the peak lasts one day then the charge for a peak therm would be the commodity charge plus the marginal cost of expanding the capacity to cope with one extra therm in the peak day. If the peak lasts for two days the capacity charge per therm delivered in the peak is halved.

British Gas's Objectives

British Gas's formal statements of objectives are usually admirably clear. For instance:

> 'a charging system devised for transportation should be set with the following objectives:...To be economically efficient, and in particular to be structured in such a way that it provided appropriate signals on the relative costs and system usage from the various supply terminals to customers at different offtake points (particularly identified as relevant to gas marketing; pipeline capacity utilization; expansion and reinforcement of the grid; location of new plant; and development and purchase of new gas fields). Additionally the pricing structure should not create barriers to entry into the gas supply market.'[10]

In view of the nature of the commodity, outlined above, one would hope to see the delivered price of the commodity itself low, except at times of peak demand, when there would be substantial price premia to reflect the incremental costs of transmission infrastructure. Infrastructure charges would directly reflect distance and other relevant attributes of infrastructure costs, such as density of customers. Because of scale effects one would expect that efficient prices would not cover costs, so there will be some form of residual cost recovery – such as standing charges – which, so far as feasible, would not depend upon volume consumed. Of course, a practical tariff must be considerably simplified and must recognise the constraints imposed by the problems, already noted, of high standing charges bearing unduly heavily on small users.

The trend towards the average

In practice, far from acting as a purely commercially motivated company, or one dedicated to developing competition and the public interest principles embodied in marginal cost pricing, British Gas appears to retain, and, until 1993 at least, to continue to develop many of the confused, 'socially concerned' objectives that one associates with a monolithic, politically influenced, nationalised

---

[10] Monopolies and Mergers Commission, *op. cit.*, Appendix 5.2, para. 2.

industry:

> 'British Gas agreed, however, that there was a trade-off between equity and strict economic efficiency, which should also take into account the cost of connecting geographically distant points regardless of peak capacity requirements. Equity turned on identifying a "fair" way of recovering total NTS accounting costs, part of which was effectively a system overhead cost. While economic efficiency considerations would suggest that the capacity: commodity structure of final charges should reflect that of the LRMC, equity arguments might suggest that a larger proportion of system overheads should be recovered through volume-related charges.'[11]

British Gas told the 1993 Monopolies and Mergers Commission investigation of its concern that competition would cause it to rebalance its tariffs to reflect the structure of its costs which would, they said, mean substantial increases to small domestic users. This was presented as an argument against competition.

The Monopolies and Mergers Commission took the longer view:

> 'In our view, a main and normal benefit of competition is to provide an incentive to relate the structure of prices to the structure of costs and to reduce the level of costs, and hence to reduce prices to users as a whole. Customers who might have to pay relatively more as a result of rebalancing could include users of small volumes of gas. The current "postalization" of prices could end. We think it likely, therefore, that competition could result in price increases to some users in the shorter term, but this would itself encourage competition in the market.'

In spite of the acceptance of the long-run marginal cost principle by British Gas there has been a steady move away from cost-based pricing towards average pricing. This seems to have occurred in all sorts of ways and, at least until very recently, it has continued since privatisation. The justifications offered are usually on the lines of an appeal to simplicity, 'understandability', 'transparency' or 'to encourage competition in the supply of gas and to allow for the extension of such competition'. The consequences have been to distort cost signals and to open up the risk of inefficient under- and over-consumption, and opportunities for competitive entry ('bypass') by gas producers. Opportunities for bypass are discussed

---

[11] Monopolies and Mergers Commission, *op. cit.*, Appendix 5.2, para. 12.

below. They have recently been acknowledged by Transco which has proposed special charges for short-haul routes, which they say are more cost reflective, to discourage it.

A trend towards national uniformity and average cost pricing is a continuation of a long-term trend. In the 19th century and first half of the 20th century gas was produced locally from coal and locally priced. There was a short period of development of production from oil feedstock. But in the 1960s natural gas was introduced. Because this was not produced locally the conversion to natural gas required the construction of a national trunk transport network. Thus a locally produced product became, at a stroke, a nationally produced and controlled product. The local municipal companies had been nationalised in 1948 and subsequently run by 12 Area Boards and co-ordinated by the Gas Council. They were replaced by a unified British Gas Council after the Gas Act 1972. The Gas Act 1986 abolished the statutory monopoly of gas supply and facilitated the offer for public sale of British Gas plc in November 1986.

The economic structure of gas supply was transformed by the technological changes. The oil-reforming process led the Area Boards to develop regional integrated supply systems. Natural gas led to a national system.

The Development of National Tariffs

The gas distribution system has four levels: the National Transmission System (NTS) and the intermediate, medium and low pressure systems which form the Regional Transmission System (RTS). The low pressure system serves domestic consumers and many commercial and industrial users. It is by far the most extensive.

In the late 1960s each Area Board had a variety of tariffs. Promotional two-part tariffs varied from one Area Board to another, in some cases to encourage higher-consuming central heating customers to switch to gas. As natural gas became established as the most economic fuel in the domestic sector British Gas's approach changed, resulting in a progressive move to harmonizing tariffs towards uniform rates around the country. British Gas told the Monopolies and Mergers Commission that

'this was based on the following considerations:

(a) the costs reflected in the standing charge in the different British Gas regions were converging following standardization of practices;

(b) the logic of the division of the country into three zones was not sustainable as there were differences in costs between the British Gas regions in each zone; and

(c) the differences in costs were not sufficient to justify the administrative cost and potential confusion arising from having different prices.

Promotional tariffs based on seasonality, time of day or domestic consumption level have not been a feature of BG's operation. Overall, BG believed that its approach had allowed the maximum number of homes in Great Britain to benefit from natural gas, whilst expanding considerably the customer base in the best interests of all customers.'[12]

Note, once again, the haziness of objectives implied here.

Until April 1989 British Gas's standing charges varied from region to region. These differences were removed and a single national standing charge now applies. There is no evidence that the standing charge has been determined according to the principles outlined above: historical accident and fear of change appear to be influential factors.

The system of uniform pricing is now, revealingly, referred to as 'postalized'.

'BG argued that a distance-related notional path approach [for the lower tiers of the distribution network] was not practically feasible for the distribution system, particularly if rapid quotation for many more customers were to be produced. BG thought that postalization on a uniform national basis had the advantage of simplicity and robustness of the underlying cost data.... there was a trade-off here between economic efficiency and equity considerations...' [13]

'Given the nature of the demand on BG's integrated system and its gas and transmission capacities, BG has to operate its system so as to

---

[12] Monopolies and Mergers Commission, *op. cit.*, Vol. 2, para. 4.19.

[13] Monopolies and Mergers Commission, *op. cit.*, Appendix 5.2, para. 19.

balance them in the most efficient way.... . Over the longer term BG has control over the development of its system by altering supply (for example, by entering into further gas purchase contracts or investing in further storage or transmission) and can influence the demands on it (for, example, by altering pricing and marketing policy).'[14]

However, there is no obvious evidence of a systematic attempt to use pricing and marketing in this way. On the contrary, the trend towards the average is a trend in the opposite direction.

There appears to be considerable confusion between costing and pricing, and between transparency and correctness:

'Several respondents comment that the proposals offered transparent pricing, not costing.'[15]

Prices should be derived from costs, but they are not the same thing. Prices may be transparent, but give completely wrong incentives, judged by the espoused principles.

The reluctance to do things in accordance with the agreed principles appears to have several causes. There is the weight of history and the traditional engineering rules of thumb; a feeling that there will be severe practical difficulties; a fear of attracting criticism for changing things – especially from and on behalf of the losers.

The underlying argument is that to have tariffs which are based on a large amount of individual detail is too administratively costly. Therefore one must revert to an alternative which is simple ('transparent'). An alternative would be to attempt something rough and ready, but on the right lines. In its evidence to the Monopolies and Mergers Commission Ofgas convincingly raised many objections to the British Gas pricing methods. For instance, on national postalization they noted that

'the important cost differences were likely to be those between urban, suburban and rural areas, rather than between BG's existing regions, which contained mixtures of such areas. Allocative efficiency implied that locational cost differences should be reflected in regional tariff

---

[14] *Ibid.*, Vol. 2, para. 2.68.

[15] *Ibid.*, Appendix 5.4, para. 12.

differences. OFGAS favoured subnational postalization, as would be implied by LRMC/EE pricing...'.[16]

Having said that postalised prices were acceptable because cost differences were so small that the complication of non-postalisation meant it was not worthwhile, British Gas responded to the Monopolies and Mergers Commission's request for cost-reflective regional prices by saying that considerable further analytical work was required to establish an agreed basis for cost-based comparisons to be made.[17]

The general effect of postalization of the RTS is to raise charges for short distances and reduce them for long distances. I show below that the same is true for the entry/exit price system on the NTS.

On the matter of peak prices:

'The introduction of a more generally available seasonal tariff would require sophisticated peak demand metering or more regular meter reading, with resultant additional costs. The potential for small tariff customers to curtail demand at peak times was limited and it was doubtful whether customers would find the benefits worthwhile when set against the inconvenience of not using gas at peak times. In BG's view, a system of seasonal prices would pose problems for certain customers (such as the elderly and those with children) for whom space heating and hot water were essential but who often had limited incomes or were dependent on state benefits. BG believed that, as the primary use for tariff gas was space heating, customers were generally concerned to maintain usage in harsh weather. To reduce demand for gas in winter, they would need to switch to another fuel, primarily to electricity, where the relative cost of peak supply was much higher than for gas.'[18]

This shows an undue willingness to substitute corporate views for people's own views of what they might or might not wish to do given the choice. It is also unimaginative about the responses individuals might make to peak prices: such as improving their insulation or heating fewer rooms – just as they used to before the advent of central heating. (Only about one in five households has

---

[16] Monopolies and Mergers Commission, *op. cit.*, Appendix 5.4, para. 11.

[17] *Ibid.*, para. 4.36.

[18] *Ibid.*, Vol. 1, para. 4.41.

any form of wall insulation.) The pay-off from the customer's point of view could be a reduction in commodity charges and standing charges during the rest of the year – because of the resource savings on capacity.

It is clearly difficult to introduce peak pricing for domestic consumers given the present lack of capabilities of installed meters. In the longer run proper consideration should be given to installing meters capable of distinguishing the time of consumption. Sophisticated electronic meters for electricity, involving two-way communication and the capability of real-time pricing, are already in the field in the United States. This degree of complexity may not be cost-effective in the case of gas, where time of year – rather than time of day – is one of the more important factors. But serious consideration should be given to the costs and benefits of improving on the rudimentary metering systems now in domestic use.

Since there is daily balancing and full metering there is no reason that the gas *shippers* could not be charged more sophisticated time-of-year tariffs than is already implicit in the system of capacity nominations. This would provide better opportunities and incentives on the shippers to make economically sensible decisions, thereby increasing the net value of the gas system. For instance, they could develop their own storage at the consumers' end of the system and thereby avoid peak capacity requirements and escape network capacity charges. This would stimulate a genuine competitive market in storage, as Ofgas seeks to do. It would give gas suppliers the incentive to persuade their customers to use less peak gas. For instance, they might provide free advice and subsidy to encourage better household insulation. There are no incentives on householders to do this at present.

An argument that there would be so little saving that the extra expense and complexity of seasonal tariffs would not be worthwhile may be acceptable, but it would carry more weight if it were adequately supported by appropriate facts.

Entry and Exit Pricing

A good example of the recent trend towards uniformity and averaging is the relatively recent development of entry and exit pricing for the transmission system. After 1986 British Gas offered transport service for other shippers' gas. Initially British Gas priced this to recover its allocated accounting costs which were distance-related. It then proposed a new system, seeking 'cost recovery, equitability, efficiency and ready applicability'. The pre-existing capacity:commodity cost allocation approach was retained. National transmission charges were replaced by a long-run marginal cost approach, with distance-related prices replaced by the entry/exit charge system.

This works by assuming all gas is injected to and withdrawn from a single 'balancing point'. Charges only depend upon which entry point and which exit points are used, not explicitly on the actual entry-exit distance.

'BG regards the "entry/exit" approach to charging as necessary if charges are to be applied to its trading activities on an even-handed basis, and if simplified procedures are to be introduced for making quotations and offers.... There is still, however, a large element of subjective judgment in BG's methods for allocating both costs and charges to different categories of customer...'[19]

To derive the charges the following procedure is used.[20] First, a sophisticated model of the physical system is used to estimate in considerable detail the long-run marginal cost of shipping peak gas from each of six input points to each one of 126 NTS offtake points.

These results are, in principle, the correct point-to-point long-run marginal costs to use as a basis for pricing. Given that the customers for transport are not the general public but sophisticated gas companies, it is hard to see why it is necessary to undertake the major simplification which follows.

First, the exit zones are amalgamated into 37 plus 22 large industrial loads. This gives a matrix of point-to-point costs, displayed in the *Ten Year Statement*.[21]

The spatial information in this table is then obfuscated by means of a systematic averaging process. This is a fixed effects regression model. It finds the average cost of transporting gas put into any one intake point, averaged across all the possible destinations. Similarly, it takes the average cost of transporting gas to each offtake point

---

[19] Monopolies and Mergers Commission, *op. cit.*, Cm. 2315, para. 28.

[20] TransCo, *Ten Year Statement*, 1996.

[21] *Ibid.*

irrespective of where the gas has come from. These averages are unweighted, except that entry/exit combinations where gas could not realistically be expected to flow at peak are excluded.

The procedures essentially calculate deviations of the averages from a reference point which must be specified to close the system. This is arbitrarily set to 10 pence per peak day therm for entry to Bacton. All others are expressed as deviations from it.

To achieve a final result yet two more pieces of averaging are used. First, the grand total of costs to be recovered is divided in two, following an established convention that capacity charges are required to recover 50 per cent of the total revenue requirement. The remaining 50 per cent is recovered from a uniform commodity charge. (This is the 50/50 rule discussed below.) Then the charges derived from the regression are uniformly scaled to produce the required 50 per cent revenue at assumed volumes (in the 10-year statement figures this scaling is a small factor: 0.974) .

The *Ten Year Statement* contains some discussion of implementing a move to a three-node procedure, as suggested in NERA.[22] In principle this looks like a considerable improvement over the single node model because it can take a more realistic view of where the gas actually flows in the network – though it is not at all clear that three is the optimum number of nodes. However, it seems that in the implementation reported in the *Ten Year Statement, 1996*, the results of the three-node model have been constrained to produce the same overall results as the one-node model. TransCo propose a fuller move to the three-node approach in their consultation report.[23]

The distortions produced by this process can be seen by inspecting Figure 4. To construct this I have worked out the point-to-point cost matrix implied by the entry and exit prices. It is then scaled to have the same overall average as does the actual cost matrix. Then Figure 4 shows the differences as a percentage of the actual values. A negative sign implies that the entry/exit system yields a lower price than the full cost matrix.

[*cont'd on p. 212*]

---

[22] NERA, *Towards a Permanent Pricing and Services Regime*, November 1995.

[23] British Gas, *The Future of Transco's Pricing and Services Regime: Consultation Report*, September 1996.

Figure 4.1: Entry / exit charges versus full cost matrix

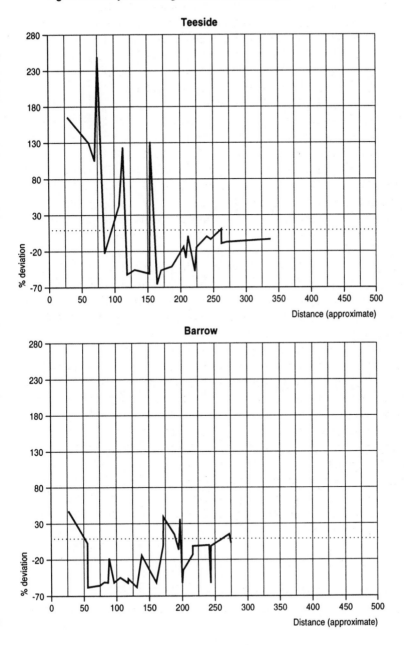

Figure 4.2: Entry / exit charges versus full cost matrix

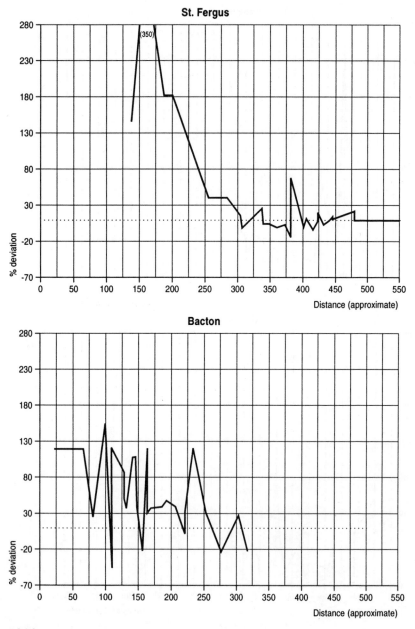

Figure 4.3: Entry / exit charges versus full cost matrix

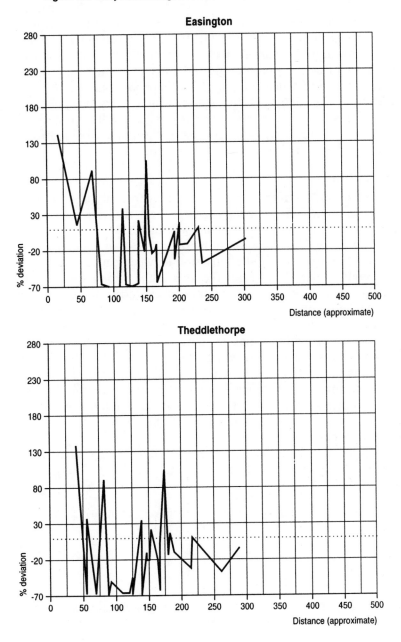

211

In general the entry/exit system raises prices out of Bacton and, particularly St Fergus (very markedly so in the case of short routes out of St Fergus). Of course, these two entry points are those which take the greatest flows of gas. The fact that the regression/averaging process is unweighted means that a flow which carries very little gas has the same effect on determining the entry/exit prices as a flow which carries a great deal of gas. It so happens that the process raises charges for some of the flows which carry very heavy volumes of gas. The prices out of Barrow are generally reduced by the process. (It is fortuitous that Barrow is the point where British Gas lands gas from the Morecambe fields, which it owns.)

The 50:50 Rule

This refers to the convention whereby 50 per cent of costs are recovered as a notional capacity charge and the remainder are recovered by increasing unit prices of commodity.

As I have noted, the long-run marginal cost methodology is adjusted to achieve a fixed 50:50 division between capacity charges and commodity charges. In principle, this is the wrong way about: one should calculate long-run marginal capacity costs and operating costs associated with volume delivered, and then recover remaining costs through a charge which, so far as is practicable, does not vary with volume. Implicitly, it has become conventional to levy the unrecovered costs in *direct proportion to volume*. This system has a doubly damaging effect on the unit cost of gas to the consumer: first, all consumers at all times are paying capacity charges which are only incurred on behalf of peak users. Secondly, volume is carrying a surcharge which should properly be recovered through a volume-independent charge.

The 50:50 rule dominates.[24] Any long-run marginal cost calculations are distorted to force them into the 50:50 straitjacket. For instance:

'The basic LRMC figures showed a cost recovery of approximately 70 per cent, so these were adjusted to the figures in the consultation

---

[24] Transco have made proposals to move in the direction of changing this balance progressively to raise the capacity proportion and reduce the commodity proportion (see below).

document to give the desired 50 per cent recovery of accounting costs.'[25]

The discussion of this illustrates the general obsession with cost allocation:

'BG told us that, in view of this earlier work and to avoid frequent changes to the cost apportionment methodology, it was still appropriate to continue with 50:50 capacity:commodity. BG told us that NTS operating costs (about 10 per cent of the capital-related costs) were allocated in the same proportions as the capital element.'[26]

Local rates paid on pipes and other areas used by the supply system (cumulo rates) are included as items 50 per cent of which are recovered in commodity charges.

Interruptible tariffs – the most obvious means of relieving the demands on the system at the peak – have atrophied.

'Long-run marginal gas costs assume that uncontracted gas comes with a particular swing, currently 143 percent. BG assumes that variations in peak demand (load factor) between markets are accommodated not by beach gas (with an assumed capacity:commodity element) but rather are met by use of storage and interruptibility.'[27]

British Gas gave the Monopolies and Mergers Commission some illustrative calculations to support the 50:50 split which are unconvincing. The particular example published in the 1993 report displays incremental cost of capacity at about 50 per cent of total capacity costs. It is then assumed that all the other 50 per cent should be recovered by a charge on commodity. The capacity costs are divided by the peak day volume to derive the peak cost per peak day therm. This implicitly assumes that the peak lasts one day. If the peak pricing were optimised then it is most unlikely that it would last so short a time: peak charges would be spread over more peak therms.

The method involves two presumptions. One is that capacity should bear no more than its incremental cost; the other is that the

---

[25] Monopolies and Mergers Commission, *op. cit.*, Appendix 5.3, para. 3.

[26] *Ibid.*, Appendix 2.4, para. 3.

[27] *Ibid.*, para. 2.98.

residual should be recovered in proportion to volume rather than in some other way such as in a standing charge (which would be more obviously closer to economic efficiency).

In any case, the examples are unconvincing as a support for such an important policy. They appear to ignore the need to keep the dimensions of analysis commensurate. The marginal cost of capacity (which is implicitly worked out on a per unit length basis) depends upon the length of pipe involved, whereas the cost of commodity depends mainly upon the volume and to a lesser extent on distance travelled (the example does not mention pumping costs). A household located at the landing point ought to be paying little more than the pure commodity cost (which would vary somewhat, reflecting the seasonal cost structure of the gas fields). A household located 400 miles from the beach ought to be paying (peak) capacity costs associated with the pipes which supply it.

Similarly, as outlined above, the correct marginal cost of capacity per unit of gas must have a time dimension, representing the length of the peak period during which it is shipped. Commodity charge does not.

Ofgas has suggested that a change to 90:10 would be an improvement – in fact, British Gas used it before 1989. This view was supported by a Coopers and Lybrand study which thought 90:10 would be more appropriate. Such a change would, it estimated, cause charges for transport of 'peaky' demand (30 per cent load factor) to rise by 25 per cent whilst for uniform demand it would fall by 16 per cent.[28]

British Gas's response to this suggestion in 1993 was not convincing:

'BG rejected some earlier suggestions that capacity:commodity costs for the NTS could be allocated 90:10 and told us that this might reflect a confusion between the ratio of fixed and variable costs and capacity and commodity. The balance of costs after the calculation of the capacity element was regarded as commodity and recovered on an annual volume basis. The commodity charge was, therefore, not the marginal variable cost of transmitting a unit of gas. It reflected the level

---

[28] Monopolies and Mergers Commission, *op. cit.*, Appendix 5.2, para. 7.

214

of costs incurred in providing system connectivity essential to meeting customers' consumption regardless of profile.'[29]

In their recent September 1996 *Consultation Report* British Gas state an intention to move to a 75/25 split by 1998.

It is not clear that *any* rule of this kind is the correct way to deal with the problem. It is certainly not consistent with the thrust of long-run marginal cost pricing. It may be that the Ofgas suggestion is a closer approximation than the present rule. It would certainly affect the prospects for competitive bypass of the British Gas network.

Before becoming further committed to this rough-and-ready rule a convincing case needs to be made to show that it is better than some form of charging consumers an approximation to genuine long-run marginal costs and recovering the residual costs through standing charges.

Planning the Capacity of the Transmission System

There are two planning standards for security of supply which have major implications for the size of the transmission infrastructure: the 1-in-20 rule and the 1-in-50 rule, defined above. It seems that these engineering rules of thumb go back a long way:

> '...variants of this criterion had long guided the former Area Boards's design standards. The current standard was consolidated in 1976 by the Gas Council so as to closely represent the views of those Area Boards. Demand on the distribution system fluctuates more than that on the higher-pressure tiers and networks are planned to meet the maximum demand that could occur over any period of six minutes.'[30]

The 1-in-50 rule also appears to originate from problems in LNG storage in the 1962/63 winter.

It is the 1-in-20 standard which is used to design the system. This is not a BG-imposed standard but a requirement of the Public Gas Transporter's (PGT) licence. Whilst one recognises that the use of standards is inevitable in practice, it seems most unlikely that standards set 30 years ago to deal with quite different technologies,

---

[29] Monopolies and Mergers Commission, Appendix 2.4, para. 4.

[30] *Ibid.*, para. 2.75.

quite different demand conditions, different regulatory and competitive régimes have any justification now, even if they had any economic justification then.

The Monopolies and Mergers Commission reports[31] that British Gas had recently appraised the criteria. To move 1-in-20 to 1-in-10 and 1-in-50 to 1-in-30 might save about £9 million per year – about 50 pence per domestic customer per year. One reason it was not more was that expensive investment in Rough storage facilities and in gas contracts had already been sunk to meet the existing standards.

The system economic model

Recently TransCo have issued an outline specification for a new system economic model. This explains that the existing, highly detailed FALCON model which is currently used to calculate marginal costs is too unwieldy for day-to-day use. The approach is firmly based on the long-run marginal cost methodology 'as agreed by Ofgas after public consultation in 1994'. The endeavour is entirely sensible and it should produce something much more useful for analysing the economics of the system.

As an *economic* model intended to translate from costs into charges it does suffer from a serious weakness: there is no consideration of the demand side, which is taken as given. As I have pointed out, if demand were really fixed there would be no particular reason to prefer marginal cost pricing over any other system of pricing from an economic efficiency point of view. In my reading of the recent documents on the gas industry I have not once come across a mention of a demand elasticity. The following sentence from the model specification document is revealing (p.19):

'The TransCost model is not for analysing the effect or the cost of adding an additional point load: it is for working out how to divide a total revenue requirement among revenue generators. The revenue generators are the entry and exit charges and, where appropriate, inter-node charges.'

---

[31] *Ibid.*, Appendix 2.1.

Competition in transmission

NERA note that in the United States the

> 'interstate pipeline industry is reasonably competitive. Almost all major gas market centres are served by at least two interstate pipelines. Indeed, when major decisions to extend the interstate gas pipeline system to New England in the Northeast and California in the West were made in the 1950s, the Federal regulators, after much discussion, certified two pipeline projects for both regions, in large part to promote competition in the future.'[32]

The historical development in the UK of a single, monolithic, state-owned gas supply system has not encouraged this kind of competition. It would have been dismissed as 'wasteful', whether or not it might have been beneficial in UK circumstances.

In fact we *do* have a large second trunk gas transmission system. This is the offshore system developed over the years by the commercial interests exploiting the oil and gas in the North Sea. Map 1 shows this in outline, with the pipes which can carry gas (as distinct from oil).

To an extent this is already competitive with the TransCo National Transmission System and it can and will be substantially developed to provide 'bypass' to the NTS if the incentives to do so remain the way they are.

Inspection of the map suggests many possibilities, bearing in mind that gas generally has to flow south, and especially the opportunities for export to be offered by the opening of the Interconnector from Bacton. The developers of Fulmar decided to ship into St Fergus when an option would have been to go to Teeside, as the later development of the Central Area Transmission System (CATS) to serve the Central North Sea illustrates. This would have bypassed the Scottish part of the NTS. There is now three-way competition between Fulmar, CATS and the NTS. Serious consideration is being given to the possibility of making major investments in offshore gas lines to shift gas from the Central North Sea to be able to reach Bacton and the Interconnector. The competitive opportunities within the Southern North Sea are obvious.

---

[32] NERA, *op. cit.*, p.18.

The offshore network has developed under commercial competition and there is a mature market structure. Producers invest in lines for their own use, but design-in redundant capacity in the expectation that they will be able to sell transport to other companies. Proper long-term contracts are used to handle the risks and hence to facilitate the financing of the investments. This is in contrast to the one-year contracts for use of the NTS which do not give TransCo a basis against which to raise finance, nor do they give the producers the assurance they require on certainty of prices and long-term capacity. If the gas can be delivered to its end-user without ever entering the TransCo system then there is more control over the characteristics of the gas (because it has not been blended) and it does not have to be odorised. Add this to the complexity of having to deal with the Network Code and it is easy to see the attraction of considering own-account transport.

The offshore industry is, of course, regulated, but under a system which appears to be more or less independent of regulation by Ofgas. The regulatory agency is the Department of Trade and Industry which, amongst other things, has to approve new investments in pipelines. The requirements are, of course, different: for instance, Transco has to meet high security of supply standards and to deliver to domestic consumers.

The DTI's regulatory régime is described in its *Energy Report, 1996*, Volume 2 , 'The Brown Book'.[33] Its overall objectives derive from the Petroleum (Production) Act 1934. They are not the same as those of the onshore régime. A formal statement of statutory duties is not shown in the document, such as one will find in Ofgas publications. When objectives are stated they clearly reflect a concern with perceived benefits to 'UK Plc' of the oil and gas exploration industry:

'A strong regulatory regime is considered important to ensure that the nation as a whole benefits from the UK's oil and gas resources, to

---

[33] This gives a great deal of fascinating detail about the oil and gas industries. It includes a review of activity in each of nearly 200 individual fields, including an entertaining explanation of the origin of all those unfamiliar new place names. Thus: 'Alwyn: a name with Scottish connotations, easily pronounced in both English and French'; 'Emerald: an emerald, being green, was considered most appropriate for an oil field'; superstitiously: 'Fife: after a character in the "Scottish Play" by Shakespeare'; and, somewhat at a loss: 'Rough: describes the sea bottom in this area'.

safeguard the environment and to ensure that optimum use is made of reserves. The regulatory regime also offers the companies involved a stable environment in which to operate and minimise disputes about drilling rights.' (para. 3.1)

There is a severe fiscal régime for the oil and gas industries involving licence fees, royalties, Petroleum Revenue Tax, Corporation Tax and Gas Levy. The objectives of the fiscal régime are stated to be:

'to extract economic rent and secure a fair share of profits for the nation, while offering stable, attractive and economically sound investment conditions to the oil industry'.[34]

The Ministerial Foreword expresses pleasure at the number of new field development approvals and at the magnitude of operators' capital investment. The document highlights oil and gas output, employment in the industry, contributions to government revenues and the contribution to exports and the balance of payments.

The regulatory régime is enforced primarily through the licensing system. It seems that whilst environmental, health and safety regulation is strict, economic regulation is light. On the whole the companies have successfully developed their trading relationships without a need being perceived by government for regulatory intervention.

New pipeline investments offshore require DTI approval. In considering this approval there are clearly significant issues which can only be satisfactorily considered by taking a view of the onshore and offshore systems as a whole. For instance, should total capacity be co-ordinated between the two systems, or should a degree of excess capacity be fostered in order to encourage competition – as in the US? And how does the setting of the various rates of tax in the financial régime relate to the pricing considerations of the Gas Regulator? There is no obvious attempt to formulate a global view on such issues and, indeed, the two responsible regulatory bodies work under differing sets of objectives.

This competitive industry has managed to find its own ways of conducting business, in particular ways of managing the problems of gaining access to one another's assets. The Minister for Industry

---

[34] Department of Trade and Industry, *Energy Report*, para. 2.7.

and Energy did have some concerns about the lack of transparency in terms of access to oil and gas infrastructure. The DTI carried out a consultation and review in 1994. The consequence has been the adoption of a voluntary Offshore Infrastructure Code of Practice which requires that the indicative offers actually made by infrastructure owners are published regularly. It also requires infrastructure owners to unbundle their services where this is requested and practical. Contractual arrangements are to be standardised and timetables are laid down for negotiations. Finally, commercial negotiations should be non-discriminatory. Owners should not attempt to exclude or prefer any potential customer in order to secure commercial or market advantage elsewhere. The DTI has undertaken to administer the code.

The Nature of Competition for Domestic Consumers

In this section I use detailed Family Expenditure Survey (FES) data to suggest the type of household likely to be an attractive target for a new competitor for domestic gas supply. Various classification systems used in the FES are compared in order to identify one which discriminates amongst potential domestic gas customers as clearly as possible and which can be closely identified in national census data. Then, by the use of a simple geographical information system a map showing the density of attractive customers is produced. This is compared with the location of existing gas supply, yielding areas of high attraction which currently do not have supply. We can thus identify potential sites for new forms of entry in competition with the existing TransCo network.

The FES is an annual survey of some 5,000 domestic households in the UK. Respondents are asked to fill out a two-week diary, recording their expenditures in very great detail. Some of the results are published in the annual publication, but considerably more detailed, unpublished information can be purchased. The published data states the average weekly expenditures on a wide selection of commodities, by various types of household, categorised in a number of ways. Just as interesting as the average expenditure, is the proportion of households which does, and does not, record any expenditure on each item. This allows us to identify high densities of households which currently are not gas consumers. It also allows a breakdown of the published average expenditure into the amount spent by those who spend something and those who spend nothing.

This is much more informative than the grand average.

Expenditure patterns on gas, electricity, and other fuels (coal, oil and paraffin are separately identified in the FES) have been analysed for the following categorisations which are available in the survey: Employment status; Professional status; Retirement and type of pension; Numbers of adults and children; Income quintile of retired households, by type of pension; Income quintile of one-adult households; Income quintile of one-adult households with children; Income quintile of two-adult households with children; Two-adult working couples; Housing tenure; and Type of dwelling.

Figure 5 displays the spending pattern for the second of these categorisations. On the right is shown the proportions of households recording some expenditure on the energy source. For electricity it is close to 100 per cent for most groups. It seems likely that a few households who have not recorded expenditure do in fact consume electricity, but have it paid for by somebody else and so their expenditure is not recorded here. Gas is consumed by between 70 and 80 per cent of households and other fuels by between 5 and 10 per cent.

The left half of the diagram shows the weekly expenditure of the households of those who spend something on the fuel. Thus, 9·86 per cent of professional households record some spending on the other fuels, and those that spend something on any one of them spend, on average, £17.87 a week.[35]

This example has features which are fairly typical of other classifications. If a household has gas then it tends to spend about the same on both gas and electricity. This feature is remarkably consistent across different classifications. Second, if a household has spending on fuels other than gas or electricity, it is substantially more than spending on electricity or gas. It is likely that this is because gas is a much cheaper fuel for space heating than the other fuels: I shall make the assumption that if the other fuels are being used it is because gas is not available. Third, there is much less variation across the classification by profession than one might have expected. Most spend between £6 and £7 per week on gas, with the exception of employers and managers who spend £8.61 per week on gas, if they have it.

[*cont'd on p. 224*]

---

[35] Those who spend on coal spend £11.30; those who spend on oil spend £7.07; and those who spend on paraffin spend £0.35.

Figure 5: Expenditure of Households on Fuel

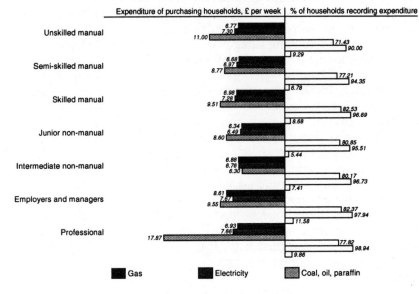

Expenditure of purchasing households, £ per week | % of households recording expenditure

Figure 6: Expenditure of Households on Fuel

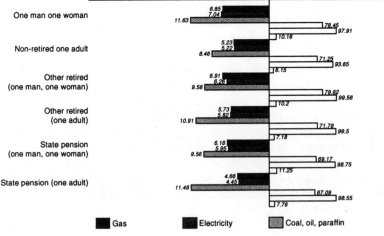

Expenditure of purchasing households, £ per week | % of households recording expenditure

Figure 7: Expenditure of Households on Fuel

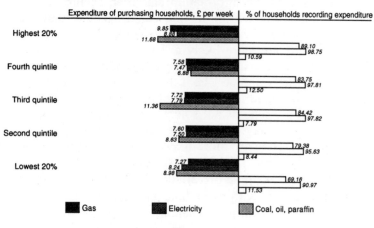

Figure 8: Expenditure of Households on Fuel

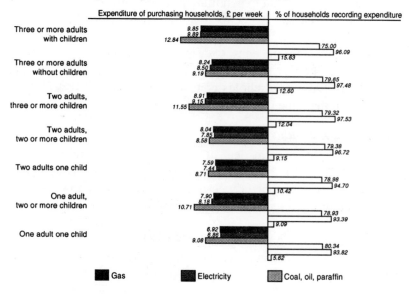

223

Figure 6 shows the information classified according to whether there is one adult or two in the household, whether they are retired and, if so, whether they are mainly dependent upon the state pension. Two adults are more likely to have gas than one. Only 67 per cent of lone state pensioners have gas and they spend under £5 per week on electricity and on gas, if they have it. State pensioners who use other fuels spend as much as £11.48 per week on them. Two-person retired households not solely dependent on the state pension are more likely to have gas and they spend much more on both gas and electricity. They are more likely to have gas than a non-retired couple and when they have it they spend more on it.

Figure 7 is an example of variation by household income, in this case for households with two adults and children. It illustrates what appears to be a general phenomenon: expenditure on fuels does not vary much with income, except the highest quintile who do spend substantially more. The lowest quintile are less likely to have gas. Of course, it follows that expenditure as a proportion of income falls as income increases. It seems that household income is not a particularly good discriminator. In any case, we could not get income directly from the census for mapping purposes.

Figure 8 shows the importance of household size and composition. Large households consume more energy, especially if there is more than one child present.

An attractiveness indicator

The FES contains a great deal of data. It is possible to attempt to find promising types of household by inspection. But it is helpful to filter the data with an objective criterion, which I will now develop. Being a quantitative index it is also useful for representation on the map.

The information we have is limited – not least because we cannot cross-classify. For instance, we can classify by retirement status or by housing tenure, but not both. Our method must be rough and ready. We assume that all households have electricity. We also assume that the main use for gas (by value consumed) is for heating. If a household is using coal or oil it must be because it does not have gas.

From the point of view of a new entrant to the market to supply domestic consumers there are two distinct types of competition: (a) between electricity and gas for heating for those who have gas and (b) between gas and other fuels for those who presently do not have gas.

Total gas sales (S) = (electricity sales (E) + gas sales for those who have it (G)

x share of gas (s)

x proportion of households that record gas sales (g).

Represent this as

$$S = (E + G). \, s \, . \, g$$

where $\quad s = G/(E + G) \, .$

A new entrant can offer an improvement to the consumer, like a reduction in the commodity charge or the standing charge, or some other attribute of the product such as quality of service or appliance maintenance. Represent this by a change in some parameter, α:

$$\frac{\partial S}{\partial \alpha} \; = \; (E \, + \, G)\beta s(1 \, - \, s)g \; + \; sg \, \frac{\partial(E + G)}{\partial \alpha}$$

$$+ \; (E + G)s \, \frac{\partial g}{\partial \alpha}$$

In the first term on the right, the expression $\beta s(1 - s)$ is imported from the logit type of market share model. β is a parameter representing the propensity of individuals to switch from electricity to gas in response to the change (it is actually the respective parameter in the generalised cost, or disutility function). We cannot know the appropriate values for this parameter in a study of this nature. For the present purpose we will assume that it is the same for all households – clearly an assumption which could be improved upon. The term $s(1 - s)$ appears because of the properties of the market share function. The expression has its highest value when s is one-half. It captures the simple idea that if s is close to one, you already have most of the market so it is going to be difficult to expand it further. If s is close to zero one starts with a small market share so the market is unresponsive to your offering and large improvements in the terms offered are going to be necessary to attract a given number of new customers.

The three terms suggest that, other things equal, the market will be responsive to the new offering if (i) $(E + G)$ is large: households purchase a lot of energy, (ii) where the share, s, is close to one-half, or (iii) the proportion of households having gas is large. Another attractive characteristic is that expenditure on other fuels is high: an indicator that gas is not currently available but there is a worthwhile target expenditure for a new gas supplier.

In view of these considerations a simple index was derived in the following manner. For each of $(E + G)$, $s(1 - s)$ and expenditure on other fuels the mean and standard deviation across all the classifications in our FES data were calculated. Then, for each category the number of standard deviations from the mean was calculated for each of the three statistics. These were then simply added to form a raw sum – though it would be easy to use a weighted average. The result is a single index value for each category, large values indicating attractive categories and negative values indicating unattractive categories.

From this it is possible to identify those methods of classification which show wide variation in the index, so they will show good discrimination. This confirmed what inspection of Figures 5 to 9 indicates. Two types of category stand out as having good discrimination. For housing tenure the index ranges from -3.6 for a 'designed flat' to +3.6 for a 'detached house'. For household composition the index ranges from 0 for one adult with one child household to + 4.9 for three or more adults with children. The range was smaller for other classifiers. In the construction of the illustrative Maps 3 and 4, housing tenure is used as the classification.

Map 2 shows those areas which are currently supplied by British Gas.

Map 3 shows the location of 1991 Census of Population wards

[*cont'd on p. 231*]

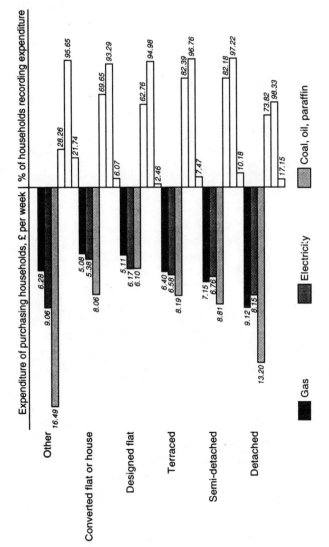

Figure 9: Expenditure of Households on Fuel

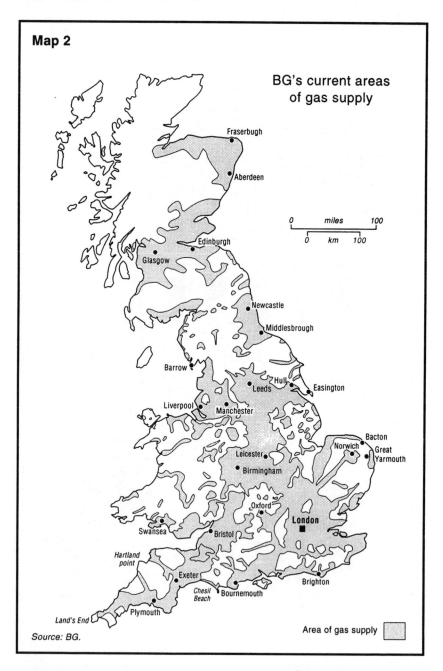

Map 2

BG's current areas
of gas supply

Fraserbugh

Aberdeen

0   miles   100

0   km   100

Edinburgh

Glasgow

Newcastle

Middlesbrough

Barrow

Hull

Leeds   Easington

Liverpool

Manchester

Bacton

Norwich   Great
Yarmouth

Leicester

Birmingham

Oxford

London

Swansea

Bristol

Hartland
point

Exeter

Chesil
Beach   Bournemouth   Brighton

Land's End   Plymouth

Area of gas supply

Source: BG.

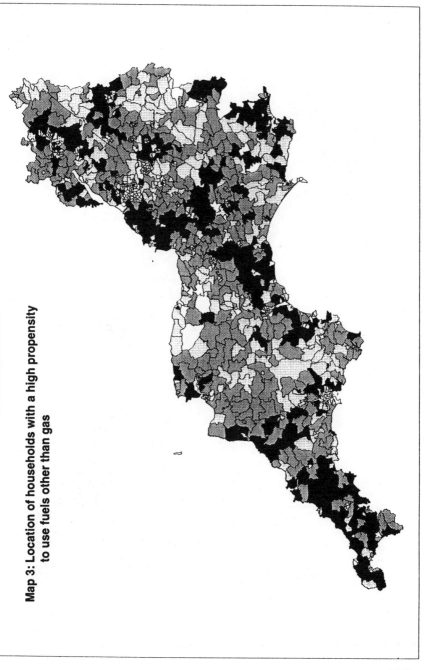

Map 3: Location of households with a high propensity to use fuels other than gas

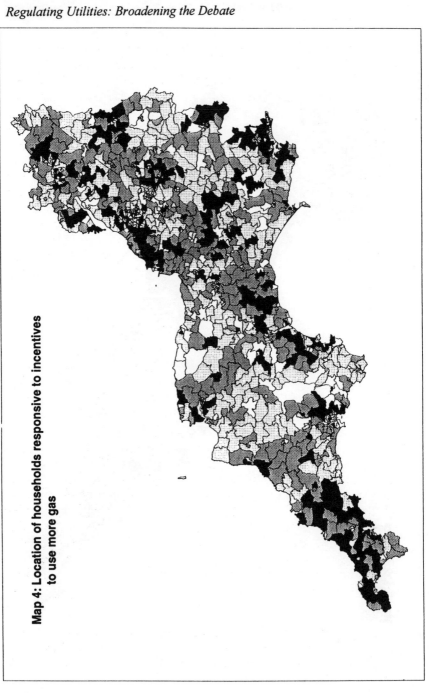

Map 4: Location of households responsive to incentives to use more gas

having households with a high propensity to use fuels other than gas or electricity. There are four shades, each shade having an equal number of wards, with darker areas having the higher propensity. On our hypothesis households will, in fact, use gas rather than other fuels if gas is available. So the interest is in finding dark areas of Map 2 which are not already supplied with gas. These would be the attractive areas for an entrant wishing to introduce gas into new territory. Generally speaking there are not many of them – British Gas already supplies most of the attractive territory in the South West. However, there are some exceptions: for instance, the area to the south west of Hartland Point and inland from Chesil Beach.

Map 4 is constructed using an index derived along the lines suggested by the above expression for the sensitivity of total gas sales to a change in some parameter. This is a way of identifying those areas which would be particularly worthy of attention to a new supplier hoping to persuade existing gas customers to switch to a cheaper supplier: the dark areas are attractive and the light ones unattractive.

In spite of the crude method of construction, Map 4 does have some interesting features. Central Bournemouth and parts of central Bristol show as unattractive, even though they have dense populations. On the other hand, most of the territory between Plymouth and Land's End, north of Bournemouth and west of Bristol shows as being attractive.

Map 2 shows that there are still areas unsupplied by British Gas, where there are domestic populations close to points where gas is landed, for example, between Easington and Middlesbrough and near Bacton. It is for discussion to what extent competitive entry at these locations is likely to occur in practice; whether there really are opportunities for independent suppliers to open up new, unsupplied domestic markets using bypass of the Transco system; to what extent this new kind of competition is a sufficient threat to drive British Gas to review its pricing structure and force it to be more cost-reflective; and what the public policy implications of these developments may be.

Conclusion

It is likely that the tendency towards average pricing has made few people better off. Gas is a cheap commodity except at peak times, yet it is made expensive for domestic consumers at all times. No incentives are given to economise on gas at the appropriate times. Geographical averaging may provide perverse incentives to locate new loads in places that are expensive to serve, and gives incentives for wasteful investment to bypass existing facilities. It is interesting to note that British Gas comments that 'The introduction of a short-haul service will avoid uneconomic by-pass of TransCo's system and inefficient investment on other parts of the system'.[36]

Introducing more competitive pricing will undoubtedly make gas cheaper for many people for much of the time, not least because it will reduce the dissipation of real resources fostered by average cost pricing. There is no escaping the fact that it would also make some groups worse off. A move to an average, 'postalized' system of prices over a number of years tends to be readily accepted by the general public because it does not perceive that there are losers. The reversal in the direction of cost-based pricing would, in this case at least, be much more controversial. As David Currie observed in a previous lecture, expecting unaccountable enterprises to administer cross-subsidy in order to deal with considerations of equity is unsatisfactory. As I have illustrated here, it leads to confusion of objectives, blunting of incentives and waste. As Currie put it:

> 'distributional objectives are better pursued through the tax and benefit system... It is best if regulators [and, I would add, the regulated] have focussed objectives, to avoid problems of regulatory capture, un-accountability and uncertainty'.[37]

---

[36] *Consultation Report*, 1996, para. 2.5.3.

[37] David Currie, 'Regulating Utilities: The Labour View', above, p. 7.

Additional Reading

British Gas, *Transportation pricing and services régime – the future,* November 1995.

British Gas, *Transco system economic model,* undated, 1996.

Ofgas, *British Gas Transco: connection and system extensions regulating for competition,* August 1996.

Ofgas, *British Gas Transco: storage regulating for competition,* August 1996.

Ofgas: Mark Higson, *A pricing structure for gas transportation and storage,* December 1993.

CHAIRMAN'S COMMENTS

Clare Spottiswoode

FIRST, OF THE RELATION BETWEEN COSTS AND PRICES: we agree that prices should derive from the cost structure and production conditions, and not vice versa. But to follow that precept we need to get the economic assumptions underlying the models each side uses right. This is not so now. Even TransCo's 10-year statement, for example, uses an 8 per cent return. We might well take issue with that, because we are using 7 per cent. More important, with respect to the asset lives, many basic economic assumptions underlie the 10-year statement with which one could disagree. Moreover, we do not yet have a really good economic model of all the transportation TransCo provides within the UK. There is a reasonable physical, engineering model but the economic model TransCo is currently producing is taking a long time. We also intend to build one if we can, difficult and complex though it is. When the model shows that price changes should be made, we shall not shirk from making them.

One of the reasons why we are considering pricing methodology now is because we are hoping that in April 1997, or fairly soon thereafter, there will be a substantial drop in transportation prices. If prices are going to go down anyway, there needs to be considerable rebalancing. Clearly there is much less pain if rebalancing coincides with a general price reduction, so we are keen indeed to put a great deal of work into this particular area. If there are changes which cannot be rolled simultaneously into major price changes, then we shall need to phase them in, to ensure that people are given plenty of warning. That is because there are substantial implications for existing industry, in particular for those who have already committed substantial sunk costs. Hence the need to take sufficient time and to plan the changes carefully.

When it comes to competition in transporting gas, I have in the past when discussing these matters used a diagram of the UK with the shoreline completely missing. It is quite clear that there is nothing sacrosanct about the shoreline. The gas system runs on shore and off shore as if there was no shoreline, and indeed there are currently plans for routing gas from the North Sea from Teesside to Bacton in response to the connector to the Continent. If it went to Bacton, then clearly it would bypass some of TransCo's UK operations, providing competition to TransCo on shore. We would say that is a good thing. Stephen may also have a point about the West Coast, when he asked why gas could not be introduced there. There have been gas finds to the north west of Ireland, and there is quite a lot of potential for gas finds further down in the Atlantic. So it is feasible that in a few years gas will come in on the West Coast, changing the pattern of flows quite significantly. We have to be aware of that in our future planning.

We have tried to introduce competition as much as we can already, for example, in new connections and in new pipelines, to even up the playing field between TransCo and other companies in new pipe building. We think it is very important for the longer term health of the UK gas infrastructure. Many pipeline developments are connected with gas-fired power stations. When decisions are made about their location, clearly it is not just gas and gas transport that matter, it is also the price of transport for electricity. We are hoping that, over time, both electricity and gas prices will reflect the economic costs of transportation. We need to get the right economic signals for both.

8

RAIL: THE ROLE OF SUBSIDY

IN PRIVATISATION

M. E. Beesley[1]

London Business School

Introduction

IN PRIVATISING AN INDUSTRY WITH A VERY IMPORTANT ELEMENT of subsidy (at least one-third of outlays arising from government subventions of one kind or another[2]), the government embarked on a most unusual course. True, there was the precedent of the local bus industry which before 1985 probably absorbed an even higher proportion of subsidy. However, one untrumpeted motive in the bus privatisation and deregulation initiative was the prospect of a rapid reduction in costs which would enable subsidy to be cut without too much damage to output. The essential difference in the rail case is that the politicians rejected the notion of leaving output largely for the market to decide; they imposed minima, through franchise conditions. Throughout the rail story the determination to preserve and if possible enhance rail output has been paramount, and forms the first plank of rail privatisation.

A second plank was the distancing of government from intervention in the consequential decisions about outputs for the railway products. This involved the substitution of one concern by contractual relations between more than 70 companies, and adopting the (by that time) well-proven UK method of applying RPI-x price

---

[1] I am grateful for discussions with Chris Bolt and Stephen Glaister on a first draft of this paper. The usual disclaimers apply.

[2] An extraordinarily difficult proportion to compute; see Annex 1.

control to the non-contestable elements – that is, track and signalling to be owned by Railtrack. Railtrack was not broken up in to its constituent geographical operations, as would have been eminently feasible. It emerged as the monopolist sandwiched between what were intended as contestable activities up- and down-stream. The initial vision was promoting competition for rights to use Railtrack's capacity. Concern to maintain at least a minimum standard output meant that hoped-for competition between the principal users – passenger services – had to be transferred to a formal system of bidding for franchises to which the rights were assigned. Subsidy would be concentrated at the stage of the franchise auctions.

Subsidy and Privatisation

In the long-running problem of controlling and rationalising the railway subsidy, privatisation can be seen as yet another, albeit extremely significant, episode. Ever since the 1968 Transport Act, determination to combine change in subsidy with increasing commercial pressure has been a common political theme. Thereafter, the change in subsidy might be up, or down, be explicit or disguised; that greater efficiency should go with it has been a constant. This time, efficiency in the rail production process was to be secured via enlisting, as far as possible, the pressures from the capital market and sharper management focus and incentives. Division into many distinct property interests brings the pressure to reduce costs closer to the points at which reductions can be made. Railway privatisation has carried these characteristics further than in earlier privatisations. But in the history of railway subsidy, the big difference, on this occasion, is that subsidy has been used to buy commitments to improving efficiency in advance by setting up the inducements via long-term contracts and taking a risk on the eventual size of the subsidy bill. In the process old Treasury constraints about certainty of commitment, and confining it to a period which will not commit future governments too heavily have been put to one side.

The original vision – of competition for railway slots with subsidy focused via the competitors for them – was seen as a means both to clarify the method of subsidy and to increase pressure, perhaps over the long run, to reduce it. What John Swift called last year the 'text-book...and blackboard designers'[3] responsible for early guidance on rail privatisation encouraged the idea that it would not be necessary for an explicit view of the extent of subsidy to be taken in advance. The expected active rivalry for subsidies would, it was thought, lead to an aggregate subsidy which would impute, in advance, the economies to be expected from the large increase in commercial pressure; so that whatever subsidy proved to be needed to float off passenger services and freight would be substantially less than the previous aggregate subsidy. But the idea of organising an auction for slots was always too optimistic. The problem was reduced to hoped-for competition for passenger franchises. This has also proved optimistic. But at least a bargaining process for subsidy with the Franchise Director was put in place. At the same time it was seen that there would have to be a sequential process, in which prospective franchise holders would have to know their service obligations and prospects and, equally important, what they would have to pay for rail access charges.

The regulator, to set access charges, had *inter alia*, to take a view of the future scale of railway operations, and so had to make implicit assumptions about the size of the subsidy underpinning total railway output. From this access charges, paid to Railtrack, could be determined in the usual way for a monopoly, to yield initial and future charges, in the RPI-x mode. It would have been possible, in principle, to have combined and made consistent forward cash flow estimates of expenditures with available subsidy, in particular for Railtrack. However, the preferred course was to concentrate subsidy on the Franchise Director's budget, thus hopefully making it possible to bargain down required subsidy in direct commercial dealings. This left the regulator with the need to estimate future operating expenditure (opex) and capital expenditure (capex) requirements without specific guidance on subsidy targets. He also decides to approve Railtrack contracts which encourage output. There were possible discrepancies in the event, between the assumed and actual activity.

Moreover, the government's intended sequence for privatisation changed significantly in 1994. Railtrack was promoted from being

---

[3] Chairman's remarks: 'Putting the Railways Back Together Again', by Dieter Helm, in M. E. Beesley: *Regulating Utilities: A Time for Change?*, IEA Readings 44, 1996, p. 184.

an ambition with uncertain timing to be the priority. The political motives are unclear; difficulty of reversing privatisation under a changed government must have been relevant. What made such a promotion feasible was that a Prospectus could be constructed in which the exposure to possible fluctuation in the overall level of subsidy for rail output could be minimised.[4] Railtrack could be made a first call on subsidy through committed contracts, isolated from the pressures influencing future governments' decisions on subsidy. So, in principle, it was necessary for the regulator to underpin revenues to construct an expected sale value, on which an appropriate rate of return could be used.[5] The Treasury's views had to be tailored to the curtailing of the subsidy risk; hence the remarkable reduction in the £6 billion or so valuation of Railtrack's assets originally mooted.

One surmises that the change in priorities put exceptional strain on what were always extremely tight timetables for privatisation. In these circumstances, it is hardly surprising that the regulator (also pressed with the need to meet EU deadlines) was able only to announce the overall levels of track access charges (January 1995) after he had pronounced on structure (November 1994), which at the time seemed to be an odd regulatory sequence for conducting regulatory price fixing. From the Franchise Director's viewpoint the result of the Judicial Review in December 1995, handed down at a process commencing in August, had the effect of raising the minimum service specifications in given cases and must have implied considerable delay in negotiation with prospective Train Operating Companies (TOCs).[6]

By the time there were serious negotiations leading to revelation of the subsidies required for the 25 passenger franchises early in 1996, would-be TOCs could focus on fairly well-defined opportunities to improve net returns and what the downside risks would be. The terms on which access would be available were known; a master lease was in place for rolling stock terms and most

---

[4] In the case of rolling stock operating companies (Roscos), the subsidy risk was likewise eliminated by selling them with a certain cashflow to cover the prospective franchise periods.

[5] In other words, he had to assume a starting regulatory asset value.

[6] Court of Appeal, *Director of Passenger Rail Franchising: ex parte Save our Railways and others*, 15 December 1995.

of the remaining costs would be open to direct control and therefore downward pressure. Minimum output levels would be required, and maximum permitted prices were known. Access charges were set with a high fixed element, but one which was favourable to achieve increasing returns, by increasing output. Why, then, was there not much more interest in franchises to enhance the Franchise Director's bargaining hand? Partly it was because of the esoteric skills thought to be needed to run railway services and partly because BR was viewed as in a highly contestable market even though it had a supply monopoly. There was also doubt about long-term prospects thrown up by the regulator's proposals for a future transition from monopoly franchises to competition through a 'Mechanism for Moderating Competition'.[7] And it took a long time to get to the point where prospects, for example, of what costs would be, could be seriously assessed; the political time-scale was simply too short.

The process so far leads to at least four interesting questions. Was privatisation worthwhile? What will the total government's subsidy bill turn out to be? Will the normal benefits of privatisation be realised? What implications for the Franchise Director and the regulator will there be?

Computing the Costs and Benefits of Privatisation

As Stephen Littlechild and I pointed out when large-scale privatisation was beginning, the decision to privatise can be seen as an exercise in (very rough) cost-benefit analysis (CBA) – will the gains be outweighed by the costs?[8] We put railways high on the list of priorities, implying prospectively a high return. Given the government's commitment to maintaining railway outputs, a CBA would measure the difference between the real resource flows with and without privatisation.

Within that, there is the narrower question of the effect on the government's net cash position – the change in the subsidies paid, less privatisation realisations. How has it turned out? In fact, there

---

[7] *Competition for Railway Passenger Services*, Office of the Rail Regulator, December 1994.

[8] M. E. Beesley and S. C. Littlechild, 'Privatisation: Principles, Problems and Priorities', *Lloyds Bank Review*, June 1993; reprinted *inter alia* in M. E. Beesley, *Privatisation, Regulation and Deregulation*, London: Routledge, 1992.

are important missing pieces in the 'CBA accounts'. Annex I tries to trace the story so far. It points out that on government account, there are three basic flows – direct yearly grant, now incorporated in the TOC franchises; future commitments to underwrite investment; and once-off reductions in future financing costs in the terms of sale of the constituent companies. It assembles what one can glean from the more readily accessible sources, but it quickly becomes clear that one cannot be comprehensive. In particular, at the time of writing, the franchise subsidy round is all but accomplished in terms of the last year of payments to BR; and what the government will receive in total for all the sales including the Railtrack float which will reduce the 'cost' is incomplete (but probably much less so than for the franchise subsidies). To put together this collection of flows and one-off adjustments one needs to standardise to an equivalent yearly flow of net government cash outlays. Up to July 1996 sales of companies, including Railtrack, give an equivalent yearly flow (at 8 per cent) of about £330 million.[9]

In 1995/96 explicit passenger grants accounted for about £1,700 million. There is an increasing, if much smaller, subsidy going into freight independently of passenger franchises. The commitments to fund future Railtrack investments are not clear but will be substantial. There will be a £680 million grant for Thameslink 2000; but the contribution to West Coast Mainline (WCML) is unknown at the time of writing (but will surely have to be settled as a condition of letting the franchise). WCML has been extremely contentious (how much of a run-down mainline from London to Glasgow will be refurbished and upgraded?); and in negotiation with the government Railtrack is arguing from a strong Prospectus statement abut the need for 'an adequate rate of return, involving the Franchise Director's exercise of Section 54 undertaking'.[10] The write-off ahead of selling companies also awaits a full account.

---

[9] The discount rate is a problem. There is a discrepancy between the rate the Franchising Director applies to his budget (6 per cent) and the 8 per cent normally thought to be more appropriate. Moreover, the 6 per cent (or 8 per cent) is certainly much lower than that applied by prospective lessees in bidding. However, the discrepancy doubtless gives useful degrees of freedom to both sides in setting the final time-path of subsidies.

[10] *Railtrack Prospectus*, pp. 42-43. Section 54 of the 1993 Act concerns the 'exercise of function for the purpose of encouraging investment in the railways'.

However, we do learn from BR's 1995/96 Annual Report that £500 million has been written off from the old Channel Tunnel contracts, presumably as a preliminary to selling the relevant business (Union Railways Ltd). Settling what the score finally is will be a big test of the commitment of government to transparency in public affairs.

In resource terms a partial score so far can be constructed by working from BR's latest full year of outlays (1995/6), to set the total resource cost per year of continued BR output. From BR's accounts we see that 'operating costs' in 1995/6 were £5,797 million, which includes the year's charges payable by Roscos and Railtrack. This, in regulators' language, stands as a fair shot at yearly 'opex' in rail; but the accounts are silent on yearly capex flow. Using Railtrack's 1995/96 accounts, a heroic estimate of what that might be can be made. What part of this represents outputs subject to market test of value we do not know; unfortunately, we do not have access to franchisees' business plans so customer payments cannot be computed. The yearly outflow is then about £6,800 million. The prospects for reduction in this flow will be reflected in the terms of the passenger franchises, dealt with in the next section.

Privatisation Benefits

Reducing subsidy?
When it comes to the likely reduction of subsidies over the next few years, it is possible plausibly to concentrate on the evidence about passenger franchises. This ignores freight, but I think it reasonable to regard the dominant passenger operations as a good marker. The franchise letting process has not, it appears, yielded much saving compared with 1995/96, the last year under BR. However, there are substantial gains in future years. Annex 2 explores these, concentrating on the next seven years common to most franchises. This involves extrapolation from the 14 franchises (covering 32 per cent of the 1995/6 subsidy) whose terms are known, to the 11 which are not known at mid-October 1996. It involves an analysis of how the sets differ. Annex 2 estimates the reduction over the seven years in the first 14 at 55 per cent.[11]

---

[11] This seems a more relevant comparison than that proposed by Mr Watts in July 1996 (Rail Franchising: A Written Parliamentary Answer, *Hansard*, 18 July 1996), where he said 'the net financial burden on the tax payer will fall by nearly £200 million by the 7th year of the

The remaining 11 will undoubtedly be much tougher propositions to franchise for subsidy reduction than the 14. A significant element in the final tally will probably be the government's timetable which calls for the completion of all sales by Christmas 1996. One cannot expect best subsidy bargains under the gun. Annex 2 considers evidence chiefly from the original description of the likely franchises given to prospective bidders in 1992 and the Office of Passenger Rail Franchising (Opraf) material since. I conclude that the comparable figure to 55 per cent is more likely to be 20 per cent. Duly weighted for the starting subsidies, my overall expectation is thus 30 per cent (the 11 are larger on average than the 14). As a minimum implied estimate of resource savings, 30 per cent is a familiar number to find in assessments of privatisation impacts. Railtrack, accounting for perhaps one-third of the final output, has an initial RPI-x of 8 per cent, and 2 per cent a year, or 16 per cent by 2001. This implies that the franchisees expect very considerable gains apart from falls in Railtrack's charges. Part will probably come from increasing the value added in services; but most must be an expected outcome of negotiations with other suppliers, including Roscos.

Land Allocation

Privatisation holds out the prospect of correcting a major and very long-standing deficiency in the allocation of railway land. British Railways was probably one of the largest land-owners in the UK. (Curiously enough, this is another number which is extremely difficult to unearth – Railtrack's Prospectus, for example, is silent on the extent of its land ownership.)

The underlying cause of this deficiency is the decline over many years in the land area required for efficient railway operation. This decline has stemmed both from the fall in volume of operations and their nature (marshalling yards are now virtually extinct, for example; yet they were the subject of intense investment in the

---

franchises' – but unfortunately added that this was in relation to BR's future budget levels, which were not disclosed. The idea of BR having a seven-year forecast of this kind is in itself a curiosity, considering the traditional difficulty of wringing out firm statements about future subsidy levels from the Treasury and when BR is due to wind up in 1997.

1960s and 1970s).[12]   All this time, the underlying value of railway land has been increasing, most notably in urban and suburban locations.

These developments have always been recognised, if only implicitly, in railway deficit financing.   Land not required for operations has, over the years, been steadily sold via the BR Property Board and used by the Treasury to compensate for outlays on subsidy.   The Treasury has also taken the benefit of developments on railway land.

During this period, up to the launching of the privatisation policy, British Rail had a key control over the quantity of land for which such property gains were possible – the definition of what or what was not 'operational' land.   This was a technical matter to be worked out by engineers, wholly dominated by BR and naturally conservative.   Moreover, deeming land 'non-operational' was predominantly a no-win decision in BR's eyes.   Any such move would not only diminish the estate but would not guarantee an improvement in the subsidy subsequently on offer.   The consequence was that the release of operational land failed to match the shift in the underlying values.

In the lead-up to privatisation (sale of BR subsidiaries, but more particularly floating Railtrack) a division of land between Railtrack and British Rail, as the residuary nationalised concern, had to be settled.   The settlement was to endow Railtrack with land at that point recognised as 'operational', with the rest remaining with British Rail.   Railtrack was obliged to offer appropriate leasing terms for railway users (for example, the track maintenance companies) and thus was committed not to make land disposals over the period of the lease terms, and to make similar commitments with respect to major stations.   However, Railtrack is free to re-negotiate when the time comes.   More important, it now decides what is, or is not, operational.   It can, if it wishes, take advantage of the shift in locational values of land to push as much as it can of its own operations (and those of its tenants by re-negotiation) down the urban rent surfaces, releasing valuable land which does not have to

---

[12] There has also been less need for maintenance depots, with technical change and technical improvement in building techniques which allow more construction over operational railways and stations.

be subject to Treasury claw-back. (Land deal claw-backs have always characterised privatisations; in this case the 'deal' was settled by the original division between BR and Railtrack.)

The critical change induced by privatisation is that Railtrack is a private sector company which, like any other, is completely free to buy land as well as sell or keep it. The old BR never could operate as a genuine land developer – to do so would have meant putting Treasury money at risk, and compromising the accepted notions of the limits to public and private sector joint venturing. Thus Railtrack has the prospect of instituting a freely contractable land development policy with an inheritance of a very large and extremely well-located portfolio.

As with all land development opportunities, there are snags – for example, the normal planning restrictions, and Railtrack has impediments such as listed buildings. Releasing operational land will take considerable time (for example, some land purchases in low rent areas will have to be found and negotiated after plans to move down the rent surface are devised). If such plans imply consequential closure of parts of the passenger network, regulatory approval must be sought.[13] Such a large and diverse portfolio must, however, be an extremely valuable base and one, moreover, which lends itself to off-balance sheet treatment, or incorporation, as seems advisable.[14]

The regulator operates a 'single till' policy in setting Railtrack access charges involving property income and gains in value.[15] 'Single till' price-fixing is an anathema to economists, as inhibiting allocative efficiency, and there must be a question about whether the complications it causes in setting price controls make it worthwhile. The amounts arising currently from property rights amount to only about 8 per cent of the basis for access charges. It is

---

[13] A current example is Wrexham Station.

[14] 'Freehold land and buildings' are valued at £1,430 million in the 1995/96 accounts. This seems a very modest indication of the potential. BR's 1995/96 Accounts have no equivalent 'freehold land and building' valuation. 'Fixed Assets' in their accounts declined from £2,748.9 million in March 1995 to £165.7 million in 1995/96; this is some reflection of the land settlement referred to above.

[15] The Act does not require this: it was one of the legacies of the period when the regulator was under 'guidance' from the Secretary of State. He does, however, appear to have embraced it willingly.

not therefore comparable in effect to the BAA's 'single till' price régime, at 28 per cent of the price control. The principal justification for the 'single till' in the BAA's case is conformity with world-wide airport charging practice. No such inhibition is present for Railtrack.

However, as just argued, the potential for raising the return from property values is now substantially greater, and will enter the 'single till'. It will be a growing source of subsidy for rail operations. The significant question here is whether this arrangement will seriously inhibit land re-allocation. The answer seems to be 'no', for two reasons. The first and less convincing reason is that the contribution to the single till is set at 25 per cent leaving, according to the regulator, 'the most powerful incentive to Railtrack to develop its property assets and to build a stronger business, without compromising its duties to concentrate and develop a better railway infrastructure'.[16] This is a tribute to the regulator's gift for putting in a favourable light the case that a tax of 25 per cent is equivalent to a tax of 0 per cent, but it did represent modification of his original position.

The better reason is that, although all forms of profit from land development, including prospective capital gains, are to be imputed into the 'single till', the 25 per cent claw-back is confined to the share in such profit which the original holding of operational land represents. In other words, the effective penalty on Railtrack will be much diminished where small parcels of its inheritance are combined with large parcels of newly acquired land. This could in principle have the drawback that too much land will be acquired. This seems, however, to be nit-picking. There has been a substantial release from governmental restrictions; and long-standing misallocation will begin to be corrected.

Freight

One substantial drawback of the privatisation process is that it has confirmed a source of probable misallocation of resources, namely in freight. The treatment of the subsidy has confirmed a long-standing bias in its favour. It will be recalled that the first explicit

---

[16] Railtrack, *Annual Report 1996*, p. 19.

attempt to put a commercial floor to BR's freight business was a consequence of the Transport Act 1968. This deregulated long distance road haulage, so that it was necessary for a Labour government to give rail unions reassurance that the odds were not to be stacked against railways in the more vigorous competition from roads to be expected. On the other hand, there had to be reassurance to road interests that railway pricing was, as we would now say, not an abuse of the monopoly's ability to differentiate its prices. The solution was found in methods of allocating costs of track and signalling, then believed to be highly unresponsive to output variation, to provide much of the justification for differential charges.

Thus the idea of allocating these costs principally according to 'prime user' was adopted. In those days, freight was found almost universally on the network, but outweighed by passenger use. From BR's point of view, the rule had the useful property of relieving freight where it shared the track with passenger services, and where most effective road competition then concentrated, whilst assigning track and signalling costs wholly to freight whenever BR's market position was strong, and where it was the sole user. A conspicuous example of this was much of coal traffic. Mark-ups over haulage costs could be set high (gross margins on different types of freight were a closely guarded secret, but 60 per cent for coal was alleged at the time, I recall).

The subsequent history of charging practices confirmed this favourable early deal, though it did little to stem the loss of traffic to road, a function of quite other factors.[17] As, successively, Inter-City passenger, Passenger Transport Executive (PTE)-oriented services and the rest of passenger services, were made to follow forms of commercial principles, individual 'deals' were done, with the result that the last-comer to be made 'accountable' commercially, provincial passengers, started life with approximately a £500 million a year 'deficit' on an £80 million a year turnover. The 1980s did not substantially change these deals, though exogenous forces, mainly road competition, continued to wreak havoc in

---

[17] Notably, road transport's service innovations due mainly to motorway building, increasing vehicle size and the decline of traditional railway customers such as steel and coal.

freight.[18] Various expedients (such as subsidy for freight install-ations) were added. The Treasury's year-on-year pressure to reduce the cash absorbed by the railways during the 1970s probably also raised the margins sought for captive freight traffic, especially coal. The coal strikes of the 1980s severely reduced the scope for this.

Privatisation included the politically correct ambition to encourage rail freight at the expense of road substitutes. As seen above, subsidy now became explicitly centred on passenger franchises only. The new holder of the subsidy budget, the Franchise Director, was divorced from the question of the terms on which freight could use railways. The regulator meanwhile was charged with defining commercially acceptable charges for freight, with the task of fitting them into the overall price structures and a level of total outlays dictated by his view of future railway expenditure. I shall describe later the problems of consistency of cost definitions and treatment to which this gave rise. However, intentionally or not, privatisation was a vehicle permanently to subsidise rail freight, in all probability backed up by the terms of the sale of the freight businesses.

One view of rail freight history is that subsidy is justifiable in terms of externalities (for instance, road congestion, pollution). I do not wish to debate that here; rather the question is the transparency of commercial transactions and future handling of the incidence of subsidy. Subsidy should be explicit; the first step is to understand what costs access charges do (or should) reflect. A more satisfactory costing procedure would reveal the present status of freight subsidy. I take this up in problems facing the regulator below. In terms of subsidy, the irony is that the Franchise Director is obliged to produce a cost-benefit account of his subsidy decisions; it seems no one has the duty to do this for freight, except to the limited extent that, where the Secretary of State, when exercising his rights under section 137 of the Railways Act, exempts freight from access charges, he must be 'satisfied that benefits of a social and environmental nature are likely to result'. Needless to say, there is no obligation to measure these, or report on them.

---

[18] The 1984 coal strike was particularly damaging to the high-margin coal traffic.

Costs and Benefits of Privatisation: A Summary

Substantial benefits of privatisation will emerge on the production side. These 'x' efficiency gains will be supplemented by consumer gains via service innovation, an aspect of 'y' efficiency gains[19] which the decentralised contract structure has helped to promote. The operation of the capital market, via actual or threatened corporate deals, will reinforce these effects on 'x' efficiency even if, as Dieter Helm predicted in last year's lecture, integration reasserts itself.[20] The non-contestable supply monopoly, in the middle of the value-added structure, might well cause more concern in terms of enhanced monopoly power. However, Railtrack will still have a fundamental effect on railway production via its ownership of the means of determining the slot structure, the train diagrams.

Exploiting monopoly from change of ownership depends on creating extra barriers to entry, based on the 'home' barriers to entry. Railtrack must be involved in any substantial building of extra market power which is the principal reason why mergers upstream and downstream of Railtrack do not, I judge, present big threats.[21] The Prospectus simply noted that the Director General of Fair Trading's remit was extended to cover railways, but it was otherwise silent on what attitudes to mergers involving Railtrack might be. No doubt such a proposal, if substantial, would attract a reference to the MMC. In terms of contracts driven by Railtrack, its powers are heavily circumscribed by the regulator's powers of scrutiny. My judgement is that the underlying assumption of privatisation – that there should be an independently owned non-contestable network, which is increasingly recognised as desirable in the privatised utilities – will be preserved. There is no serious risk of dissipation of consumer gains through building on Railtrack's monopoly.

---

[19] My term for recognition of, and action on, demand-side (service) improvements hitherto neglected.

[20] Dieter Helm, 'Putting the Railways Back Together Again: Rail Privatisation, Franchising and Regulation', in M. E. Beesley (ed.), *Regulating Utilities: A Time for Change?*, IEA Readings 44, 1996.

[21] The Secretary of State's decision on the Stagecoach/Porterbrook merger was awaited as this was written. The former operates passenger franchises; the latter owns the three rolling stock companies.

Implications for the Franchise Director's Function

Annex 2's calculations suggest that, at 2003/4, despite the anticipated 30 per cent reduction in passenger subsidies, there will still be a passenger subsidy of about £1,200 or £1,300 million a year. By then, the Franchise Director's office may have been abolished, but the functions will have to be performed somewhere, perhaps by re-integration with the Department of Transport.

These functions are both to negotiate the level of subsidy and to monitor performance. The latter task has been sharpened in its impact by the formal contractual procedure; experience in dealing with direct contractors to the government can be brought to bear. In this case the apt analogy is with London Transport's bus service contracting in the late 1980s and in the 1990s, and the Franchise Director's office is benefiting accordingly, not least because the franchise holders are heavily populated by companies with bus service roots. It will be unfortunate if this expertise is lost by absorption of the office.

The privatisation process, with the independent rail regulator setting important contract terms ahead and the Franchise Director negotiating to lessen the cost of the government's open-ended use of subsidy, has had considerable merits. However, one can well envisage eventual discontent with taking most of the risks into subsidy. Also, subsidy will be called 'uncontrollable', not without some substance. Subsidy comes in many guises; it is not concentrated in the Franchise Director's budget; and it is fixed only for three years ahead, though no doubt subject to *ad hoc* adjustment. Subsidy for investment involves *inter alia* an independent force, Railtrack, and franchise contracts are renewable at irregular intervals, up to 15 years ahead.

Renewing of Rosco contracts, now concentrated in single hands, may well be a challenge. It is certain there will be productivity improvements during the Rosco contracts' span, but the terms may prove to have incorporated a large capitalisation of subsidy up front. Whoever is responsible for renewing the contracts will be faced with a private sector operator with great bargaining strength. This would be of no moment if one could assume contestability in supply at that point. But that is a doubtful assumption, not because of present concentration in supply, but because of incumbent advantage to commitment to investment in rolling stock during the

251

life of the present contracts. To commit is not to be left with unsaleable assets with long unexpired lives.

There is a continuing, shared political commitment to subsidy and increased, or at least maintained, railway output. There are negligible alternative uses for rolling stock outside the UK, and to perform in the UK, one will have to have appropriately aged British vehicles. Even if some device to create truly rival customers can be engineered, the vehicles will command an appropriate price, based on relatively certain prospects in the UK.[22] It is also notable that there has been an increased willingness for franchise passenger operation to commit to new vehicles. Experience in a still highly subsidised bus industry has created a specially knowledgeable set of bus entrepreneurs comfortable with government influence on contracts. It is significant in this connection that successful bus operators were prominent in the earliest organised group of interests in future franchises in 1992.

All this will not surprise those who believe a principal function of privatisation is to disclose the real market risks. But unfortunately, as I see it, the emphasis will be on 'windfall gains' not foreseen at the time, if this will not prevent forces in government strongly arguing to rationalise, predict and control government's commitment to subsidy. Also, there is almost certain to be pressure to raise the function of cost-benefit analysis in particular in justifying subsidy. As indicated earlier, the basis for this is laid down in the Franchise Director's obligations and implicitly in the Secretary of State's in Section 54 of the Act.

As an approach to assessing the factors which should underlie broad policy choices, CBA is a useful means of shaping discussion but I see nothing but trouble arising out of attempting to elevate it to underpin specific subsidy provision. Annex 1 comments on what the National Audit Office found in pursuing the topic with respect to freight grants; this does not augur well. There are formidable technical problems too. The two principal sources for absorbing subsidy are freight and passenger services. To standardise CBA measurements across these, for the purpose of setting the total subsidy and its division between them, constitutes a task which has so far eluded analysts.

---

[22] This is a consideration in the proposed Stagecoach/Porterbrook Merger.

Nevertheless, CBA will doubtless have a role to play in the deliberations about subsidy. Its use in practical applications to individual contracts is likely to be confined to lesser matters of variation of contracts in mid-term. Here again, bus precedents are useful indicators. CBA became a practical tool in bus affairs when London Transport Executive (LTE) was able to devise a workable proxy – £s per passenger mile gained – used as a pass mark for proposed changes in fares and services. It turned out to be a reasonably good proxy for external benefits, notably relief of road congestion;[23] but it was not a tool for justifying absolute subsidy levels.

The Franchise Director's office does not have the built-in deterrents to re-absorption in the government's machine which Ofrail has. Its *de facto* independence is at the will of the Secretary of State of the day. Its strength lies in its singular focus on subsidy granting and monitoring. It has a professional interest in developing, as far as it can, rationalisation of subsidy. Its (*de facto*) independence has led to an unprecedented transparency in the subject industry's affairs. It will be a great pity if this accumulating expertise is weakened by arguments which see the 'solution' to a problem of government's expenditures as chiefly a matter of reorganisation to 'improve co-ordination' in railway affairs.

Emerging Problems for the Regulator

The price control

It is worthwhile to raise the question of what is needed to found the basis of track access charges more securely, for two reasons: they will have to be reviewed by 2001, and there may well be a need to consider the cost implications of possible changes in current franchises within the franchise time limits. The second will call for what the regulator has termed 'what-if' calculations to adjust track charges in response to proposed franchise output changes. Now that the charges have been settled for at least most franchises, and no-one has yet sought a 'what if' calculation, this is a good time to

---

[23] Compare the study by Beesley, Gist and Glaister, 'Cost Benefit Analysis and London's Transport Policies', *Progress in Planning*, Vol. 19, Part 3, 1983.

attempt to foresee what may be needed to improve the cost side of the calculations.

As far as can be judged from public pronouncements, the regulator took an orthodox line in approaching his original task of fixing access charges by Railtrack. All the normal utility ingredients are present: emphasis on what should turn up in future cash outlays (opex and capex), efficiency targets expressed in an x in an RPI-x incentive control, and scepticism about accepting accounting conventions like 'depreciation'. In order to represent what would be due to the continuing ownership interest, emphasis was laid on a target return. Unsurprisingly, there was more emphasis on achieving an appropriate financial profile for the company in terms of cash flow and financial indicators than on justifying a particular value to which this flow and financial indicators would apply. Potentially most important, in my view, the concept of a 'control total' for a forward-looking run of outlays was formulated to focus on the charges for the passenger franchises. [24]

Less happily, this 'control total' was struck after deducting 'excluded activities' – the effect of the 'single till' policy, freight revenues, and open access revenues. Thus the 'control total' was a 'revenue required' total, not the 'control total' of future total Railtrack outlays needed to underpin any attempts to assign costs to the various users. As I shall argue in Annex 3, the need to treat freight in particular differently from passengers – clearly foreshadowed in the Department of Transport's original paper on 'Gaining Access to the Railway Network' (February 1993) and thus followed by the regulator – leads to a quite unsustainable confusion about the nature, measurement and use of information about Railtrack's costs. However, the principal duty of a regulator is always to try to get his or her sights on achievable total outlays; the regulator was, it seems, determined not to lose sight of this. The relevant 'control total' is the left-hand side of Figure 1. The first question for a future review therefore is: what problems is the sequential process likely to have left with respect to this 'control total'?

---

[24] Office of the Rail Regulator, *Framework for the Approval of Railtrack Access Charges for Franchised Passenger Services*, July 1994, Fig. 2.1. The years taken were 1994/5 – 1997/8.

Figure 1: Railtrack Revenues and Costs

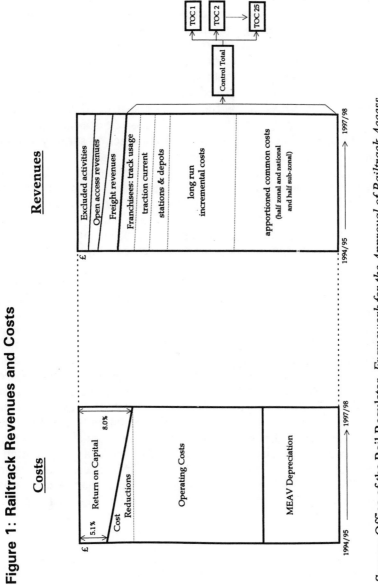

Source: Office of the Rail Regulator, *Framework for the Approval of Railtrack Access Charges for Franchised Passenger Services*, July 1994.

First is the open-ended nature of the subsidy. From Railtrack's point of view – and that of defining the 'control total' relevant for regulation – what quantity of subsidy in the event is realised principally affects achieved or prospective outputs. Access charges were fixed with a target output in view. Franchisees have signed up for minimum levels of output, on terms encouraging increases. If actual subsidy turns out to be considerably higher in the event, this may prove to have raised outputs, so the output assumptions on which the 'control total' is based will need to be raised. Railtrack will presumably stress that extra opex is justified. But this, or any other prospective output change, should cause no special difficulty, since the basic effect of the open-ended approach to subsidy will be to confirm outputs already determined.

Railtrack's outlays on investment will be influenced, in the event, by further government support, as yet undecided, on major projects such as WCML. Railtrack's gross investment outlays over a future review period will be affected by vagaries of subsidy of this kind. True, far the largest outlays concern replacing existing assets, part of the normal interchange between a regulator and utility at Review time.

The more important practical issue, as the regulator has pointed out on several occasions, is trying to ensure that committed investment of all kinds is carried out, including delivery on core maintenance and renewal, which in WCML's case includes complete re-signalling. The regulator's tasks are more complex than those of other utility regulators because of the uncertain effects of bargaining about subsidy. Though the Prospectus did not say so explicitly, the regulator has presumably reserved the right to alter charges in specific cases like WCML if assumed investment does not materialise; but Railtrack will be able to bargain directly with government with the cash from servicing capital and some equivalent of depreciation already in the bank as negotiations proceed.[25] Moreover, *de facto* modifications of access charges in mid-RPI-x period will make it even more difficult than usual to sort out efficiency gains at the next Review – that is, how far a given

---

[25] Had BR been privatised in the way some of us thought more sensible, *viz.* by creating separate geographically integrated companies, the difficulties stemming from run-down lines would have been better focused. It would also have been easier to have approached this problem via setting up specific penalties against failure to reach investment targets.

shortfall in achieved investment is due to exogenous events and how far to management's unpredicted gains in efficiency.

Probably the most important fall-out of the 'sequential process' of privatisation is the likely impact of realised flotation proceeds. There are two reasons why the element in the access charges relating to the existing assets is unlikely to have been confirmed in the event. *First*, there was a substantial shift in the Treasury target implicit in the negotiations leading up to the float. For example, the last-minute bargaining on Railtrack's opening debt led to a settlement of £600 million compared with an alleged Treasury target of £1.5 billion.[26] *Second*, the final decision about the price at which Railtrack could be floated was necessarily made very late.

In the 'Framework' what the flotation proceeds or the other terms of Railtrack's financing might be did not feature at all directly. The decision to make Railtrack a privatisation priority clearly introduced a new dimension in regulator/government dealings, whose effect on the access charge which emerged must be unclear to an outsider. If one's experience of previous privatisations is relevant, however, the target realisations for the 'punters' money' on flotation were subject to frantic interchanges between relevant parties right up to the final decision on share quantities, and particularly strike price. The regulator had already been obliged to make his own assessments about what levels of return on what assets were appropriate. As a consequence, a gap may well have opened up between the 'regulatory asset value' on which predicted returns to the ownership interests were based, and what happened in the event.

If the rail regulator follows the precedents, the flotation value will assume an important part of his future judgements on what revenue to allow. I would guess that the realisation was probably less than that explicitly or implicitly included in the 'control total'. If that is true, then Railtrack has even more reason to be satisfied about its 'balance sheet strength' than it was in the Annual Report (p. 24). But the other side of this coin is that the regulator has greater reason to press for downward adjustments, whether or not involving higher gearing, and for backing up pressure to see the fulfilment of original investment assumptions. This, in turn, will make more difficult his assessment of what part of realised cost-savings, below the targets

---

[26] *Financial Times*, 26 May 1996.

set, will rank for unanticipated efficiency gains, and thus candidates for inclusion to greater or lesser degree in returns to shareholders.

The points just made bear on the size of the 'control total' of future outlays which will be set in forthcoming reviews of track access charges. A control total of outlays (covering opex, capex and shareholders' requirements) has another very important aspect. It acts as the basis for calculations of what costs should be attributed to particular kinds of users of Railtrack's network, and, since there are inevitably considerable elements of non-attributable, or 'common costs',[27] in the control total, what needs to be raised from users. The non-attributable elements will also include the amounts needed to satisfy shareholders' claims. Some principle for setting what I term 'mark-up' on the attributable costs has to be selected. These issues are taken up in the next section.

Annex 3 argues in detail for a fresh approach to the problems of measuring attributable costs and assessing required mark-ups. The essential features are, first, that cost attribution should start from a 'control total' comprising the aggregate revenues in the price control. Attribution implies considering what changes in the control total would occur were specific changes in outputs associated with the differing customer sets made. The sets to be recognised initially should, I believe, be the 25 TOCs and freight operators (viewed as a whole). There would be two useful hypothetical changes in output to consider – a 20 per cent reduction in output in each group, and the withdrawal of each of them. These would give two levels of attribution, one at total group level, and one applicable within each group. Non-attributed costs, or 'common costs', would have to be the subject of mark-up rules, to ensure that all outlays in the control total are accounted for.

A principal effect of this revised approach would, I believe, be to reveal the degree to which this is, or is not, a cross-subsidy to rail freight, measured in terms of resource use, and if so, its extent. More important for the regulator's immediate concerns, it would provide for a much less irksome way of setting track access agreements.

---

[27] The term used by the regulator.

Track Access Agreements

An important, time-consuming task for the regulator is to approve track access agreements involving freight operations. Both the level and the structure of the charges are of concern and subject to scrutiny. In 1995/96 the regulator approved 129 freight track access agreements to add to the 200 agreements affecting freight yards, sidings and light maintenance.[28] In marked contrast to passenger agreements, the freight access agreements range from three months to 10 years, so renewals will be frequent; the hope is that freight competition will grow, with more activity, under open access agreements. It is timely to ask how far this work-load is really necessary and what simplifications could usefully be made.

The regulator's concerns (largely enjoined upon him) are threefold:

- there is a public interest in the allocation of the rail slots on the network where these truly involve rival operators, including freight;

- Railtrack shall not inhibit rail freight's competitive position with road by inappropriate charging; and

- competition between freight operators shall be fair and not lead to a misallocation of resources.

I shall not attempt to comment on the first concern here, because from rail freight's viewpoint it seems a relatively minor problem. (It may well emerge later on, especially in the form of concerns about the degree of subsidy of freight.)

The second and third concerns are tackled in the 'Framework' policy statement on freight in February 1995. This is not the tidiest document conceptually because the two sets of objectives are largely mutually inconsistent. Wearing his 'pro railway freight' hat the regulator must condone any and every encouragement of price discrimination on Railtrack's part which is calculated to increase rail freight, including prices reflecting what the traffic will bear and those which, at the other end of the spectrum, will just cover a highly favourable view of attributable costs. Wearing his resource

---

[28] Railtrack, *Annual Report 1996, op. cit.,* pp. 14-15.

allocation/fair competition hat, such discrimination must be bounded. Minimum prices are needed, it is said, to avoid 'waste', and perhaps to avoid raising too much suspicion about the amount of the relative subsidy landing up in freight. Maxima are needed because 'too high' charges may smack of 'exploitation' and, more specifically, because there is the possibility of (a) rail-user-on-rail-user competition being 'distorted', and (b) similarly, rail *versus* road freight, in the case where a road operator uses rail in part (for example, piggy-back operations *versus* plain road operations). Distortion implies that the least-cost competition may not win.

My first reaction (clearly sometimes shared by the regulator) is that, in the long-term losing game played by rail against road freight, rail needs to be able to deploy all the pricing tricks it can. However, regulators must suppress these feelings. But could simplifications reduce the conflicts?

The obvious way to avoid so much enforced nannying about commercial contracts is to adopt a reactive stance, based on the need simply to be able to intervene if parties have substantial complaints about Railtrack behaviour – that is, essentially to concentrate on the traditional anti-monopoly role common to general competition authorities. The regulator's *ex ante* role will then boil down to constructing a guideline maximum charge, for reasons I hope to show.

What are the basic competition concerns which might merit attention? The principal worry about a monopoly in the middle of the supply chain which, as here, has an overall price control on RPI-x lines, is that market power will be used either to prevent entry of a rival supplier, or to influence competitive relations upstream and downstream to the monopolist's benefit. Railtrack's direct competitors as a railway track and signalling owner will predictably remain few; entry is quite unlikely to be profitable. Rather the arguments will be about acquisition or divestiture involving parties upstream and downstream, should they perceive profit in integration. These must fall to be considered in the usual way, via the MMC. Upstream, concerning Railtrack's inputs, conditions will be competitive, so Railtrack's possible gain is to drive down rewards below a competitive level, but this is hardly likely to be in Railtrack's own commercial interest. One cannot in the long run beat competitively determined prices.

Downstream, there may be more concern. What limits should be placed on its ability, where possible, to discriminate between its rail freight customers? First, we may dismiss the need for minima in this context. Railtrack must be presumed to have its own financial well-being at heart. The regulator's great concern to monitor and establish minima could be interpreted as uncertainty as to whether Railtrack knows enough about its costs to be left alone. However that may have been before privatisation, we can be sure that it will be remedied now. Thus Railtrack will not charge a loss-making price unless it has reason to gain from such behaviour indirectly. With no ownership interests downstream, it cannot gain from predatory behaviour in the downstream market, which is the traditional reason for accepting losses. Equally, there is no reason to intervene in the 'structure' of prices charged (the proportion of 'standing' charges, incentive marginal contracts, and the rest). Railtrack for years to come will have spare capacity, and will be keen to fill it, by whatever contracts yielding some profit it can persuade its customers to make.

This leaves the possibility that 'too much' may be charged to a 'captive' customer, for instance, a piggy-back operator, or that there may be too much 'unfairness' as between freight customers in general. It makes good sense in a generally reactive system to issue an indicator of a limit, so as to provide guidance within which contracts can be freely and individually struck. Thus all details of contracts can be left to the parties, always subject to particular powers of investigation on a complaint. How should the guideline be formulated?

The use of such a calculation would be in complaints about prices. The regulator would have to consider all relevant circumstances in the normal competition authority mode. As to the prices involved, the present view on the maximum is that it should be a 'stand-alone' price, derived from considering what an independent rail operator's charge would be to enter the market to provide the flow concerned. Such a marker has a very respectable foundation in this literature, but it is likely to be quite impracticable in this case. The dilemma is well put at page 15 of the February 1995 ORR paper.[29] Even an 'efficient' new operator may well be

---

[29] *Framework for the Approval of Railtrack's Track Access Charges for Freight Services*, Office of the Rail Regulator, February 1995.

unable to beat the present value of Railtrack's costs for the same service, because Railtrack generally is facing declining demand, and has a large accumulation of sunk but still relevant assets. The better approach seems to be to extend the analysis of Railtrack's own costs for freight, and to consider implicit mark-ups or failures to do so over attributable avoidable costs in the case at hand. The issue is not correctness of the charge in relation to costs *per se*, but the effect on competitive relationships, in the specific case at hand.

The basis should, I argue, be the approach to attributable costs and mark-ups sketched in Annex 3. Using this approach, it is highly likely that the sum of allowed revenue for freight access charges will fail to yield a mark-up over attributable freight costs when computed at the freight/passenger service level. It is likely that some will fail to contribute to common or joint costs within freight operations also. But these results should not indicate that the tests must be abandoned in favour of new specific definitions of costs which look to yield more respectable prices. This would be to recreate the confusion described in Annex 3 (pp. 279-286). The proper course is to recognise the revealed subsidies as a reduction of the non-attributable costs that have to be considered, or indeed an 'aggregate mark-down' on total attributed costs. Then the comparisons designed to set standards for plausible competitive behaviour can proceed.

One implication is that an externally devised stand-alone price for the permitted maximum is even less relevant. Any control total representing actual outlays would have to be diminished by whatever subsidy level is appropriate. What level this should be cannot logically be underpinned by objective evidence in the absence of detailed CBA studies about the values of individual freight flows derived from effects external to railways. I have already stressed the difficulties.

In order to set the level for an individual freight flow, a limit based on the real facts of attributed costs should be substituted. I suggest this should reflect a price allowing upwards deviation from the set of prices which suffice to cover the control total for freight, ignoring subsidy. Thus, I think a more readily agreed limit might well be that price which, if applied to all freight flows, would eliminate the failure to cover all freight attributable costs plus freight common costs, revealed from a process which starts from the total set of passenger and freight flows. At that level, the attribution process across the 26 groups (25 TOCs plus the freight sector) will throw up avoidable unattributed costs. A notional mark-up to represent these, on principles common to passenger and freight, could be added – for example, a mark-up proportional to the individual attributed costs for the 26.

The principal function of such a limit would be to provide guidance to Railtrack when considering what limits to put on negotiations about prices. If and when competition disputes arise, the regulator would not be bound by the rule but would, in the usual general competition regulatory mode, take into account all aspects of the behaviour complained of.

In an important sense, the exposition of the regulator's likely thinking on principles of assessment is much more important than giving express guidance. Having a general principle of non-discriminatory behaviour in the licence, the regulator (like his fellow-regulators) has the advantage that the burden of proof to show relevant information to refute a complaint lies with Railtrack. When a case is brought, the principles on which Railtrack must respond with evidence about costs and margins are established; Railtrack must produce the evidence or lose the case. But I think the incidence of cases will not be great. With this reactive mechanism, the industry and the regulator can be relieved of much tedious and intrusive interference in commercial affairs; and, of equal importance, Railtrack's management will be freer to get on with developing the means to increase its traffic.

Conclusions

I have tried to explore some of the distinctive problems which arise out of a bold attempt to privatise an industry with substantial ongoing needs for subsidy to sustain an output which is, by and large, the subject of a political consensus. The whole is mind-bogglingly complex, but I have sought to indicate ways forward for some of the problems the Franchise Director and the regulator face or will face.

I have characterised this privatisation as one in which, partly by design and partly by accident, the supply monopoly's prices were fixed independently ahead of its flotation and without being governed by consequences for expenditure on subsidy. The government in effect shouldered the subsidy risk, both in Railtrack's case and that in selling off other industry producers. I was one of those who wished to see a privatisation of a different character based on regionally separated integrated companies. I have to admit, however, that circumstances – markedly different, I believe, from what the architects themselves foresaw – promise to yield substantial benefits, particularly in the form of increased productive efficiency and use of land. The jury is out on the eventual costs to the public purse, but the prospect is for a substantial fall in subsidy levels in future, with no reduction in output.

Especially in a time of political change, this 'model' of a process which, in many ways, is another stage in the 40-year-old battle to contain railway subsidy, looks particularly frail. The frailty will partly stem from a renewed concern to control and rationalise subsidy, and partly from suspicions about such an obviously divided structure. Depending on the political scenario, there will be pressure to reincarnate the integrated control of railways, opening up a renewed battle for funds, backed by quantified subsidy justification. I would hope, however, that before the demolition of the present structure is put in hand, due consideration will be given to the possibility of repeating the essentials of the process, *viz.* independent assessment of required railway output, and its consequent independent translation into required subsidy. The one-off deals associated with privatisation, now causing considerable irritation, will be over the dam. Continuing subsidy will cost less, because of the prospective increases in efficiency, albeit on a lesser scale. The innovation of shouldering the subsidy risk could be repeated, with less net cost overall to the Treasury next time around.

The output of rail passenger services, whether franchised or not, will always be driven by public conceptions of 'need'. Subsidy has to adapt to these perceptions. I would like this to be recognised in facing the question of what is to be done when franchises fall in. One implication is that a vision of the future in which there can be effective competition for railway slots is mistaken. Hence I depart from the regulator's view expressed in his policy statement.[30] I think a more desirable approach is to retain the general structure that the regulator sets the prices of the non-contestable elements, with a Franchise Director (or his equivalent) charged with securing value for money from letting out monopoly franchises for services. The

---

[30] *Competition for Railway Passenger Services*, Office of the Rail Regulator, December 1994.

Treasury would again be 'at risk' in its budgetary provisions, but would retain the advantage that, once a franchise item is set, further extra subventions will be avoided. There are also strong practical reasons.

The franchises will fall in at periods between 5 and 15 years. The practical need is to create a system which will cope. My vision is that the Franchise Director, when entering a negotiation, will be armed with a much better knowledge of what will face new franchises than on the first round. With respect to costs, I have suggested a revision of costing procedure in which Railtrack's outlays can be attributed to franchises much more certainly. The Franchise Director will also know more about other aspects of costs. He will perhaps have some useful input for his cost-benefit deliberations. The regulator, meanwhile, will have to reset Railtrack's prices, in the normal RPI-x mode. I have also suggested that the regulator should perform his functions as general competition arbiter for freight in a way which avoids the present nannying of contracts. In this also, a proper approach to costing will be essential.

In short, my argument is that we should now concentrate on effective competition for passenger franchise monopolies. Admirers of Harold Demsetz should approve. I think we could do a lot better in the railway area than was apparent in US cable franchising which has caused so much scepticism about his insight. Particularly because of the continuing role of subsidy, this is a fresh challenge to economists, which I hope will be relished.[31]

---

[31] For example, Robert Baldwin and Martin Cave's review of 'Franchising as a Tool of Government', April 1996, while most useful, does not focus the problem of combining franchising with a continuing commitment to subsidy.

Annex 1

Subsidies

'Subsidy' can be manifest in many forms. The 'headline' figure often quoted for the current annual rail subsidy is £2 billion, representing Passenger (OPRAF support grants) and PTE yearly grants, paid in the last accounting year.[32] These are the figures which will be most affected by the franchise round proceeding in late 1996. PTE grants are not part of the Franchise Director's remit, but the authority for them is the 1968 Transport Act. Earlier this year PTEs and government were in conflict about the implications of Track Access Charges. PTEs considered the terms of payment to be too stringent, requiring payments for services beyond the typical rail access agreement. In settling the matter, the Minister in effect much improved the terms payable for existing services, but made the terms for underwriting further services much more onerous. The net effect of the settlement was to leave the PTEs with an increased potential to buy more services for their money.

The creation of subsidiaries (including Railtrack) in the run up to privatisation means that there are additional sources of subsidy which will appear in BR's accounts only as further revenue, because routed to them, not to BR via Passenger Grants. For example, in 1995/96 Railtrack received £57 million in revenue grants from the Department of Transport (DOT) towards the cost of maintaining level crossings, foot bridges and underpasses.[33]

Promises of subsidy for current operations extend beyond passenger-oriented services. The Railtrack prospectus (p. 99) notes £18.5 million a year is to be made available to Freightline, to be 'coterminous with its principal track access agreement'. This was made under section 137, Railways Act, in which the Secretary of State may pay any or all of track access charges. The criteria to justify his decisions are broad. He has to be assured that 'benefits of a social or environmental nature are likely to result'. An interesting

---

[32] BR's Annual Accounts has the subsidy at £1,983 million (p. 51), all included in BR turnover, accounted for as sales.

[33] Railtrack Annual Report, p. 24.

contrast with the criteria for grants to assist the provision of facilities for freight haulage (Section 139) is taken up below. £18.5 million is a small sum compared to £2 billion, but far more significant in terms of Freightliner's turnover which was £87.9 million in 1995/6, with a £20.2 million 'loss' (BR Annual Report, p. 22). Sweeping up the grants for the cost of operating and maintaining level crossings, footbridges and underpasses into the TOC grants also implies some relief, albeit small, for freight.

A second way to grant subsidy is by underwriting future investment. The amounts which will eventually be promised are also unknown. Project 2000 (Thameslink) is the first; project costs are estimated around £600 million (Prospectus, p. 45). How much of this will fall on the Franchise Director's budget depends on how far outside capital can be attracted, and the terms the Franchise Director secures from franchisees in pursuit of his power under Section 54 of the Act. Section 54 does not mention criteria to judge how far he should go in 'encouraging railway investment'.

His statement in the Prospectus, however, says that 'there must be a substantial gain in financial value for money to be obtained in making such an investment' and refers to 'the best value for money option for securing investment'. This seems to indicate that in respect of Section 54 grants, it is intended to start off the negotiations without invoking the criteria relevant to grants for freight (Section 139). But doubtless a future directive from a Secretary of State can alter the negotiation; Section 54 is not constraining. Moreover, in negotiation with the private sector one cannot 'shift risk' without paying for it up front.

The most contentious and potentially largest scheme will be the West Coast Main Line improvements, the dimensions of which are uncertain now. The Railtrack Prospectus points to another source of subsidy in this connection, *viz.* the £7 million from the EU in 1995 for the WCML feasibility study, which it points out will be available in the future. The DOT expects to make additional applications on behalf of Railtrack for further funding (p. 100). Other grants may come from the European Development Fund. These EU sources in principle could offset UK-based funding. It is highly unlikely they will wholly do so.

Though the focus in dealing with these larger future subventions is the Franchise Director, they will also serve, if only in a minor way, freight. In response to an explicit intention to shift freight traffic to rail, these sources seem to have been stepped up. Freight facilities grants under Section 139 have been the prime focus of a National Audit Office report.[34] These route capital costs subsidies via customers of Railtrack. The report details the difficulties in finding and awarding applicants in a declining business. In 1995/6 only £4 million was awarded from a budget of £14 million, much stepped up from the budget of about £3 million in 1993. For 1996/7 £13 million is budgeted. This again is a trivial addition to overall subsidy, but not negligible in the rail freight business.

Privatising Railtrack gave the opportunity to cancel future obligations for payments by writing them off up front. Two outstanding examples of this were in freight. BR's Annual Report writes off £300 million of its Channel Tunnel freight assets (p. 61), presumably as a preliminary to selling the Rail Freight Distribution (RFD) business, stripped down to Channel Tunnel freight after the separation of Freightliner. Apparently the Treasury will also shoulder the future losses likely on the minimum usage charges which BR had notoriously negotiated in the heady days when the Tunnel was to be a saviour. It writes off £200 million for these which will of course mainly relate to passenger services. The Annual Report makes the laconic statement 'In certain circumstances Channel Passenger services may fully recover the minimum usage charges...for this to occur passenger carryings would have to attain approximately 4 times their reported 1995/6 level'. Something similar apparently happened with coal contracts; Railtrack's Annual Report remarks on the 'renegotiation' – a £40 million a year reduction from 1994/5 to reflect the 'commercial reality' of coal haulage agreements expiring in 1998, taken into the accounts in 1995/6.

Selling Roscos, and since then other BR subsidiaries, and the privatisation of Railtrack involved decisions about what value to set on the businesses. The subsequent flows of cash to be realised from users are affected accordingly. In principle, this is a matter of how subsidies are focused; a loss of value taken now can relieve the flow of subsidy later. The decision was taken to focus (most of) subsidy via the Franchise Director/TOC route and express it as conventional year-on-year flows. Having fixed contracts for Roscos and for track

---

[34] Department of Transport, *Freight Facilitation Grants in England*, National Audit Office, HC 632, Session 1995-96, 2 August 1996.

access charges ahead of Railtrack's float, imputing subsidies, and with an expected flow of outlays for opex and capex, a margin could have been foreseen which, at the appropriate cost of capital, would have determined the price shareholders were asked to pay. However, even if this model was followed, which is doubtful, the interval between fixing the track access charges and the float gave the opportunity for minor (or major) tuning. A reduction in the target sale value would enable the subsequent elements in year-on-year charges (which would then reflect shareholders' returns) to be lowered.

So many adjustments were going on in this period on so many dimensions that it will probably be impossible ever to track down the precise role played by this degree of freedom. However, it is known that the Treasury's public pronouncements about Railtrack's 'value' moved substantially downwards from the £6 billion or so original ambition to the actuality of a float of £2.5 billion. At most, at 7 per cent, this could be described as a prospective yearly outlay difference of about £245 million or perhaps a difference of 10 per cent in equivalent yearly subsidy on £2 billion plus.

Some of this difference is accounted for by injecting greater value into the scale and timing of required future investment and maintenance flows which would doubtless have indicated £6 billion as having considerable capitalised rents. A much more realistic view must have been taken in the actual estimates made, as explained in the text, for cash needs underlying rail access charges. But, to an extent impossible to trace with figures in the public domain, subsidy was doubtless shifted into the capital structure and commitments that finally emerged from Railtrack. For example, describing Railtrack's balance sheet as 'strong' the Annual Report for 1995/6 reports the Group's debt at £585 million. Creditors included £1,216 million in various forms of capital grants and deferred income, Asset Maintenance Plan accruals and Property Maintenance back-log accruals, to be fed into profit and loss account in later years. The Prospectus performance accounts at 31 September 1995 show a comparable, smaller, figure of £1,103 million. This implies about a £100 million increase in the six months leading up to the float. The 'strength' included a cash balance of £504 million.

In so far as subsidy was, in effect, transferred to the terms of the float, it decreases the need to raise subsidy later, but this leaves the bulk of subsidy for all sources still to be determined. The realised float introduces a potential gap between the implicit 'opening regulatory value' inherent in the original calculations for access charges, and the opening market values (shareholders' payments plus debt) always influential in settling the amount to be allowed for the shareholders' interests at the next Review. The size of this and indeed, in principle, its sign is not known to outsiders.

For all these reasons, to compute a sum which could be the net effect of privatisation on government subsidy, would make a fascinating PhD study, beginning, say, in late 1997. The government received proceeds to set against this outlay, of course. A Parliamentary Answer on 11 July 1996 gave the figures for the three Rosco sales, some other sales, and the first instalment for Railtrack shares. £1,822 million is recorded for Roscos, £1,054 million for the Railtrack instalment, in a total of £3,513.7 million in nominal terms. The additional 75p a share from investors raises the figure to about £4,140 million. At 8 per cent government borrowing rates, this represents, so far, a yearly equivalent flow of £331.2 million. BR's Annual Report 1995/96 records 'operating expenditure' of £5,797.2 million, including the year's charges payable to Roscos and Railtrack. In it the figure for payments to Railtrack, £2,155.5 million, closely mirrors Railtrack's turnover for 1995/96 for passenger and freight of £2,161 million (Annual Report 1995/6). No detail is recorded for BR's investment outlays; but Railtrack has the usual cash flow statement about purchase of tangible fixed assets of £437 million. A heroic (foolhardy?) attempt at the 'score' so far is to suppose that BR's expenditure on assets was in the same ratio to operating costs as Railtrack's. This would give yearly capex of:

$$\frac{5,797.2 \ \times \ 437}{2,155} = £1,176 \quad \text{million}$$

Arguably, Railtrack is the notably capital-intensive part of a 'reassembled' BR operation. So this figure has to be lowered. Let us write in capex of £900 million, giving a yearly flow of cash to be met of above £6,800 million for the equivalent BR total output. So far, sales of companies promise to contribute £331 million a year; passenger subsidies alone were about £1,700 million for 1995/6, a figure yet to be confirmed. Many gaps remain to be filled in the story about the net effect on government outlays. On the 'benefits' side, more can be said about the likely future change in subsidies, as noted in Annex 2.

The National Audit Office Report also throws an interesting side-light on the evaluation of subsidies. The Franchise Director is obliged to reveal his criteria soon, and will have to include 'value for money' in financial terms. The 1993 Act offers, as seen earlier, different versions for criteria as they affect freight. Both are, however, expressly tests for externalities of railway activity, and it seems very likely the Franchise Director will feel obliged to align with them in the criteria he adopts.

The National Audit Office reveals the Department's ways of evaluating freight facilities grants. To an old hand at social cost-benefit analysis, these read extremely oddly. 'Environmental benefits' to date are compressed to a tariff per lorry mile displaced by rail running from £0.5 per lorry on motorways to £1.50 for urban single carriageways (p. 23). In 1990 it was decided that 'reducing road congestion should not be taken into account because grants were to deal with environmental concerns'. In 1994 the Department relented so far as the least congested routes (motorways and dual carriageways) were concerned 'to reflect the benefits of reduced traffic congestion and accident savings from removing heavy lorries'.

Discounting was introduced in 1990, after schemes had run since 1974. A commissioned report in 1995 on the 'Valuation of Environmental Externalities' reported a very wide range of 'noise costs' in the UK from £2 billion to £4 billion a year. Further research would be required for the case at hand (p. 24). One wonders what has happened to the last 30 years' efforts to evaluate road externalities in CBA terms! The Franchise Director's rationale for support will be much more important than these small schemes; but one has great concerns about the practicalities of applying the criteria, as well as their definition.

Annex 2

The Franchising Process and the Subsidy Outturn

This annex attempts to estimate what the total franchise subsidy outlay will be by the 7th year, on the basis of information in the public domain about the 14 franchises let to 20 September 1996.[35]

Though only 11 of the 25 franchises remain to be announced at the time of writing, they cover some 68 per cent of the subsidies to BR. Whether subsidies to the remainder can be extrapolated from the first 14 depends on how far their characteristics differ. One would expect that given the very limited time-scale for the negotiations, the more difficult cases would appear later.

Table 1 lists the 'deals' in chronological order, as suggested by the OPRAF Annual Report (Column i) which describes different stages, from those whose terms were announced in the Report, through those listed and awarded to 24 June, those for which the sale processes had 'commenced', those where 'invitations to tender' had been sent out. The rest are divided into two sets: at the foot of the table are those which press reports of 12 June describe as 'the last five offered' and the remainder, labelled 'post 24 June'. Column (ii) records the nearest equivalent FRPS description ('profit centres') and (iii) the figures from that source showing employees per million 'revenue' ('fare box', to use a bus term for cash as opposed to subsidy). For each franchise, column (iv) gives the total claim for support by BR for the companies (then owned by BR) and column (vi) the element of (iv) which is accounted for by PTE grants (grants most heavily influenced by the authorities in the big urban concentrations). Sub totals and percentages are given in columns (v) and (vii).

Table 2 includes somewhat later information for the 14 franchises let to 1 October 1996. They include all the first three categories in Table 1's list, plus Thames Trains. For the earliest three franchises, OPRAF's Annual Report gives the full year-on-year support story. Column (i) gives the name and date of announcement, Column (ii) gives the contract length and Columns (iii) to (v) the House of Commons (HC) 1995/96 figures. These are split in each case into two elements: 'Total claim' plus 'Administered profit'.This division

[*cont'd on p. 276*]

---

[35] OPRAF *Annual Report*, 1995/96; OPRAF *News Releases*; Transport Committee on Railway Safety, Vol. II, *Minutes of Evidence with Appendices*, H of C, July 1996.

TABLE 1
Franchise Data, £millions

Opraf Annual Report 1995/96	1992 'Profit Centres'	FRPS Employees per £miln revenue 1992	Total Claim for Support £miln 1995/6	Sub Totals £miln 1995/96	% of Total Support	PTE S20 Element £miln
(i)	(ii)	(iii)	(iv)	(v)	(vi)	(vii)
First Franchises:						
S West Trains	S Western	32·5	63·52			
Great Western Trains	Great Western	42·6	47·27			
I. C. East Coast	East Coast	35·0	47·88	158·67	9·4	
'Awarded to 24 June':						
Midland Main Line			8·59			
Gatwick Express	Gatwick Express	14·5	-3·14			
Network South Central	South Central	37·5	80·79			
LTS Rail	LTS		27·98			
Chiltern Railway	Thames Chiltern		14·99	129·21	7·6	
'Sales Process Commences'						
Cardiff Railway Co			20·68			
South Wales & West	South Wales & W.		70·51			
South East Train Co	South East	36·4	124·90	216·09	12·8	
Invitations to Tender						
Thames Trains			37·35			
Anglia Railways	Anglia	17·8	32·98	70·33	4·2	
Post 24 June						
Cross Country Trains	Midland X Country	21·4	91·92			43·13
Great Eastern	Great Eastern	41·6	30·25			
Island Line			2·47			
Mersey Rail Electric			48·74			44·81
ScotRail	ScotRail	114·5	231·49			115·03
Thameslink	Thameslink	11·5	11·26			
West Anglia Great N	W Anglia Great N	23·9	57·76	473·89	28·0	
'Last five' offered Reported 12 June						
Central Trains	Central Trains	90·5	162·92			43·13
I C W Coast	West Coast	40·4	68·29			
North London	Net North	26·7	46·16			
Norwest Regional	N. W. Regional	140·7	179·57			83·24
Regional North East	Regional North East	102·3	187·53	644·47	38·1	67·58
			1692·66	1692·66		

TABLE 2
Franchise Predictions, £ millions (except for contract length)

Franchise Date, 1995/6		Length of Contract (yrs)	BR Subsidy,1995/6 H of C Transport Committe		
	(i)	(ii)	Administered Profit (iii)	Passenger Claim (iv)	Tota (v
19 Dec	S W Trains	7	19·89	63·52	83·4
20 Dec	G W Trains	10	14·51	47·27	61·7
29 Mar	ICEC	7	18·35	47·88	66·2.
20 Dec	LTS Rail	15	4·13	27·98	32·1
3 Apr	Gatwick	14	3·14	-3·14	0·
12 April	Net S Central	7	13·67	80·79	94·4
22 Apr	Midland Main Line	10	5·87	8·59	14·4
9 May	LTS	15[1]	4·13	27·98	32·1
25 June	Chiltern	7	2·26	14·99	17·2
21 Aug	South East	15	18·03	124·09	142·93
17 Sept	S Wales	7	4·38	70·51	74·89
17 Sept	Cardiff	7	0·69	20·68	21·37
19 Sept	Thames	7	4·67	37·35	42·02
20 Sept	Island	5	0·12	2·47	2·59
	TOTALS		107·56	577·24	685·61

[1] Conditional on Rolling Stock.

TABLE 2
(Continued)

BR Subsidy,Opraf Annual Report:Press Releases			Franchise 1st yr Payments	7th year (2002/03)	Average Yearly Payments	Latest Year
Administered Profit (vi)	Passenger Claim (vii)	Total (viii)	(ix)	(x)	(xi)	(xii)
19·5	65·9	85·4	54·7	40·3	47·46	
15·1	45·7	60·8	53·2	38·2	46·8	31·6
19·4	56·9	76·3	64·6	0·0	32·3	
4·1	28·0	32·1	29·0	23·9	Av. 26·1	(2011) -22·6
-3·9 (prov)	-		-4·6	-12·3	-13·5	
13·3	93·0	106·3	85·3	34·6	51·4	
7·0	10·1	17·1	16·5	-1·8	-1	(2006) -10
3·2	31·4	34·6	29·5	24·6	18·4	(2011) 11·2
2·1	16·5	18·6	16·5	2·9	Av 8·9	
18·3	120·8	139·1	125·4	60·5	35·7	(2011) -2·8
4·8	80·0	84·8	(1997/98) 70·9	(2003/04) 38·1	53·9	
0·7	21·5	22·2	(1997/98) 19·9	(2003/04) 13·3	16·3	
5·1	38·7	43·8	(1997/98) 33·2	(2003/04) 0·0	16·6	
0·1	2·3	2·5	2·1	1·8	1·9	
112·7	610·9	723·6				

is also reported in the OPRAF material at columns (vi) to (viii). 'Administered profit' amounts for all services to about 15 per cent of the 'total claim' which includes PTE contributions, in the HC material for 1995/96. It is unclear whether the OPRAF reader is supposed to compare the franchise letting with this book-keeping addition included. It of course improves the story about the relation of the payment to the franchise compared with what is deemed to be the BR equivalent for 1995/96. A further complication is that (one assumes) the figures are nominal. If we raise the total for 1995/96 by 2·1 per cent, the August 1996 on August 1995 all items retail index increase, the HC figures for 1995/96 for the 14 services become £583.78 million plus administered profit £116.23 million = £700 million. This compares with the grand total for 1996/97 of £723.55 million. OPRAF's figures thus indicate a small increase in the 1996/97 base compared with 1995/96. OPRAF's Annual Report, recording the first three franchises, also shows 1995/96 figures which are different from and somewhat larger than the HC source. This was no doubt a later Treasury estimate for 1995/96. These minor discrepancies do not invalidate the general conclusion about how the seven-year total will work out.

OPRAF's material for the 14 reports runs in terms of 'current prices' so the change over the years is best approached via these data. Column (ix) gives the 1st year franchise amount. The latest common future figure is for 2002/3, Column (x). Column (xi) gives the average franchise outlay over the years of the contract; column (xii) the amount in the final year. As can be seen, five are for seven years; others up to 15. For the last four the reported base year shifts to 1997/98 as the end date moves out. The last, Island Line, is exceptional; it is the shortest at five years, ending in 2002/3.

When the contract terminates later than 2003 in cases after the first four, we have to interpolate the 2002/3 data. From the three we do know, no consistent pattern of the rates of change (downwards) emerges. I have therefore simply assumed a constant yearly decline. To standardise for the elapsed period, I have taken the 1997/8 to 2003/4 figures for South Wales, Cardiff and Thames. The result is a starting point total subsidy of about £596 million, falling to £269 million, or a 55 per cent decline.

Whether this will be characteristic of the rest depends on how alike they are. Table 1 indicates that the remaining 11 are very different. First, they are on average biassed towards the North and

North West. The 14 contain most of the more buoyant demand prospects – and the two eventual major negative subsidy cases, Gatwick and Inter City East Coast (ICEC). This geographical bias is reflected in the deals the Franchise Director has managed to obtain for service improvements above the required minimum and commitments to renewal and refurbishment of railway stock. Thus, the five leading franchises in terms of percentage reductions in subsidy (up to 80 per cent) are Midland Mainline, ICEC, Chiltern and Thames, with Gatwick sharply increasing its profit (negative subsidy). The last 14 contain all the cases of PTE involvement. As seen in the text, their timing owes something to the technical difficulties surrounding PTE (or Franchise Director's equivalent) support. Nevertheless, they are subject to greater constraints on the franchises than average. For example, the biggest is Scotrail, both in absolute subsidy terms and in PTE involvement. Strathclyde PTE has in the past insisted on preserving its own views of what contributions are appropriate to ensure passenger safety. Table 1 also indicates that among the 14 are those most dependent on subsidy as a source of income, with the highest ratio of employees per £ million revenue, from the 'fare box' in 1992. This ratio is of course two-sided; it can also indicate larger scope for cost reduction via manpower savings. But it is also associated with PTEs having a background of low public fare preferences.

It would be optimistic indeed to extrapolate the 55 per cent reduction to the remaining 68 per cent of subsidy. My guess is that 20 per cent would be a fair assessment, duly weighting for size of passenger subsidy in 1995/96. This makes a prediction of around 30 per cent overall, well in line with what one has come to expect from the effect of exposure to capital markets and management rivalry. The Railtrack price control calls for an aggregate 16 per cent reduction to 2001 so a very substantial part of the savings must be from franchisees' action to reduce other costs, including those originating in Roscos. When this 'prediction' is held up to critical scrutiny when the final results are known, I would hope we know more about the ways in which the subsidy 'cat' can be skinned.

Applied to the 1995/96 figures the 30 per cent reduction would indicate a passenger subsidy of about £1,200 to £1,300 million a year in current prices. Two conclusions may be drawn. First the 'costs' of privatisation discussed in Annex 1 will have very substantial benefits in subsidy reduction. This time one can predict a continued reduction in public expenditure, far more certainly than in the last 40 years. But this rate of reduction cannot be expected to be repeated with sustained outputs. There will still be a very substantial requirement for subsidy. Second, the regulator, in fixing his sights for the revision of the price control, will have an uncertain, but significant, question of future subsidy levels to contend with.

Annex 3

Cost Attribution and Mark-Ups

Arguably, the most impenetrable part of the whole rail regulatory process so far is the question of assigning Railtrack costs to operators, whether TOCs or freight companies. It is not disputed that charges must reflect costs; the question is how can this be achieved? The regulator has frequently expressed his conviction that charges to all parties must reflect good economic reasoning. I would argue that this is not simply a maxim for seeking economic efficiency; it is also critical to effective regulatory operation in the long run. This is because better regulatory information depends on the commercial interest of the regulated in needing that same information to run his business effectively – to be able to judge the more profitable from the less profitable course of action. In newly privatised utilities, the firm's inheritance of financially relevant accounts for decision making is typically very poor, so that the goad provided by the regulator to develop them, alongside the pressures from the capital market, are important. Railtrack is no exception. The specific context in which questions about attribution of costs arise is in the regulator's duty to encourage competition. So far as costs are concerned, the regulator's role seems difficult, to say the least.

A review of the regulator's publications in the area since November 1994 serves to indicate the problem. A reader of the five publications[36] will find a bewildering array of descriptions about what constitutes 'costs'. Compare the following:

'Short-run variable costs': *Structure*, November 1994
'Long-run incremental costs': *Structure*, November 1994
'Common costs': *Structure*, November 1994
'Short-run costs': *Structure*, November 1994
'Variable costs': *Structure*, November 1994

---

[36] November 1994 on Structure: 'Railtrack's Track Access Charges for Franchised Passenger Services: Developing the Structure of Charges', Office of the Rail Regulator; December 1994 on Competition: 'Competition for Railway Passenger Services', Office of the Rail Regulator; January 1995 on Level of Charges: 'Railtrack's Access Charges for Franchised Passenger Services. The Future Level of Charges', Office of the Rail Regulator; February 1995 on Track Access: 'Framework for the Approval of Railtrack Access Charges for Freight Services', Office of the Rail Regulator; March 1996 on Investment: 'Investment in the Enhancement of the Rail Network', Office of the Rail Regulator.

'Short-run variable costs': *Structure*, November 1994
'Short-run incremental costs': *Structure*, November 1994
'Short-run track usage cost': *Structure*, November 1994
'Avoidable costs': *Track Access*, February 1995
'Truly avoidable costs': *Structure*, November 1994
'Long-run avoidable costs': *Structure*, November 1994
'Stand-alone cost': *Level of Charges*, January 1995
'Freight specific costs': *Level of Charges*, January 1995
'Avoidable costs of freight only lines': *Level of Charges*, January 1995
'Avoidable costs in enhancing network': *Investment*, March 1995

The list probably does not fully represent the variety of terminology and usage in Ofrail's output, which does not maintain a consistent view about what is meant by 'costs'. Consistency is important both for judgements about the applications of subsidy and for understanding how and why Railtrack makes its margins. Most of all, it is necessary for the regulator to be able to understand what underpins the 'control total', so that the competitive aspects of approvals to track usage agreements can be articulated with the question of how much revenue in total to allow. It may be this need was recognised when the oddity of trying to settle the 'structure' ahead of 'levels' of charges was recognised. These papers were issued, respectively, in November 1994 and January 1995 when 'levels of charges' meant deciding where the 'control total' should be. The practical question is what now to do about it.

The reasons for the confusion must be recognised before progress can be made. I would single out the following:

- Largely because of the perceived need in the past to endow increasingly subsidised rail freight operations with some commercial respectability, a cardinal error in the approach to 'costs' has been perpetuated. 'Costs' and thus the terminology used, have driven prices charged, that is, they have been decided with respect to revenue implications. Hence the need to invent new labels to justify outcomes. But 'costs' must always be viewed independently of revenue issues: they are one side of the information (potential outlays) needed to confront revenues (potential sources of cash inflow). If economic advice is to be used, issues concerning supply (costs) must be kept separate from issues concerning demand (revenues).

- An unfortunate by-product is that the connection to the required control total (all Railtrack outlays) is fudged. If one is not consistent in the treatment of all Railtrack outputs, as potential cost drivers, imputation of cost to passenger services is compromised. The awkward question – is the sum of recognised 'costs' equal to the total of allowed revenue? – does not get asked or, if asked, is abandoned as hopelessly difficult. Real commercial pressures always drive out such observations; even if the answers are very rough, the consequences of particular changes of prospective outlay and income have to add up to a viable financial condition for the company as a whole. That is the inevitable consequence of shifting from public to private operation.

- Railway operations have always produced intellectual controversy about 'costs', from the time of the 'traveller to Calais' problem. One can always imagine circumstances in which the 'cost' to the railways saved of not having an extra passenger is the production cost of the ticket (and, we would say nowadays, the associated transactions costs). But in commercial terms this is not a sensible scenario to imagine, so one does not pose the question. Detection and measurement of costs must relate to a decision which can be feasibly made by the regulated company and is relevant for future decisions. I shall suggest later what seems a plausible way of doing this.

- Economics text books are less than helpful in defining 'costs' in a way useful for business decisions. The maxim 'bygones are bygones' is indispensable; the central question for affecting future financial outcomes (cash flows) is what outlays can be avoided, because only outlays presenting a prospect of change by management action can affect future cash flows. What is 'avoidable' is a general quality underlying *all* costs which must be considered before measurement of 'costs' is attempted. There are no 'true' costs which are waiting to be found: costs are what the feasible options allow. This sets up a conflict with general economic advice about what conduces to a 'good allocation' of resources. A regulator must get at the commercial base of costs before entertaining problems of welfare.

- This necessary view of what is or is not a 'cost' does not normally add up to the 'control total' critical for the regulator. Future outlays to be allowed in the revenue (opex and capex) will pass the test of 'avoidability'. But there is always the problem of the remainder of outlays – largely obligations to recognise past investment – which must be included in the control total. Their treatment is part of the question of attributable costs and mark-ups, where the obligation is regarded as a sum to be recouped in the mark-up (see below).

- In short, there is a need to devise a practical approach to measurement of Railtrack costs which will make major questions about franchise change and renewal relate to the allowable total revenue. This requires a fresh approach to measuring those parts of avoidable costs which are attributable to changes in output by franchisees, to rationalise the mark-ups needed to cover remaining avoidable costs, and to extend that treatment to the mark-up to cover the financial commitments (shareholders and others). How far this will involve adoption of existing information and how far the generation of new information, necessarily in conjunction with Railtrack, must be judged after a specification is attempted. I sketch such an approach below.

A consistent procedure for cost attribution and mark-up

The indispensable starting point is the 'control total' of allowed revenue in the current control, for several reasons. It aligns the regulator's needs with the practical needs of Railtrack to know more about its business. Second, it embodies correct notions of avoidability as a necessary characteristic for measuring cost. The 'control total' is , on the outlay side, a set of cash flows representing two principal elements – capex and opex – to keep Railtrack output at the required levels, plus an outlay representing past and present ownership commitments carried forward into the future. The aim is a set of attributable costs plus mark-ups which are relevant to deciding what individual customers should pay and which, when added up, will leave no unexplained gaps between the charges and the original control total. Third, though access charges are committed for the current franchise periods, in practice one needs to work on the present control numbers to test the feasibility of any new approach. Furthermore, at some point, variations in current franchises have to be considered.

The correct approach takes the starting point that Railtrack has an infinite life. No limit is in principle set on the time period over which costs are to be measured. Thus the costs concerned are the sum of future discounted costs. The practical effect is that a sufficiently long period is selected for all important variations in terms of outlays explicitly to be included. In particular, long lasting capital expenditures come into the reckoning, even if fairly distant, and certainly if they occur in the period of the next review, beginning 2002. This treatment abolishes false dichotomies like 'short' and 'long' period as independent constraints on measuring costs. Some 'costs' simply have the characteristic that they occur repeatedly; others are lumpy.[37]

The first attack on the problem therefore treats all costs as if they were fully subject to contractual revision. The manipulation to derive attributable costs should be performed as if this were true of the present control. There are, to be sure, entering any real commercial situation, costs which cannot be changed tomorrow (a firm needs time to hire or fire labour, or supplant one supplier with another). These are deviations which can be grafted on to the basic calculations where deemed necessary; realistically there is a good deal of fluidity in shifting such contracts.

No 'cost' can be measured (attributed to a customer) unless a change of output (services) is predicated. There is no limit in principle to the number of such changes in service. The commercial (and regulatory) needs are to focus on a limited number of feasible and important changes and build up to further cost estimations from there. I would judge that the obvious candidates to start with concern the 25 TOCs and the principal freight operations, the latter viewed initially at least as a group. An appealing test for

---

[37] Once the consistent framework is set up, it becomes possible from the regulator's viewpoint to make controllable variations – for example, in the treatment of competition issues. (A particular case could be argued that a proposed pricing offer for access is made in the light of a firm intention to abandon the relevant costs generators at a definite future point, so a profitable withdrawal strategy is available in particular cases.)

measurement of cost is to select a given percentage reduction in each of these customers' activities, say 20 per cent, and calculate what the effect on the control total and future outlays is of such a reduction in each case. A further test is also relevant: what happens to these outlays if a TOC or freight operation were to be withdrawn entirely? The first calculation will be appropriate for variation in franchises; the sum of each will be relevant for complete changes in customers (such as re-auctioning franchises).

Calculations for each customer set in turn will yield 'attributable' costs. In each case, the sum of such 'attributable' costs together with some extension to the small residual of customers deducted from the total (control plus later) outlays will give (rough) estimates of the 'common' costs which must be the subject of some mark-up rule. The juxtaposition of the 20 per cent and the total withdrawal tests will indicate to what extent economies of system fill are present. In the context of reviewing all future costs, it would be surprising if these displayed much deviance from a proportionate relationship.

The 20 per cent reduction would itself be an average of the activities which characterise a particular TOC or freight operation. Thus in the appropriate cases there will be a mixture of fast and slow trains which will be reduced. This raises a very important point: the costs measured here do not attack directly the question of the gains or losses of any optimising procedure of reallocation of slots, for example, from faster to slower operations. When a given 20 per cent reduction is made, all the rest of operators' outputs are deemed to stay as they are. What the shadow prices of the slots are in postulated different mixes of traffic is not germane to this exercise. That is an interesting question to be approached only with far better knowledge than we now have both of the attributed costs in the sense taken here and the prices which could be extracted from alternative users of slots.[38]

The test of a reduction (or complete withdrawal) of a customer's demands is taken, again, as a result of commercial judgement. The opposite test, of similar increases, seems to me quite inappropriate in this industry. There is no believable prospect of a generally

---

[38] There are echoes of the old short- *versus* long-run marginal cost pricing controversies here. SRMC pricing on today's railways would yield a rather low sum of prices relative to the present sum of any reasonable view of actual outlays.

expanded set of Railtrack services, taking the system as a whole. On the other hand, there is a far more believable prospect of substituting at the present overall level of services, or somewhat lower. This in turn will raise the objection that there are already plans for extension to parts of the system. When these are predicted to occur, they can be added to the forward-looking calculations, thus perhaps raising (net) the level of the relevant control total. The operator sets may be revised in parallel. The larger set is still best treated by the 'reduction' tests.

What percentage of total outlays is likely to be revealed as 'attributable' or 'common' respectively by these tests? My guess is that the latter will be, in traditional railway terms, surprisingly low. Some indication of lower limits is perhaps given by the percentages of 'apportioned' common costs appearing on page 37 of the Framework as 43 per cent.[39] My reason for predicting the outcomes of the exercises sketched here to be lower is a result first of including all future outlays in the calculation, and second of the marked geographical differentiation of the UK railway system. There are very considerable parts of customers' demands which do not overlap geographically. There are still strong influences from the old separate company systems, which overlap rather little. To the extent that they do not, they will be attributed with all future relevant costs.

The central fact of geographical differentiation will also lend itself to further treatment of the rather rare instances of genuine competition between operators for the use of particular bottleneck sections. These essentially occur in the approaches to London. There it may be sensible to carve out 'London approaches' as a region in which one might relax the general rules on taking the existing pattern of use as simply reducing, in turn, the operations involved in holding other things constant. The procedure I have described in a sense systematises what Ofrail has termed 'what-if' exercises in cost determination. The London approaches could be made the subject of 'what-if' exercises of a rather different kind, linked to possible variations in system operation and investment.

---

[39] This is reached by deduction from 100 per cent of 'short-term variable costs', 'stations and depot access charges', and 'long-run incremental costs' which reflect allocation conventions rather than the tests proposed here.

Having started the process of cost attribution and mark-up in this way, it will be possible to proceed to lower levels of attribution and mark-ups within the 26 groups, nested in the higher-level calculations. In each case, the essential 'control' total from which to start will be that indicated by applying the attribution costs plus the required mark-up to sum to the highest level control total. At, say, the total freight business level, the 'control total' will include the mark-up representing its share of non-attributable costs calculated at the 26 group level. The 'Freight business' itself can be expected to have its own set of non-attributable costs which will be revealed by repeating the tests of attribution for each set of freight services comprising the freight business. Assertions about 'cross-subsidy' can then be put in the proper context of a level of attribution and mark-up to which they are intended to refer. The text makes a suggestion about basing the indicative limit for particular freight charges on the freight business control total, which is derived at the 26 group freight business control total level, and which will necessarily include the result of applying a mark-up rule at that level. The calculations will also, when developed for all 26, form a consistent context in which particular 'what-if' calculations – directed to system or service charges – can be assessed.

Finally, it should be noted that if the Franchise Director is contemplating a thorough-going CBA analysis of the justification of subsidies, the cost exercises I have described are an essential input to his work.

CHAIRMAN'S COMMENTS

John Swift QC

THAT WAS A MOST STIMULATING PAPER. As one who has been near the centre of the institutional framework for almost three years as regulator, I am delighted to find that Michael Beesley is broadly positive in his endorsement of the means by which this privatisation programme has been executed. I share with him his conclusion that what we have at the end of 1996 is not necessarily what those people who thought it all up in 1992/93 had in mind. I apologise for those who have heard this reference before, but about two and half years ago I joined Jimmy Knapp at a seminar, at a time when the tide of public opinion was flowing very strongly against the whole policy for the privatisation of the railways. I put forward the argument, which seemed non-contentious, that the government would not have embarked on the most difficult privatisation of all had it not gained experience since 1984 from the privatisations of telecommunications, gas, electricity and water. So, said Jimmy, 'it's just an act of faith, is it?'

Two years ago, privatisation was an act of faith that in the process of reconstruction sufficiently strong commercial organisations either existed, or could be created, which would take over the massive burden which British Rail had handled since 1947 or thereabouts. A year ago, no franchises had been awarded. Although, as Michael said, the government took the ultimate risk on the subsidy, it was a black time for those who believed their faith in market processes would be rewarded. Yet within a period of less than a year, fairly robust markets have been developed in supply of infrastructure, maintenance and renewal services to Railtrack, and in the markets for acquisition of the franchises.

Recently, when French representatives of the Assemblée Nationale and the Senate were listening to my explanation of the process of privatisation in this country and what had been achieved, I was met with stark incredulity that anybody could embark upon any such process. But who should be among the new arrivals on the scene but a subsidiary of Société Genérale des Eaux connected to the water industry which has already acquired two of the rail franchises? These are critically important franchises, supplying central commuter services into London and associated markets. This sparks confidence that the British programme could well be exported. The deficits that so far have been accumulated by other member states of the union to commit to the maintenance and extension of the national railway network are now coming under increasing scrutiny, not least as a result of Maastricht.

As Michael has said, there is a prospect of x-efficiencies through better use of capital and labour in privatised markets. This will be of major importance in the development of our own railways. But I differ from Michael in one point of emphasis. He says the process which has been followed is in many ways another stage in a 40 year battle to contain railway subsidy, and that we are engaged in a continuing battle to raise the share of rail against competing modes of travel. We have emphasised that the various contracts, the licences, and the subsidy are means to an end to enable the industry to deliver better products and better services to the benefit of passengers. That is the goal which we have set ourselves at the Office of the Rail Regulator since December 1993. It has been a slow and uncomfortable process, but I really do believe that we now see prospects for the delivery of that better performance upon which the whole political justification of the Railways Act 1993 depends.

So, Michael is setting a good example to other economists and to political commentators in trying to extend the intellectual arguments that are necessary to derive the appropriate mechanisms for the future. I will not seek in this instance to defend my setting of the prices of the monopoly supplier, which according to you arose partly by design and partly by accident. I would like to believe they were a result of rational decisions by me and my advisers and my employees. It was a difficult decision. Most regulators who deal with privatised utilities look at the four legs of regulation of prices – namely operating expenditure, capital expenditure, the regulatory asset value and the rate of return. They are, as Alec Douglas Home might have said, the match-sticks of regulatory control. As an independent regulator for Railtrack, we had to set prices with only two of them. We had views about operating expenditure and capital expenditure, based on Railtrack's plans; but as for rates of return, assessments of cost of capital risk, the regulatory asset value and how these would be taken into the market view of Railtrack, we did not know either the timetable of privatisation, or the market acceptability of what we were doing. There again, the Treasury and the Government took the risk. In May 1996 Railtrack was floated as a corporation not needing to earn a rate of return calculated at 8 per cent on the modern equivalent value of its assets as had earlier been advocated. When one has estimates of asset value that vary as widely as £6.5 billion to £10.5 billion, then regulators should stick to the two matchsticks with which they are reasonably familiar.

The role of the railway regulator is not limited to the regulation of the network prices of the monopoly controller of the infrastructure. So long as we have a subsidised railway, many political and social considerations are within the scope of a regulator; for example, fares, passenger service requirements, inter-availability, network benefits, conditions of carriage and provision of special facilities for disabled persons. This is not a simple industry to which one can apply the standard rules of economically efficient regulation. There is a great deal of balancing, experiment and risk-taking to be done. As a lawyer coming into regulation, I can say that these are part of the fun of the job!

9

REGULATION, DIVERSIFICATION AND

THE SEPARATE LISTING OF UTILITIES[1]

Tim Jenkinson

Keble College, Oxford

and

Colin Mayer

School of Management Studies, University of Oxford

Introduction

ACCOUNTING, STOCK MARKET AND BOND MARKET INFORMATION are key ingredients in the regulation of utilities. Diversification of utilities out of their core regulated activities into related and unrelated businesses diminishes the quality of information available to regulators. This is particularly acute where utilities are subject to acquisitions by other firms and mergers with other utilities. At a conference at the Adam Smith Institute on 13 December 1995, Mr Ian Byatt, the Director General of Water Services, called for separate Stock Exchange listings for all regulated water companies following take-overs or mergers. Writing in the *Financial Times* on 9 January 1996, Mr Byatt argued that a stock exchange listing would provide valuable information about a utility's market valuation and increase transparency by requiring the publication of separate accounts for the regulated business. He noted that a condition for a stock exchange listing of a subsidiary is that a majority of directors are independent of the parent and argued that this would be beneficial in ensuring that decisions taken by a utility's board were in its shareholders' interests.

---

[1] The paper was presented by Colin Mayer.

Mr Byatt's proposal evoked a storm of protest from the industry. Mr Michael Hoffman, the President of the Water Services Association, argued in a letter to the *Financial Times* on 4 January 1996 that utilities are 'already elaborately "ringfenced"...and provide the regulator with all the information which he might wish to have'. Concern was expressed by him and others about the cost of separate listings and the loss of control for parent firms which they would entail. Even so, separate listings or their closely related 'tracker' shares have been discussed in relation to a number of acquisitions since then.

The issue is one that goes to the heart of the regulatory process. As the paper will argue, it touches on two key issues in regulation: access to information and the control rights of different parties. The purpose of this paper is, first, to consider the effect of diversifications on utility regulation and, second, to evaluate the merits and deficiencies of separate listings and tracker shares as responses to resulting regulatory problems. It describes listing rules in the UK, considers the pricing and trading of separately listed shares, discusses their impact on control exercised by parent firms, and considers their implications for utility regulation. Conclusions are then drawn.

The Problem

The recent spate of acquisitions of utilities has brought to the fore a generic problem in regulation which to date has only received limited attention. Following privatisation, many utilities diversified their activities out of their core business. In some cases diversification involved an expansion into closely related businesses, such as waste management in the water companies, and in others took utilities further away from their core activities (for example into foreign markets). Much diversification was achieved through acquisitions and mergers, some through joint ventures and some through green field site developments. In all cases the effect was to create companies only part of whose activities corresponded with their core utilities.

This raised a number of regulatory issues. *First*, there was a concern that where there were transactions between the utility and the remainder of the business they may not occur at commercial prices. By setting prices above or below those available elsewhere in the market, resources could be transferred from the utility to the group and out of the reach of the regulator.

Second, share price information is an important part of the information available to the regulator. It is used in determining the cost of capital of utilities through, for example, computing the beta coefficient of companies in the Capital Asset Pricing Model. Share price information is also a central component in the determination of the past performance of firms. Much of the debate about returns to investors has focused on share price performance.

Still more significantly, share prices can be used as indicators of whether regulation is unduly onerous or lax. The ratio of a firm's market valuation to its replacement cost (Tobin's q) is widely used as a performance measure. Where the valuation is in excess of unity then a firm is expected to earn a rate of return on the replacement cost of its assets which is greater than its cost of capital. In the case of a regulated firm, the relevant cost base is that used by the regulator in setting price caps. A ratio of market to regulatory asset valuations which is in excess of unity implies that the market anticipates a rate of return on the regulatory asset base which is in excess of the cost of capital and a ratio of less than unity implies that anticipated rates of return are less than the cost of capital. Immediately after a regulatory settlement, the ratio therefore provides a succinct measure of the stance of regulation without requiring the identification of the cost of capital: a value greater than unity signifies that regulation is more lax than was intended and a value less than unity indicates unduly onerous regulation.

The difficulty which diversifications present is that share prices relate to group rather than core activities of the utility. As diversification proceeded, the relevance of share prices to the regulation gradually diminished. Even prior to the recent wave of take-overs, share price evidence became increasingly difficult to interpret.

The response of regulators to diversification was twofold. *First*, where possible, rules were introduced requiring companies to subject their transactions to market testing. Contracting out to third parties avoided potential conflicts but where trades between related firms occurred then they should be transacted at commercial prices. *Second*, regulators sought the ring-fencing of core from other activities and companies were required to lodge regulatory accounts for their utilities distinct from published accounts for the group.

These responses raise several difficulties for regulators. *First*, strict enforcement of market testing involves the regulator in detailed and costly monitoring. *Second*, there are numerous problems in interpreting accounting information. Accounting profits and asset valuations are particularly subjective in capital intensive companies such as utilities with long-lived assets. *Third*, the above responses do not deal with the diminishing significance of share price information. The natural response of the regulator to diminishing quality of information is to seek more and to become more directly involved in auditing information supplied.

While these problems have been present for several years, the recent spate of acquisitions has significantly magnified their severity. Most of the Regional Electricity Companies (RECs) have been recently acquired and multi-utilities have been created from firms in one utility sector taking over utilities in other sectors (for example, in electricity and water). Instead of share prices being somewhat distorted by diversifications, they bear little relation to core activities at all in utilities which are acquired by larger groups. Typically in an acquisition, the acquiror is around 10 times the size of the target firm. This will not, in general, apply to acquisition of utilities but it is still true that the share price of the target firm is effectively extinguished.

In addition, concerns about transfer pricing are intensified where utilities are acquired by others. It is true that potential divergence of interests between core and group is possible wherever there is diversification but until recently diversified firms were essentially utilities with a few other activities. Where they are acquired by other firms, they are generally only one of a range of activities performed by the parent.

As mentioned above, the response will be for regulation to become increasingly interventionist in seeking more information and further controls. In addition, the potential for incorrect decisions based on incomplete information increases. For example, where there is a suspicion that resources are being withdrawn from utilities there will be a natural tendency to seek draconian restrictions on dividend distributions from subsidiary to parent.

It is against the background that some regulatory response to the changing structure of utilities will occur that the proposal for separate listing should be considered.

Listing Rules

The London Stock Exchange lays down a set of rules regarding the listing of companies. The minimum size of a company (including a subsidiary) to be floated on the exchange is £700,000 and at least 25 per cent of the company's shares must be in public hands. Accounting information must be provided for at least three years prior to the issue.

While the above are generally applicable to listings, two sets of rules which are particularly relevant to the listing of subsidiaries are those concerning controlling shareholders (sections 3.12 and 3.13) and transactions with related parties (Chapter 11 of the Stock Exchange rules).

Where there is a controlling shareholder, the applicant (that is, the subsidiary seeking a listing) 'must be capable at all times of operating and making decisions independently of any controlling shareholder and all transactions and relationships in the future between the applicant and any controlling shareholder must be at arm's length and on a normal commercial basis' (section 3.13). A majority of the directors of the board of the subsidiary must be independent of the parent firm.

Shareholders have to be notified about transactions with the parent firm and their approval has to be sought in advance with the related party abstaining from voting on the transaction (sections 11.4 and 11.5). Minority shareholders therefore have the right to be consulted about and approve transactions with the parent firm.

These rules are quite different from those in several other countries. For example, in Germany if a company controls at least 75 per cent of another company's share capital then it can pass a resolution at the subsidiary's AGM to enter into a control and profit-transfer contract which allows the parent to issue instructions to the subsidiary's management board (Vorstand). Such a contract must 'adequately compensate' minority shareholders and provide them with an option to tender their shares at a reasonable price. Where they feel aggrieved shareholders can appeal to regional courts and if successful have the control and profit-transfer contract cancelled. There is therefore a minimum level of minority protection in Germany. However, it falls far short of that in the UK where regulation requires that the board reflects minority rather than controlling shareholder interests in the event of disputes between the parties.

Pricing and Trading

Approximately one-fifth of the German stock market comprises listed firms with a super-majority-listed corporate shareholder holding at least 75 per cent of voting share capital. Listing subsidiaries is particularly common amongst banks, breweries, insurance companies and some industrial conglomerates. There are several regional utilities which are owned by larger utilities (for example, RWE, VEBA and Bayernwerk) or by public sectors (for example, towns and counties).

Many of the subsidiary listings result from take-overs and mergers by parent firms which acquired less than 100 per cent of equity. In some cases these result in free floats which are less than 5 per cent of equity; in other cases, free floats are in excess of 20 per cent.

What information do partial listings supply about the valuation of subsidiaries and how does this compare with the valuations of widely held firms? There are two considerations. The first is the liquidity of partial listings and the second is the take-over bid premium. Where a substantial proportion of shares is held by a controlling shareholder and not available for trade, free floats may be highly illiquid. This clearly applies to the very small free floats in Germany. However, Stock Exchange rules in the UK are designed to protect minorities and encourage trading in partial listings.

Most utilities are large firms with high market capitalisations. As Table 1 records, 25 per cent of their market capitalisation places most of them within the top 400 firms on the UK stock market. For example, 25 per cent of Norweb's shares would have a value equal to that

TABLE 1:
Market Capitalizations

Company	Market Capital (£ millions)	Rank*	0·25xMarket Capital	Rank
Southern Electricity	2,449	73 (79)	612	196
Midlands Electricity	1,860	94 (104)	465	231
Norweb	1,690	102 (115)	422	243
Manweb	1,074	151 (147)	268	329
South Wales Electricity	853	174 (169)	213	367
Northern Electricity	772	181 (148)	193	394
Northumbria Water	692	189 (219)	173	419

Note to Table 1:
*Rank refers to the ranking of firms by market capitalisation at end-1995. Since rankings could have been affected by bid premia during the year, they are also shown at end-1994 in brackets.

of the 243rd largest firm on the stock market, making the value of its free float greater than that of Taylor Woodrow, National Express, Stagecoach Holdings and George Wimpey. Utilities are prominent firms with strong name recognition, suggesting that they will be widely held and traded even as partial listings. There are several examples of firms with dominant shareholders which have been widely traded, not least Wellcome before its take-over by Glaxo and many of the utilities, such as BT, that were sold in separate tranches.

Since it will not be possible to acquire partially listed utilities through tender offers in the market, share prices will not incorporate bid premia associated with potential changes in control. Instead, they will reflect the value of the dividend stream under existing management. However, that is precisely the valuation which is relevant for regulatory purposes. The stock market capitalisation of a partially listed utility will reflect the present value of the dividend stream to its owners, both majority and minority shareholders.

In that regard, it has been suggested that stock exchange listings increase the cost of acquisitions: the price at which the utility is purchased includes a bid premium while the price at which the minority shareholding is sold on the stock market does not. However, this argument is quite misleading. The initial purchase includes a premium to account for the control rights which the acquiring company enjoys. When a sale of shares occurs the bidder loses a claim on the dividend stream of the subsidiary but not the control rights which the acquisition conferred. To the extent that regulation limits parent company control and protects minorities, it sustains a higher dividend stream for minorities and therefore a higher share valuation at which the minority shares will be sold off. Bidders cannot be made worse off by a fairly priced disposal of shares in a subsidiary. Furthermore, the information imparted about the valuation of the utility from a separate listing may actually encourage a more active take-over market.

It has also been suggested that there are significant transaction costs in organising a flotation. However, all that is required is for the subsidiary to allow trading to take place in some of its shares – an introduction to the stock market rather than an offer for sale. There is a particularly straightforward way in which these could be organised – that is, through a *pro rata* distribution of shares in the subsidiary to the parent firm shareholders. This is equivalent to a scrip issue but in shares of the subsidiary instead of the parent firm. Like a scrip issue it avoids any possibility of dilution of value of existing shareholder investments.

The direct costs of listings are modest. There is an initial listing cost of £31,000 for issues of less than £200 million and of £45,000 for issues of less than £500 million. Thereafter, there is an annual expenditure of £14,000 for issues with a nominal value of less than £200 million and of £17,000 for issues of less than £500 million.

Control

A subsidiary listing can take two forms. *First*, parent firms could be left to determine how they treat minority shareholders. The share price would then simply reflect the value which investors attach to a company in the knowledge that the parent firm can exploit the value of the subsidiary. In that case, the listing of the subsidiary would have information but no control implications. This is the process which operates in Germany; disputes between shareholders have been commonplace. For example, in the case of Paulaner-Salvator-Thomasbrau AG, the Bavarian High Court ruled in favour of minority shareholders in a dispute about compensation following a take-over. The case cost DM75 million and lasted about 14 years. In a large majority of cases, the final judgement favours minority interests by, for example, requiring payment of higher levels of compensation. However, the parent firm may not wish to exploit minority interests for several reasons. It may use the subsidiary as a way of raising share capital and therefore be concerned about maintaining the value of the subsidiary's shares. It may also use the valuation as a way of setting objectives for the management of the subsidiary.

The *second* form which a listing could take is to require the parent firm to protect the interests of minority shareholders. This would involve the parent firm in taking decisions which are to the benefit of the minority as well as the controlling shareholder. In this case, there are control as well as information implications limiting the extent to which parent firms are able to control the activities of the subsidiary.

Stock Exchange rules in the UK impose the second form of listing: there are control as well as information consequences. They prevent wealth transfers occurring from subsidiary to parent firm. They do not prevent large shareholders from exercising control in the interests of the shareholding population as a whole. However, where there is a divergence of interest between minority and parent firm they allocate control to the minority interests.

Tracker Shares

In the US, General Motors (GM) created shareholding classes with control rights which were similar to those of separate listings in the UK. In 1984, GM took over EDS, an electronics company, and issued a new class of common stock, GM 'E'. In 1985 it took over Hughes, an aviation firm, and issued a similar class of stock, GM 'H'. These shares were designed to 'track' the performance of the subsidiaries and provide management and employees with share-price-related incentives. Approximately 12 US companies have introduced tracker shares.

The subsidiaries were owned and controlled by GM. Class E and H shareholders received dividends based on the earnings of their respective subsidiaries. The earnings of the subsidiaries were excluded from the income base available for distribution to the main class of shares in GM. Dividend distributions to all shareholders, including those in the subsidiaries, were determined by the main board of GM. Shareholders in GM 'E' and GM 'H' class shares had voting rights in GM, initially on the basis of one vote for every two shares held. The board of directors in EDS comprised eight directors from the subsidiary and four from GM and there was a similar arrangement in Hughes. In addition, there was a Capital Stock Committee of the General Board of GM which was concerned with ensuring equitable treatment of all classes of GM shareholders. Amendments which affected the rights, powers or privileges of one of the classes of stock had to be agreed by that class. Any increase in the number of authorised shares had to be approved by all shareholders voting together as a class and the individual classes voting on their own. There were 483·7 million GM 'E' shares outstanding and daily trading volume on the New York Stock Exchange was usually between 600,000 and 700,000 shares.

The main distinction between the GM classes and separate listings was that shares in the former related to the parent firm and in the latter to the subsidiary. Ownership and control of the GM subsidiaries resided in the parent in which there were several classes of shares with different voting rights attached. However, the Capital Stock Committee of the main board and the independent directors of the subsidiary boards offered a degree of protection to shareholders which was similar to that of UK Stock Exchange rules.

There are several drawbacks to the use of tracker shares relative to separate listings in the context of utilities:

1. Shareholders in the subsidiary have reduced voting rights. This is designed to reflect their lower proportionate interests in the total assets of the parent firm. However, it means that minorities are still prone to abuse by majorities. A motion to transfer assets from the subsidiary to the parent could be carried on a simple majority vote. While nothing as blatant as this could be expected to be passed, it illustrates the balance of interests which the board represents.

2. The voting rights attached to different classes of shares should alter as the proportion of assets in different parts of the business changes. This will present particular difficulties in utilities which are just in the process of building up their non-core businesses.

3. It is difficult to imagine creating tracker shares in utilities as they are currently constituted. Utility assets comprise a high proportion of the assets of groups. The tracker shares would therefore represent a majority of the total shares of the group and nearly all of the votes would have to be allocated to shareholders in the subsidiary. This will create an unbalanced and somewhat perverse voting structure.

4. Tracker shares could only be introduced in the context of utilities which have been acquired by other firms and thereby become components of larger businesses. In other utilities, the application of tracker shares would require holdings to be reversed, that is, instead of having groups owning utilities and other businesses, utilities would have to become the parent firms owning subsidiaries operating in other areas. But this undermines the ring-fencing of utilities from other businesses.

Tracker shares were designed to monitor and provide high-powered incentives to managers of subsidiaries. They are not well suited to situations in which there is concern about regulation creating divergences of interest between shareholders in parent firms and stakeholders (including customers) in subsidiaries.

Problems of Separate Listings

Separate listings are not without their problems too. Consider the following examples:

Example 1: The parent firm wishes to rationalise the arrangements for billing customers by merging the billing systems of the parent and subsidiary firm.

Both companies derive cost savings as a consequence of the rationalisation. However, the allocation of cost savings between the two firms may differ appreciably. In the event of the rationalisation being agreed through arm's length arrangements between independent firms (through, for example, setting up a joint billing company), there might be an extended period of negotiation regarding the allocation of costs between the two firms. The minority shareholders or the independent directors could object to the allocation of benefits between parent and subsidiary and thereby delay or prevent a cost-saving rationalisation from taking place. Outright ownership of the subsidiary could therefore reduce negotiation costs and ensure that value-enhancing transactions occur.

Example 2: The parent firm wishes to arrange the provision of engineering or construction services for the subsidiary. Regulatory rules require that such services are put out to market testing. The parent firm undercuts alternative bids but minority shareholders object to the conduct of the tendering process.

There are several reasons why minorities may object. *First*, they may be concerned about the extent to which supply from the parent firm will increase dependency to the possible detriment of the long-term performance of the subsidiary. *Second*, minority interests may be concerned about the conduct of such competitive bids and suspect that influence has been brought to bear on management. Objections may therefore be lodged with the Stock Exchange giving rise to protracted periods of negotiation.

Example 3: Minorities object to the payment of a dividend.

The parent firm may wish to fund some of its own activities out of resources from the subsidiary. The tax implications of a distribution may be different for minority shareholders from those of the parent firm or its investors.

In summary, while Stock Exchange rules, which require that the board of directors should be able to make decisions independently of the majority shareholder, are designed to limit the scope for abuse by controlling shareholders of minorities, they do not remove the possibility of *conflicts of interests* and increased *transaction costs* between the parent and subsidiary in respect of related party transactions. These are potentially the most significant costs of separate listings but it is unclear how quantitatively significant they are.

Implications for Utility Regulation

The presence of minority shareholders is therefore potentially costly for controlling shareholders. However, the proposal to introduce separate listings for targets of bids has to be considered in the context of the operation of the regulatory system.

Regulators require information on which they can establish whether transactions between utilities and their parents are being undertaken on normal commercial criteria. They need to have the power to intervene and prevent transfers of resources from taking place where they believe these are acting to the detriment of the utility and its customers. They are therefore concerned about similar issues to those which affect the minority shareholders in a publicly listed firm. There will be disputes between the regulator and the company analogous to those between minority and majority shareholders.

The key question that therefore arises is not whether share prices of partially listed subsidiaries are perfect indicators of utility performance or whether there are limitations imposed on parent firm control by the presence of separate listings. It is whether the information provided by the stock market is superior to that which would otherwise be available to regulators, and whether exercise of control by minority shareholders is superior to control by regulators.

A key principle guiding privatisation is that market processes dominate government and regulation. The valuation attributed by a large number of independent investors is superior to that of a single regulator and private investors are better placed to establish when a controlling shareholder is acting against their interests. The separate listing proposal is therefore attractive, both to those who wish to reduce the scope of regulation and enhance the function of the market, and to those who wish to support the regulator in protecting customer interests.

It should not furthermore be regarded as necessarily unhelpful to utilities or their new owners. The benchmark against which the separate listing proposal should be compared is not one where unlimited control can be exercised over the subsidiary. In the absence of separate listings, the regulator will have to perform the function of minority shareholders in avoiding wealth transfers from subsidiary to parent. Clearly, one of the concerns which utilities may have about the proposal is that minority shareholders will be better placed to do this than the regulator. It is, however, unlikely that on average there will be greater abuse under one system than the other. As suggested above, the real risk which uninformed regulation poses is of arbitrary and periodically draconian judgements. Directors of subsidiaries who are required to reflect the interests of shareholders broadly defined are better placed to make informed judgements than arm's-length regulators. Furthermore, the requirement to publish separate accounts opens the process to public scrutiny.

Companies which have already completed acquisitions of utilities will feel understandably aggrieved if the rules of the game are changed after the event. All of the acquisitions of utilities have involved the payment of substantial bid premia, frequently in excess of 20 per cent. One possible explanation for such high premia (which are not dissimilar to those generally observed in acquisitions of unregulated firms) is that bidders earn substantial rents from control of subsidiaries. If they are subsequently forced to abide by rules which limit their potential control, they could reasonably claim that they have overpaid for the acquisition and that compensation is required. However, it is unclear that this claim would be justified.

As noted above, the price of the minority shares will reflect the dividend stream which the parent firm is forgoing. The greater is the protection which Stock Exchange rules offer minorities, the higher will be the predicted stream of dividends and therefore the greater the share price of the subsidiary. If revenue is raised from the listing the parent will be appropriately rewarded for the loss of control, and if shares are simply distributed to existing shareholders then the value of the distribution should be exactly equal to the reduction in value of the parent firm. Either way there is no cost imposed on the parent firm's shareholders.

Separate listings are relevant to a number of other more general debates about utilities. The suggestion has been made that utilities should be run in the interests of a broader constituency than their shareholders. They have responsibilities which extend to their customers and communities and this should be reflected in the way in which they are managed and controlled. The difficulty which acquisitions and diversification present for this view is that they blur the distinction between utilities and other companies. It would, for example, be difficult to appoint stakeholder representatives to the board of Hanson plc (at least in its integrated form) simply because it controls Eastern Electricity. However, they could be appointed to a separate board of the subsidiary.

Partial listings also go to the heart of the concept of a utility. To date, the definition of a utility has corresponded to the range of services set out in the regulatory contract; for example, a water company is a bundle of contracts to supply water and sewerage services. But acquisitions raise the issue of whether a utility is a cost base or a collection of services. The formation of United Utilities out of Norweb and North West Water reflects a belief that electricity and water services can be delivered more cheaply in combination than separately. On that basis, it could be argued that the creation of separate boards is a wholly inappropriate response and firms should instead be allowed to determine the bundling of services which achieves lowest costs.

Were it possible to determine the price at which services should be supplied without reference to underlying costs, there would be a great deal of substance to this argument. Regulators would determine a set of services and prices, and firms would be free to choose how and in what combination they provided them. The difficulty with this argument is that the regulator cannot in practice determine prices for services independently of the cost structure of firms. A key element in regulation is to be able to measure the value of capital inputs. The regulator or the government therefore takes a view about the appropriate bundling of services, for example that water and sewerage services should be considered in combination, and then draws a ring-fence around that particular bundle. Over time the appropriate bundling may alter as technologies change to include, for example, electricity distribution with the provision of water services, but the regulatory process means that this decision cannot be left entirely to the discretion of firms. The partial listing then relates to the bundle of services defined by the regulatory contract.

Conclusion

Diversifications of utilities out of their core activities have posed problems for regulators. Those problems are particularly acute where utilities have been acquired by other companies. Responses from regulators in trying to ring-fence regulated activities, requiring the submission of regulatory accounts and enforcing market testing of transactions with related parties, are difficult to implement.

This paper investigates the claim that the partial listing of utilities which have been acquired by other companies would assist in the regulatory process. Stock Exchange rules in the UK require that a listed subsidiary should be able to take decisions independently of the controlling shareholder. Minority shareholders have to be informed and have the right to vote on transactions with the parent firm. These rules are designed to avoid abuse of minority shareholder interests and, where such abuse can take place, to confer control on the minority rather than the majority shareholders. They do not limit the exercise of control to increase shareholder wealth as a whole. However, they also do not eliminate potential conflicts between different classes of shareholders. Negotiation and bargaining costs may increase and it is possible that mutually advantageous transactions may not always take place. We consider these to be the main potential costs of separate listings.

The paper has also evaluated a number of alternative arguments, namely that partial listings will be (i) illiquid, (ii) costly to organise, (iii) underpriced relative to widely held utilities, and (iv) a disincentive to the acquisition of utilities. It has not found these arguments compelling. It records that (i) the market capitalisations of the free floats of utilities would be substantial, (ii) they can be distributed at low cost in the forms of scrip issues to existing shareholders, (iii) their share price is an appropriate measure of their value to investors, and (iv) partial listing should not reduce shareholder value and hence not affect incentives to acquisitions.

Instead, the paper argues that the main question that partial listings raise is whether they provide superior information on performance to that which would otherwise be available to regulators and whether they can more effectively control wealth transfers from the utility than the regulator. There is a strong political as well as economic appeal in using market rather than regulatory mechanisms to limit potential abuse and there may be significant advantages to utilities in reducing arbitrary and ill-informed regulatory interventions which may otherwise result from acquisitions. These benefits have to be set against the increased negotiation and bargaining costs which separate listings may entail.

CHAIRMAN'S COMMENTS

Professor Geoffrey Whittington

I CONGRATULATE COLIN MAYER ON GIVING AN EXCELLENT PAPER. He has explained the implications of separate listings for the cost of capital but he offered bonuses as well in measuring profitability, transfer pricing and so on.

My first response on reading the paper was to think that it is persuasive. Why was I so foolish as a member of the MMC Panel on the proposed take-over of South West Water to reject Severn Trent's argument that a separate listing would be a suitable remedy for its take-over of South West Water? The issue concerned a water-on-water merger. This raised the regulator's problem of identifying potential efficiencies in the industry through comparative competition.

The arguments usually made for mergers are anticipated economies of scope arising from common management, such as closing one head office, or imposing a particular management or engineering style that is alleged to be successful. That inevitably reduces variety in the industry. In that case separate listing is not going to give the regulator independent observations. There are going to be two similar listed water companies rather than two dissimilar ones. Severn Trent, of course, will say that it is going to be a much better water company, but regulators are interested in the nature of the separateness. This depends on independence of operation, enabling companies to reveal the different types of efficiency which are possible within an industry, so I do not have to disagree with Colin on those grounds. He was talking about something different, the case of diversification. That is not a case where two companies of the same industry come together, diminishing the regulator's ability to observe variety of practice and efficiency in the industry, but rather the case where two utilities in different industries are merged.

Where you get diversification, as with electricity companies taking over water companies, the interest of the regulator is in observing the two separate operations, to identify that in which the regulator is

307

particularly interested, rather than the draconian view that you should not allow take-overs at all because they suppress diversity in a particular industry. Separate listing might seem to be an appealing solution to the problem of observing the separate activity. Take-overs are the standard mechanism for inducing efficiency in firms listed on the Stock Exchange, and separate listing allows take-overs, whilst preserving accounting separation. Even if a take-over does not happen, there is at least a threat of take-over happening which keeps people on their toes. If you remove that, you remove a spur to efficiency.

Superficially at least, the solution the paper offered is very appealing. The idea is that the regulator does not have to do all the work, such as getting transparent accounting, and having to estimate costs of capital by unscrambling the cost of capital in one big firm. Instead, the minority shareholders will do it. They are expected to ensure that the regulator can observe the separate performance and valuation of the regulated company. Colin made a number of assertions about how good shareholders are at doing this and that this is a superior solution to having interfering regulators getting in the way. When I was at the MMC, I expect I was an 'interfering regulator', so I naturally think of possible reasons why that would not happen. I am going to raise three possible problems with this model. I will then make a couple of more detailed observations.

First, is there congruence between the regulator's interest and the minority shareholders' interests? If I am a minority shareholder, what I want is money, dividends, capital gains and earnings per share. I want my shares to grow and be prosperous. I do not care how they grow or prosper; whether from the regulated industry or elsewhere is irrelevant so long as the company gives me a good deal. But the regulator is interested in the balance between the customer and the shareholder. As a shareholder I am not interested in that at all. I may be a customer as well which may restrain me, but I am mainly interested in my returns. So why should I work to enable the regulator to restrain my company and possibly allow lower dividends in the future?

Colin argues that this is not the case because it is in the interests of the shareholder to maximise profits, and profit incentives arise through the regulator's activity in fixing the pricing formula. Nevertheless, suppose, for instance, there is a pass through of costs in the pricing formula, and the holding company charges 'too much' for managing the subsidiary (that is, the regulator has wrongly allowed an excessive amount through the regulatory formula). As a shareholder, I do not care because it is all going to be passed on to consumers. I do not mind if the costs are 'too much', so long as the costs are passed on to the consumer. There is not a direct congruence between the interests of the shareholder, even the minority shareholder, and the interests of the regulator. There are similarities and overlaps but they are by no means identical. An important issue is the extent to which they are congruent in practice.

The *second* issue is the nature of shareholders' information for monitoring companies. Shareholders receive financial accounts, not management accounts. There has been a lot of controversy about financial accounting recently, associated with issues of corporate governance. It has improved a lot (I hope) because of the activities of the Accounting Standards Board, of which I am a member, but it is still far from perfect. On issues such as related party transactions, directly related to Colin's concerns, there was extreme opposition from some firms. A great deal of criticism was directed at the Board. It may not have forced through transparency on the scale that Colin would like to see or that his system would require. The regulator, on the other hand, has access to management accounting data, and can request additional information which the receiver of financial statements cannot do. This information is usually backed up by the threat of using the regulator's power to enforce licence amendments. Many shareholders would like to be able to enforce licence amendments in order to increase their dividends, reduce directors' pay, to do all sorts of things they have been grumbling about lately, not least in regulated utilities. Shareholders do not have this power and we must not put too much extra weight on the shareholder, already struggling to keep our system of governance effective.

The *third* question fits in with the sort of pro-market approach the paper was advocating. If shareholders are more effective than regulators, why has separate listing not happened already? Why do more companies not have listed subsidiaries on the Stock Exchange? They are not regarded with great favour in the City. Now, maybe the City is wrong or maybe the City is ignorant, but it is the City and investors who are going to have to operate the system. At the moment they vote with their feet. It seems that listed subsidiaries do not fit easily into the way in which the stock market works. The fact that company law has to deal with oppression of minorities shows that

309

minority shareholders can have a harsh deal. Colin very fairly referred to some of these things, but he might have under-estimated them.

He also used the analogy of the German system. The German system is different, in several ways, such as the structure of shareholding, corporate governance, the role of banks and the existence of many more closely held companies. Comparison with, or transition to, that system is not easy. He could have referred to other countries where listed subsidiaries are quite common, for example Sweden. They have rather a small number of very large companies and tend to have chain holdings in subsidiaries and sub-subsidiaries. It also happens in South Africa, for the same reason; big companies like Anglo-American have subsidiaries listed on the Johannesburg Stock Exchange. But again the way shares are held in those countries, and the way the system is operated, are different. In short, it is not clear to me that separate listings would fit easily into the way that things are done in the UK.

But I do see the sense in what Colin is saying. When I first read his paper, I asked myself why, instead of having a listed subsidiary, the other utility could not be constrained to have a minority interest? Then, the holding company would be minority. It could still have a big stake, up to 49 per cent. I expect the answer is that, although it would lead to a more genuine arm's length relationship, it would not actually give the holding company or the investor companies the same incentive or power to reorganise the company. When people take over companies they usually think, rightly or wrongly, that they can run them better. In an associated company, the stake holder does not have quite the same power to shake up management and change things.

Thus, there is a spectrum of possible structures. At one extreme you have the wholly owned subsidiary where the parent can do basically what it likes. It can reorganise it as it sees fit and we would probably see the maximum benefit. On the other hand, the regulator will not have transparency. Then there is Colin's ingeniously interposed idea of the listed subsidiary where there is at least a minority of independent shareholders and there is possibly a degree of transparency and information for the regulator. Then you have the associated company where the investor has less incentive to reorganise things and less power, so that it would be less effective, although the independence and transparency of the associate would be greater. This arrangement would effectively insulate utilities from the take-over threat, which might be a very important issue. None of the solutions is perfect and determining which is best is substantially an empirical issue.

I have two specific questions. One is the issue of the control premium. Colin took that up twice. First of all he talked about it in the context of whether the value of the holding company would be diminished by issuing minority shares. The answer was no, because either they would get a good price for the minority shares or they would get a lower price and the value of the control premium would remain in the holding company. Later on he explained how the holding company would perhaps actually generate extra dividends in the subsidiary. That, of course, should increase the price that they received for selling the minority anyway and the holding company shareholders would also benefit from this, so nobody would be worse off. The puzzle I have is, what is the nature of this control premium? It seems to me that, if the holding company does not succeed in generating extra returns from controlling the subsidiary, there may be no control premium, because control is held in the hands of somebody who is not very good at getting returns on their investment. There is then control but no associated return. It might be argued that the company might see the light and sell it to somebody who can manage it better, and there then might be a control premium in the price. But personally I would not like to be a shareholder in a company that could not justify its control premium by generating appropriate returns.

A second detailed issue is that Colin said that, although his talk is on the cost of capital, we can bypass that by looking at market value by just reading off the share price and comparing it with the current cost of assets, in other words, what some people call the 'valuation ratio' and other people call 'Tobin's q'. That is true in a sense because it is what regulators tend to do when they use the cost of capital to discount possible returns. This does worry me a bit because it is getting very mechanistic. As an accountant I worry about how we assess cost. Cost is a very flexible concept to apply. I worry about the whole issue of focusing on the cost of capital and looking at the rate of return in the regulatory process. I think it runs the danger, particularly when you put it in the clear way that Colin did, of lapsing into the rate of return regulation that they have in the United States which is pretty much a dead hand on regulated industry.

Markets in the Firm

A Market-Process Approach to Management

Tyler Cowen and David Parker

1. Information is now the critical factor of production: firms need to be able to sense the need for change and respond before their competitors do.

2. Use of market principles within a firm can help it learn and adapt.

3. The days are numbered when rigid 'Taylorist scientific management' principles could usefully be applied. Markets now demand more variety and quality. Companies are decentralising to cope with the uncertainty and pace of change of markets.

4. 'Looser-coupled' firms, however, run the risk of anarchy. Means of maintaining the 'coherence and strategic direction of the firm' are required.

5. Economists from Ronald Coase onwards have been interested in why firms exist. Viewing the firm as a 'nexus of contracts' focuses attention on the similarities between resource allocation in markets and in firms.

6. Some companies have applied market principles '...to unlock the problems of management.' Koch Industries Inc. in Kansas has been particularly successful.

7. Its success appears to have been achieved by an integrated system of mission statements, decentralised management (profit centres and cross-functional teams), and definition of property rights within the firm so as to provide appropriate incentives.

8. 'Command-and-control' methods are as inappropriate within a firm as they have proved to be outside it. Firms need to harness the ability of markets to 'flex and change, assimilating and processing information speedily and accurately, attributes that are essential to the learning organisation.' (p 73).

9. The 'command firm' is '...subject to all the disincentives of planned economies, including the hiding of resources, aggravated shortages, the over- or under-use of inputs and the resulting inefficiencies of production.' (p78).

10. Market economies have been effective in '...encouraging learning, adaptation and innovation'. The challenge is to '...design firms that can mimic these attributes of the market economy.' (p80).

The Institute of Economic Affairs

2 Lord North Street, Westminster, London SW1P 3LB
Telephone: 0171 799 3745 Facsimile: 0171 799 2137
E-mail: iea@iea.org.uk Internet: http://www.iea.org.uk   ISBN 0-255 36405-9

£8.00

How Markets Work:

Disequilibrium, Entrepreneurship and Discovery

Israel M. Kirzner

1. Mainstream neo-classical economics focusses on already attained states of equilibrium. It is silent about the processes of adjustment to equilibrium.

2. Human action consists of '...grappling with an essentially unknown future', not being confronted with clearly-specified objectives, known resources and defined courses of action as mainstream theory assumes.

3. Critics of the market economy find ammunition in neo-classical theory: they '...merely need to tick off the respects in which real world capitalism departs from the requirements for perfectly competitive optimality'.

4. The theory of entrepreneurial discovery allows economists to escape from the 'analytical box' in which 'choice' simply consists of computing a solution implicit in given data.

5. An entrepreneurial act of discovery consists in '...realising the existence of market value that has hitherto been overlooked'. Scope for entrepreneurial discovery occurs in a world of disequilibrium – which is quite different from the equilibrium world of mainstream economics where market outcomes are foreordained.

6. Entrepreneurial discovery explains why one price tends to prevail in a market. Though new causes of price differences continually appear, entrepreneurs exploit the resulting profit opportunities and produce a tendency towards a single price.

7. Only with the introduction of entrepreneurship is it possible to appreciate how markets work. Without entrepreneurship, there would be no market co-ordination.

8. So-called 'imperfections' of competition are often '...crucial elements in the market process of discovery and correction of earlier entrepreneurial errors'.

9. Advertising expenditures, for example, are means of alerting consumers to 'what they do not know that they do not know'. Anti-trust laws may hamper market processes and prevent competitive entry to markets.

10. Entrepreneurial profit, far from generating injustice, is a 'created gain'. It is not '...sliced from a pre-existing pie...it is a portion which has been created in the very act of grasping it'.

The Institute of Economic Affairs

2 Lord North Street, Westminster, London SW1P 3LB
Telephone: 0171 799 3745 Facsimile: 0171 799 2137
E-mail: iea@iea.org.uk Internet: http://www.iea.org.uk   ISBN 0-255 36404-0

£8.00

Less Than Zero

The Case for a Falling Price Level in a Growing Economy

George Selgin

1. Most economists now accept that monetary policy should not aim at 'full employment': central banks should aim instead at limiting movements in the general price level.

2. Zero inflation is often viewed as an ideal. But there is a case for allowing the price level to vary so as to reflect changes in unit production costs.

3. Under such a 'productivity norm', monetary policy would allow 'permanent improvements in productivity...to lower prices permanently' and adverse supply shocks (such as wars and failed harvests) to bring about temporary price increases. The overall result would be '...secular deflation interrupted by occasional negative supply shocks'.

4. United States consumer prices would have halved in the 30 years after the Second World War (instead of almost tripling), had a productivity norm policy been in operation.

5. In an economy with rising productivity a constant price level cannot be relied upon to avoid '..."unnatural" fluctuations in output and employment'.

6. A productivity norm should involve lower 'menu' costs of price adjustment, minimise 'monetary misperception' effects, achieve more efficient outcomes using fixed money contracts and keep the real money stock closer to its 'optimum'.

7. The theory supporting the productivity norm runs counter to conventional macro-economic wisdom. For example, it suggests that a falling price level is not synonymous with depression. The 'Great Depression' of 1873-1896 was actually a period of '...unprecedented advances in factor productivity'.

8. In practice, implementing a productivity norm would mean choosing between a labour productivity and a total factor productivity norm. Using the latter might be preferable and would involve setting the growth rate of nominal income equal to a weighted average of labour and capital input growth rates.

9. Achieving a predetermined growth rate of nominal income would be easier under a free banking régime which tends automatically to stabilise nominal income.

10. Many countries now have inflation rates not too far from zero. But zero inflation should be recognised not as the ideal but '...as the stepping-stone towards something even better'.

The Institute of Economic Affairs

2 Lord North Street, Westminster, London SW1P 3LB
Telephone: 0171 799 3745 Facsimile: 0171 799 2137
E-mail: iea@iea.org.uk Internet: http://www.iea.org.uk

ISBN 0-255 36402-4

£8.00

Back From the Brink: An Appeal to Fellow Europeans Over Monetary Union

Pedro Schwartz

1. European Monetary Union is an 'unprecedented experiment', a 'huge gamble' which produces mixed reactions among Europeans.

2. There are many possible pitfalls before monetary union can come into being. One particular problem is that from 1998 to 2001, national currencies will remain legal tender. The currencies of 'misbehaving countries' may therefore be '…pounced upon by speculators and marauders…'

3. A monetary zone can function effectively only if it encompasses a single market, especially a single labour market. Establishing a monetary union when there is no hope of removing some of the barriers to a single market means '…applying perpetual fetters'.

4. The labour market of the European Union is '…far from being integrated'. The entry into monetary union of countries with rigid labour markets would warp the functioning of the union: moreover, those countries would probably demand subsidies to alleviate unemployment.

5. European Monetary Union therefore faces 'a bumpy road' before and after 2002. Before 2002 there may be 'speculative storms'; after 2002 large pockets of unemployment may persist, undermining European unity.

6. If European politicians had really wanted a stable currency they would have linked their currencies to the Deutschmark and turned their Central Banks into currency boards.

7. Monetary competition among existing European currencies plus the euro would offer a better long run prospect of monetary stability than monetary union.

8. Competitive devaluation is less of a problem than industrial lobbies claim. Over-valuation is more of a danger: '…fake converts from easy virtue love the prestige of a strong currency'.

9. In practice, careful economic analysis of European Monetary Union 'counts for nothing'. The proposed union is a 'dangerous experiment…' to build a certain kind of Europe surreptitiously' and to give a '…huge boost to centralisation'.

10. If monetary union goes ahead, Britain should go it alone and '…set an example from within the European Union of what can be achieved by a competitive, deregulated, private economy with a floating and well-managed currency'.

The Institute of Economic Affairs

2 Lord North Street, Westminster, London SW1P 3LB
Telephone: 0171 799 3745 Facsimile: 0171 799 2137
E-mail: iea@iea.org.uk Internet: http://www.iea.org.uk   ISBN 0-255 36401-6

£4.00

New Zealand's Remarkable Reforms

iea

Donald T Brash

1. New Zealand's economy has revived in the last few years, following '...one of the most remarkable economic liberalisations in modern times' since 1984. There is little public enthusiasm for reversing the reforms.

2. Once one of the most regulated OECD economies, New Zealand is now one of the least regulated. Unemployment has recently fallen sharply. The estimated sustainable annual growth rate of real GDP is now 3-3½ per cent.

3. The transformation of New Zealand – from a protectionist, regulated society with 'cradle-to-grave' welfare to an open, market-based economy operating under the rule of law – has a 'Hayekian flavour'.

4. Under the guidance of Roger (now Sir Roger) Douglas, New Zealand adopted a 'big bang' approach to reform, though the pace of reform slackened for a time in the late 1980s.

5. Micro-economic reforms included removal of controls on wages, prices, and foreign exchange and floating of the New Zealand dollar. Import quotas have been removed and tariffs reduced. Agricultural and industrial subsidies have virtually disappeared.

6. '...the most remarkable liberalisation' has been that of the labour market where from 1991 contracts have been on '...almost the same basis as other commercial contracts'. By December 1995 only 17 per cent of the workforce had union-negotiated collective contracts.

7. High marginal rates of income tax have been reduced and a broad-based Value Added Tax introduced. The tax structure is now '<None>the least distorting of any in an OECD country'.

8. State-owned companies have been 'corporatised' and many have been privatised. Privatisation has generally not taken place until a corporation entered a contestable market: privatised companies are lightly regulated under the general powers of the Commerce Act.

9. A Fiscal Responsibility Act promotes sound fiscal policies and requires governments to explain present and projected budgetary positions.

10. Under the Reserve Bank of New Zealand Act of 1989, the government specifies an inflation target and the Bank Governor is left to implement it. The Governor can be dismissed for 'inadequate performance'. So far the monetary framework has been very successful in reducing inflation and inflationary expectations.

The Institute of Economic Affairs

2 Lord North Street, Westminster, London SW1P 3LB
Telephone: 0171 799 3745 Facsimile: 0171 799 2137
E-mail: iea@iea.org.uk Internet: http://www.iea.org.uk

ISBN 0-255 36400-8

£5.00